Life Writing Series

Life Writing Series

In the **Life Writing Series**, Wilfrid Laurier University Press publishes life writing and new life-writing criticism in order to promote autobiographical accounts, diaries, letters and testimonials written and/or told by women and men whose political, literary or philosophical purposes are central to their lives. **Life Writing** features the accounts of ordinary people, written in English, or translated into English from French or the languages of the First Nations or from any of the languages of immigration to Canada. **Life Writing** will also publish original theoretical investigations about life writing, as long as they are not limited to one author or text.

Priority is given to manuscripts that provide access to those voices that have not traditionally had access to the publication process.

Manuscripts of social, cultural and historical interest that are considered for the series, but are not published, are maintained in the **Life Writing Archive** of Wilfrid Laurier University Library.

Series Editor
Marlene Kadar
Humanities Division, York University

Manuscripts to be sent to
Brian Henderson, Director
Wilfrid Laurier University Press
75 University Avenue West
Waterloo, Ontario, Canada N2L 3C5

Repossessing the World

Reading Memoirs by
Contemporary Women

Helen M. Buss

WILFRID LAURIER
UNIVERSITY PRESS

This book has been published with the help of a grant from the Humanities and Social Sciences Federation of Canada, using funds provided by the Social Sciences and Humanities Research Council of Canada. We acknowledge the financial support of the Government of Canada through the Book Publishing Industry Development Program for our publishing activities.

National Library of Canada Cataloguing in Publication Data

Buss, Helen M. (Helen Margaret)
  Repossessing the world : reading memoirs by contemporary women

(Life writing series)
Includes bibliographical references and index.
ISBN 0-88920-408-X (bound)

  1. Autobiography—Women authors.   2. Literature, Modern—20th century—History and criticism.   I. Title.   II. Series.

CT25.B88 2002   809'.93592072   C2001-903198-X

© 2002 Helen M. Buss

Cover design by Leslie Macredie,
using a photograph by Brian Henderson.

All rights reserved. No part of this work covered by the copyrights hereon may be reproduced or used in any form or by any means—graphic, electronic, or mechanical—without the prior written permission of the publisher. Any request for photocopying, recording, taping, or reproducing in information storage and retrieval systems of any part of this book shall be directed in writing to the Canadian Reprography Collective, 214 King Street West, Suite 312, Toronto, Ontario M5H 3S6.

Dedication

Over the years of researching and writing this book many individuals have contributed to my thinking on the memoir form as practised by women. Mentioning them by name would inevitably leave someone out. Instead, I would like to dedicate this book to the various communities they represent for me:

> ∼ to my family for continuing to tell their lives to me and for listening to mine
>
> ∼ to feminist colleagues for the inspiration of their intelligence, courage and persistence
>
> ∼ to the graduate students whom I have supervised for being my teachers
>
> ∼ to students in my classes on life writing for hearing me out and speaking up
>
> ∼ to the first readers of my manuscript who gave good advice
>
> ∼ to memoirists, both those who have written and those who desire to write

Contents

Acknowledgements ix

An Autobiocritical Preface
Writing As a Memoirist xi

Chapter 1
Introduction
   Memoir As a Life-Writing Discourse 1

Chapter 2
Memoir with an Attitude
   One Reader Reads *The Woman Warrior:*
   Memoirs of a Girlhood among Ghosts 27

Chapter 3
Identity As a Balancing Act
   Memoirs' Practice of Non-Sacrificial
   Rituals of Self-Performance 57

Chapter 4
Dancing with Our Mothers
   Reading and Writing Memoirs
   As a Mother and a Daughter 85

Chapter 5
"Scenes of Language"
  Trauma and the Search for Form
  in Women's Memoirs 121

Chapter 6
Joining Heart and Head
  Contemporary Academic Women's
  Uses of the Memoir Form 163

Conclusion
  Repossessing a Relational Autonomy
  That Resists Appropriation 183

Works Cited 191

Index 201

Acknowledgements

I would like to thank the Social Sciences and Humanities Research Council of Canada for their support during the research phase of this project, the Calgary Institute for the Humanities for the research time provided by a fellowship to the Institute, and the Killam Resident Fellowships program for the time provided for the writing of this book. I am grateful to the Department of English, University of Calgary, where I have had opportunities to teach courses related to my research. I would like to thank Richard Buss for composing the index of this book.

An earlier version of chapter 2 appeared in *a/b Auto/Biography Studies* 12, 2 (Fall 1997).

An Autobiocritical Preface

Writing As a Memoirist

Memoir: personal history; the personalizing of history; the historicizing of the personal. Memoir: the personal act of repossessing a public world, historical, institutional, collective....The memoirs are *of* a person, but they are "really" of an event, an era, an institution, a class identity.

—Francis Russell Hart, "History Talking to Itself"

ONE OF the first stumbling blocks I encountered after I tentatively admitted to family members that I was writing a memoir of my childhood in Newfoundland was that the family stories began to change—to clean themselves up, so to speak, for public consumption. This was especially the case with my mother's stories. *Memoirs from Away: A New Found Land Girlhood* was dependent on the stories my mother told me of the traumatic times around my birth in 1941, when my family began to be affected by the events of the Second World War. Her changing stories created a serious problem for me, because I was engaged, as Francis Russell Hart puts it, in "the personal act of repossessing a public world" (195). In trying to regain a public history that had left me out, dispossessed me of a sense of my self as connected to the world, I felt that my mother's personal memory of wartime was an essential part of that repossession, as essential as a history book. In writing my chapter about these times, entitled "War: Mother's Child," my original impetus was to tell how the great immorality that is war reaches into the lives and psyches of the most ordinary people, even those who are distant from the scenes of battle, like those of my mother and her children in Newfoundland. Although our family did not have a particularly dangerous war, our experience was dislocating and often very distressing, especially for my mother and her little ones. By writing about those times I felt I would be "repossessing" my childhood self as a psychological entity and reclaiming a female identity from the male-based disciplines of medicine and psychology, history and literature that had "possessed" femaleness. I also felt I would be "repossessing" a history of the war that had edited out the lives of people like my mother and her children, people on the so-called home front.

Early in my writing, because I saw my project as being historical as well as personal, I needed to believe that the stories my mother told me about that time were her authentic memories of events. I do not mean that they constituted a factually complete record. I knew that memory doesn't work that way—my mother would inevitably leave out some facts and tailor her interpretations of events to her own particular psychological and social position in the larger culture. But to find my mother actually contradicting previously stated facts when she knew that her daughter might publish some of what she said was, to say the least, unnerving. I reacted by attempting to find a way to accommodate my mother's revision of her memory in the text of my memoir, and in doing so I made discoveries concerning the memoir form. I want to illustrate this by quoting from "War: Mother's Child":

> My dad says that my birth cry was a scream of absolute anger. The story of my absolute anger at birth has become a family joke. My brothers have been known to elaborate on the birth story, honing the figure of anger into a lifetime of inappropriate behaviour. But that's another story. When you dig behind the anger at birth as metaphor, there is a history. There is always a history. You just have to find it and shape it to your needs.
>
> It seems that at the beginning of her ninth month of pregnancy my mother wanted to borrow something from the next-door neighbour who had a very vicious dog. I would like to tell you she was trying to borrow a gravy boat or a fruit bowl or some other grail-like object, suitable to a birth story, but I am afraid I cannot tell you the exact goal of her mission. Anyway, she approached the yard and yes, there was the dog, full of teeth and growling. Kathleen was certain that she could just make it to the neighbour's door before the dog got her, and she really did need whatever it was she wanted to borrow. Halfway up the pathway she saw that her certainty was mistaken and the dog was going to get her if she didn't change her plans quickly. She leapt for the fence and hurdled it, feeling the painful pull of tearing in her eight-month pregnant belly as she did so. She went home and cried. Her water broke that night and I came angrily into the world the next afternoon at six o'clock, one month early, and have continued to be pretty angry, by all accounts, for a number of decades. I have always made it a point to avoid dogs. As a child I would go blocks out of my way to do so. After I had therapy I learned to stare dogs down, but I still don't like them and neither does Kathleen.
>
> Just recently my mother told me another version of this story. In it she is not off on any borrowing adventures, does not jump any fences. She is hanging out clothes in her own back yard and the neighbour calls her to the fence to talk. She is terribly afraid of the wolf-like dog, but the neighbour says not to worry, he's harmless. The dog jumps the fence, leaps up my mother's body to her throat, the neighbour still insisting on her doggie's good nature. Kathleen is so traumatized she gives birth the next day. I

don't like this second story, preferring mother the guilty but self-empowered risk-taker to mother the innocent victim. I'm almost certain that years ago she used to tell the other version. Surely I have not imagined this. I have noticed that since I've become a writer Kathleen is more careful with her stories. I don't want to lie to you so I let you make what you will of both versions. (34)

The narration of both versions of the birth story in my memoirs was part of my continuing education in the memoir form. It is a form in which one cannot rely only on the facts of official history, yet it is a form in which one cannot dispense with historical narrative. It is a form in which one must respect one's sources, respect the others that make one's own story; yet it is a form in which one must suspect one's sources, doubt them while affirming them. It is a form in which one cannot be entirely in control of self-construction, but must come to see that act of self-making as a process of *performing* the self. This self changes and grows, leaves parts of the old self behind, gains new performances that become more completely one's self as they become habitual. Most important, the memoir is a form in which history must come into concourse with literature in order to make a self, a life, and to locate that living self in a history, an era, a relational and communal identity. Gender (like race, nationality, class, sexual orientation, and a other factors) inflects each of our lives in different ways, and women's memories of life events are often different from men's. I chose the memoir form just because of this difference. The memoir is so dependent on the personal recollection and interpretation of private and public events that it would allow me a performance of self that would accomodate this difference. Alice Kaplan, one of the memoirists whose work is taken up in this study, says that we cannot just dismiss the memoir from serious consideration as a form by labelling it "personal writing," because "memoir is a genre, with its habits, its rules and its codes" (quoted in Williams 163). In studying the form before I practised it, I learned that my gender would make a difference, because of the specificity of my person and my experiences.

An Autobiocritical Preface

Even when memoir is highly researched, as, one assumes, are the memoirs of major public figures, memoirs plead special cases. They give primacy to the viewpoint of their narrators over the literary aesthetic to show rather than tell. Memoir narrators tell you as well as show you. They also refuse the historical narrative's dictum to objectify the personal interpretation through the device of documentation of many sources. Memoirs, because of the very nature of their form, admit the limitation of their sources. Because of their dependence on narrators who are never fully impartial, and often highly opinionated, memoirs have been considered to be both bad history (which assumes objectivity) and inferior literature (which prefers narratives that show rather than tell). Despite what would be viewed as disadvantages, by some readers and writers, I found in the memoir the perfect medium to embroider my own rebellious discourse. I liked that it was a marginal form, even a marginal form of a marginal discourse, Life Writing. I felt marginalized myself, so the marginal nature of the discourse suited me. This does not mean that I found the memoir easier to write than any other form I have practised, whether it be the novel, poem, short story, essay, or academic article. Each, as Kaplan would put it, has its own habits, rules, and codes.

One of the things that I had not counted on in my memoir writing was the infirmity of my mother's memory, or my own infirmity in remembering her memory. Indeed, I had built an identity around the first version of her birth story. Now, even as I wrote I had to revise that version of myself. Fortunately, the memoir form also facilitates the changing nature of memory. What the memoir allows me and increasing numbers of other contemporary women to do is to assert our versions of reality and revise them as we assert them, by questioning our own reality, pointing to the ways all memory and documentation rest on precarious foundations.

In writing the two versions of my mother's story of my birth and inviting the reader to mediate, I wanted to point to the way in which all recollections are profoundly influenced by contexts in the present moment. Did my mother change her story to make it more respectable for publication, or did I imagine it differently over the years because of my desire for a rebellious mother? Did my mother let me imagine it differently, as long as it remained private, because she liked my more heroic view of her? Did she change it to make herself more respectably compliant as a woman? The opportunity to tangle with these inconsistencies allows the reader to be a more active participant, to understand the very tentative and multi-directional nature of reality. I think one of the great attractions of memoirs is the way we, as readers, are drawn actively into the narrator's reality-building process. We have an intense relationship with the narrator, because as witness of and participant in the events she relates, she is the narrator we depend on as readers, as well as the main character with whom we often identify. The narrator is our "guide," as Kate Adams puts it, our "participant observer [who] lends the history she chronicles significance, humanity, insight" (8).

I tried to let the reader participate in the narrative inconsistencies set up by the two versions of my mother's stories. Yet, there are consistencies between the two stories that draw attention to and, indeed, reinforce the fact that what does not change is my premature (and for my mother) traumatic birth when my parents are about to undertake a stressful move in wartime. In writing memoir certain basic historical and personal facts must be present or the account loses its mandate as memoir. But other "facts," such as my father's perception of my anger at birth, are really perceptions of fact. However, through time and repetition such perceptions take on the value of facts. My father's perception of anger in my birth cry begins the family's belief in my identity as an angry female person, a condition that I, as well as my whole family, have believed to be my most prominent characteristic for much of my life. Memoir writing becomes my way of turning the anger into a more useful personal motivation in that it can, with practice, become art. As a result of the play of the facts of events with the perceptions of events in memoir, memory in this form is not proposed as either simple recall or pure imagination. It is both, operating in a process of identity making. In the case of childhood events and perceptions, memory is made up of more than one's own recall, more than one person's imaginative reconstruction. Indeed, memory is a dialogue between the self and others, and it is caught up in the process of identity making in the present moment of writing.

While my first motive in writing memoir was concerned with this play of recall and imagination, self and other, my second motive in writing memoir was to use the memoir form to suggest how historical narratives change when read through women's lives. In writing the chapter "War: Mother's Child," it was my original intention to make the traumatic events of my mother's wartime isolation, after a move to a small Nova Scotia town where she knew no one, as compelling and significant as other war stories. I wanted to show her predicament, and therefore mine, as she carried a third child (my younger brother) alone, while believing that her husband was off to some dangerous front of the war. I wanted to give these events and struggles, as examples of ordinary women's wartime experiences, an equal footing with the historical narrative that paralleled her life and filled my early education. This historical narrative taught us about the Battle for the North Atlantic, the part of the public war in which we Newfoundlanders participated most directly. I wanted to write a woman's experience of public history—the different way a mother experiences war. Historian Gerda Lerner has suggested that by making women's personal stories into "documents" for study, which show women's lives as different from those of men in a specific era, we can also show how women's lives are significant to the era. I wanted to make my mother's story, and mine as her girl child, part of these "documents" of difference. But once again, as with memory, there were surprises waiting for me when I began to write. I wasn't even finished telling my birth story, not even on to the main theme of wartime, when another kind of history started to insert itself into my story. I suddenly found my memoir of wartime becoming conscious of a different context, a different personal and public history. This is illustrated in the paragraphs that immediately follow the story of my mother's premature labour which resulted in my birth:

One fact I can be sure of is that the day I was born was March 28, 1941. I found my original birth certificate this very morning as I checked my childhood history book, *The Story of Newfoundland*....However, no history book will tell you why March 28, 1941, is an important date for me and lots of other women. I'm sure there are all sorts of things that were happening that day and an encyclopedia yearbook will tell you about them if you want to look. But it will not tell you what I am about to tell you. To know the importance of March 28, 1941, you have to have lived a woman's life in the latter days of capitalism in the West, learned its workloads for middle-class females, the compromises it enforces, the betrayals it encourages and the smallness of the rebellions that class privilege makes possible, learned them with such sureness that you pretty well break under the load. Then you have to make your damaged self well enough to learn how to study. Harder still, you have to disobey the rules when you study, seeking illogical adjacencies, remote occurrences and unlikely contingencies that are considered of no relevance whatsoever to whatever your subject of study is.

That's what I did. One day when I was forty and working as a graduate student in a university library on an annotated bibliography of the works by and about a famous male poet, a class assignment which needed to be done right there and then, I left my assignment to wander the library bookshelves and find a reason to be distracted. I did. I found Virginia Woolf. Years earlier, when I was an undergraduate in the late fifties and early sixties we had studied Joyce and Eliot until we thought Modernists were the only thing that mattered in literature, outside of Shakespeare. But at that time Virginia was mentioned only occasionally, as a sort of writer manqué, a talented woman who just didn't make the Eliot/Joyce-defined grade, like people such as Elizabeth Barrett Browning and Emily Dickinson. Later, when I returned after a career as a high school teacher to do graduate work, I discovered Woolf had become fashionable in feminist circles, so I read her works on my own. But I had never read about her life.

On this occasion, looking for an excuse to further delay working on my assignment, I took a book off the shelf that gave a brief biography of Woolf. There, right in the chronology of her life, was the important fact that nobody had told me. At eleven o'clock on the morning of March 28th, 1941, Virginia stuffed rocks in her pockets and walked into the River Ouse and drowned. I didn't find out about the rocks until years later, but I like the detail. If you are going to do it, do it right and let them know you did it, that it was no silly slip of the foot, fainting in madness or heartbreak, no

Ophelia or Lady of Shalott, bleating when they should have tried swimming.

I have calculated the time differential between England and Newfoundland, and reckon that it was around dawn of March 28th, 1941, just when Kathleen must have been getting really scared that this baby was going to come too early for its own good, that Virginia did it. I want you to know that my ego is not so inflated that I believe that all of Virginia's spirit rushed across the Atlantic, and like some jet-stream incubus flew up my mother's vagina and into the little baby vagina of yours truly. There was too much of Virginia for that. It may have taken months, years, for all the energy in Virginia to get properly accommodated in various little girl bodies around the globe. It may have taken a thousand little girl babies, maybe a million, to use up the suppressed anger that a life like hers must have gathered. I meet these little girls every now and then, all aging now. They pass me in hallways, in stairwells, in streets; we make eye contact, but do not speak. We are a generation trained to keep quiet about what we really think, but our eyes tell each other that we serve the same lady.

I like to think that there in Britain's oldest colony my mother's distress went out like Marconi's first wireless message, shooting out from Signal Hill into the ether of the universe. I like to believe it was picked up loud and clear by some part of the energy that Virginia never got to use, and one small distilled drop of her most suppressed anger—maybe the part that could never admit it hated doctors who shut her up in dark rooms and forbade her books; maybe the part that didn't like to admit that Leonard was not God's gift of a perfect husband to a female writer; maybe the part that wished her mother had loved her more than that demanding old man, her father. Some tiny pearl of anger, pressed as tight as matter in a dark hole in the universe—I like to think I got that bit. (35-36)

What I found in writing this portion of my memoir was that when I tried to write my woman's history of the war years, fantasy immediately intervened. Making a fantasy may seem to have no relation to making history, but to make history look at what it has ignored, it may be necessary to resort to an imaginative fantasy. Just as the racial, ethnic, and national histories that dominate public discourse are mandated, informed, and shaped by originating myths, the highlighting and special interpretations of events that give public purpose to private lives, so a woman's history must make such myths also. In my life the coincidence of my birth a few hours after Virginia Woolf's death created a private fantasy of empowerment that got me, as a rather ancient student, through the rigours of graduate school and the task of finding gainful employment in a bad market. Until the moment I wrote about my birth I did not know that I would use such a private fantasy to inform either my personal life story or my version of the war. But I should not have been surprised. For that is exactly what memoirs by women in recent times are doing. Take, for example, the way in which Maxine Hong Kingston negotiates myth, memory, and history in *The Woman Warrior: Memoirs of a Girlhood among Ghosts*. On rereading Kingston's book, I discover that the very wordings I have used in speaking of Virginia Woolf in the passage quoted above—"I like to think...," "I like to believe..."—are the phrases that twenty years ago Kingston used as she went about the task of revising her received Chinese and American cultures to insert her woman's story.

In adopting Virginia Woolf as a kind of surrogate "mother" for the creativity I needed to write my memoirs, I discovered that I was using exactly the figure that inspired critic Shari Benstock in her consideration of Woolf's memoir work. This figure helps her explain important psychological and linguistic female differences in autobiographical production. Woolf stands at the beginning of many feminist projects, both creative and critical. Benstock, along with Estelle Jelinek, Domna Stanton, Sidonie Smith, Bella Brodski, and Celeste Schenck, all published books between 1986 and 1988 that have become the foundation of later critical work on women's autobiographical production. However, it is Benstock's use of Woolf as the symbol of women autobiographers who have trouble looking into the "abyss" of a divided self that resonates with my current work on memoirs. Benstock says that Woolf's fictions "were in some sense a pretense against the primordial split subject" and that when Woolf took up memoir writing it "posed the question of selfhood directly; it forced Virginia Woolf to look into the abyss—something she could not do" (28). Perhaps she could not do it because the age she lived in lacked a fully articulated sense of what memoir can be for women. What I want to do in this book is show how the memoir form, as it is evolving in the hands of contemporary women, does allow for a fuller performance of female self. I want to show that such a fuller performance allows women to access that very "private self" (that is the title of Benstock's collection), while joining that sense of self to "the concerns with gender, race, class and historical and political conditions" (Benstock 11). Women need to seam together the "private" self with these "conditions" of the public world in order to be able to accept the multiplicity of the self while gaining a self that is empowered to act in both private and public worlds. The first public world in which Virginia Woolf tried out her memoir writing—which contained an account of her half-brother as a sexual abuser—was the "memoir club," made up of her Bloomsbury friends. The silence and avoidance with which her male friends greeted her work caused her great pain. When a writer, especially a woman writer, breaks taboos, a poor reception can be the spur that drives the experiment back into the private world. Silence is a particularly strong form of negative reception. Virginia Woolf did not live to complete her memoirs. The fact that she wrote several memoir stories that possess the style and content now familiar in women's memoirs places her at the beginning of a tradition of contemporary women memoirists, and at the beginning of the contemporary critical and theoretical process devoted to women's self-writing.

The implied connection between Woolf and war in my writing is that she represents my war dead just as much as any soldier who died in the war. She is part of my history as a woman in our culture. She is also part of my tradition as a memoirist who brings the content of the private world in connection with the contexts of the larger world. In a more contemporary moment Sara Suleri, in her memoir *Meatless Days*, interweaves private and public history through a kind of poeticized working of fact into metaphor. In telling of her beginnings in the civil wars and religious and ethnic violence that marked the birth of Pakistan, Suleri parallels her public narration with the story of various household accidents, mishaps, and tragedies of her personal family. The public and private narratives are so well interwoven that, without Suleri ever announcing the parallels, the reader is allowed to read the private and public narratives as metaphorically joined, even though traditional history teaches us they are separate. Women such as Kingston and Suleri radically revise the memoir form as a tool for rewriting reality through women's performance of the process of memory as well as their revision of history. It was comforting for me, when I began to see the seemingly strange contexts my memoir stories seemed to be taking, to know that I was already working within a tradition. What I needed to do was to find ways to establish that tradition in the face of a critical community that now mistrusts the whole idea of tradition. As a writer who felt marginalized by old traditions, I nevertheless knew that the idea of a tradition that feeds rather than starves could be empowering. As a critic I wanted to find ways to let other women know that they could write and read in a tradition of women's memoirs. This growing tradition of writing needs to be assessed in a way that is more informed by a knowledge of how the memoir form works. Reviewers, critics, and readers are beginning to read these texts with more frequency, as the memoir begins to challenge the novel as a preferred reading choice for large numbers of people and as more and more life writers call their texts "memoirs" rather than "autobiographies." It is my hope that my study will help establish appropriate reading strategies for the memoir form.

When I first began writing fiction back in the late seventies and early eighties, my imagined reader was often a woman like myself—overworked, with a career, kids, and marriage—seeking some view of herself that didn't devalue the very tasks that her woman's life and identity were made from. She was, to my mind, in need of positive views of women's ordinary lives, and she especially needed to know that friendship between women, between mother and daughter, between female contemporaries of different backgrounds, was both possible and laudable. These were my desires, and I wrote them into my novels for the readers I imagined. I now like to call my novels "feminist fantasies," and I don't mean to demean them by that term; I mean to imply that I wrote of possibilities as if they were real. But I realize as I write this that my idea of my reader has changed, and thus the form I work in has changed. I think that when I wrote fiction I wrote for a specific kind of reader to receive some shock of recognition, to see her life mirrored, her fantasies of female solidarity made real. Now that I am writing memoir, I write to initiate a certain process, one that cannot be "received" through the shock of the mirrored reality, but must be "performed" through an active participation of the reader's own revision of history and memory. Since the publication of my memoir, some friends have told me that it made them think about how they have arrived at their own versions of their childhood selves. Others have written me long letters constructing their own recall of some event or era significant to their lives. I think that this reaction is encouraged because my views, my reflections, my reflexivity to my own life, and the revisions I make to that life in writing, are very much on the surface of my memoir. Because its narrator addresses herself directly to the reader, others seem to have been inspired to offer me their direct address, based on their own life experiences. With these readers I have succeeded, because active revision has begun for them as a result of reading.

I also write memoir because I have come to understand that the bonding I would like to see between women of different races, classes, and generations is not possible just out of good will on all sides. The forces of division caused by the tradition of misogyny that we inherit are so great that such solidarity must be grounded in finding a common reality-making process, a common experience of making identity. By that I do not mean a common reality or a common identity. I think for women to find a solidarity that can bridge the differences caused by factors such as race, class, generation, and sexual orientation, they must recognize and understand their diversity. But at the same time they can also discover a similarity in reliable and repeatable processes of revision of received history and memory which can help them to perform effective and satisfying selves in their time and place. Through those acts they can begin to repossess the public world for themselves and for other women. I think that performing acts of memoir can make that happen.

But to make that performance of many selves possible it is necessary to begin to take the category "memoir" seriously, as writers, critics and readers, and that is what I intend to do in the following chapters. Chapter 1 compares and contrasts the development of the memoir form with the allied history of the traditional forms of confession and autobiography, but also locates it in terms of other allied literary forms such as lyric poetry, biography, drama, and the essay. This introductory chapter describes both the rhetorical strategies that writers need in writing memoirs and the critical reading assumptions that readers need if we are to understand the memoir form as a contemporary social discourse that can have a profound political impact on the way we make our culture.

Chapter 2 concentrates on the reading act by taking up my own process of reading what is perhaps the most famous memoir text of contemporary times, Maxine Hong Kingston's *The Woman Warrior: Memoirs of a Girlhood among Ghosts*. Ironically, despite Kingston's naming of her book as "memoirs," this fact has not been the subject of critical inquiry. Through undertaking a reading of the book as an example of the memoir form and describing the active readership that implies, I theorize that reading memoirs, because of the nature of our relationship with the narrator, requires an especially participant stance on the part of the reader.

Chapter 3 proposes that the form of memoir is closely related to the kind of identity formation that feminist theory sees as the chief challenge that women face, the challenge of avoiding the dichotomization of identity as either entirely autonomous or entirely relational in nature. I take up Allison Weir's analysis of the "sacrificial logics" of such a dichotomy and work through memoirs of women entering and leaving important stages of female life. In these memoirs women insist on repossessing a world in which both autonomy and relational aspects are part of their self-performance, making identities that are "balancing acts."

Chapter 4 explores the phenomenon of the many contemporary memoirs that are concerned with the mother/daughter relationship. In examining my own history of reading these texts as both a daughter and a mother, I am interested in how the sometimes troubled nature of these relationships as they are portrayed in memoirs tells us much about what remains silent and unexamined in our public culture.

Many contemporary memoirs originate in devastating public and private instances of trauma in our times. In chapter 5 I explore trauma, not only as the site of injury, but also as the site of new knowledge that the trauma victim, in negotiating her own survival, offers to the larger culture, a wisdom that works toward healing both the individual and the public history.

In chapter 6 I look at the texts of a growing list of academic women who have undertaken memoirs. I speculate on the usefulness of the form for such women, and show how academic women are well located as human subjects to use the memoir to repossess a sense of themselves as women without sacrificing their identities as intellectuals. I want to show that memoir offers a mode to repossess ways of knowing the world and the self that does not divide the heart from the head.

Introduction

Memoir As a Life-Writing Discourse

> In general, what does a memoir do? It encapsulates, through the telling of an individual's story, a particular moment or era. A mix of the personal with the contextual, an autobiographical narrative intersecting with history, memoir gives its readers an author as guide, an informant whose presence lends a unique perspective to the historical moment or event or actor being recorded; the author's status as a participant observer lends the history she chronicles significance, humanity, insight.
>
> —Kate Adams, "The Way We Were"

"MEMOIR" IS a much older term in English than is "autobiography." The *Oxford English Dictionary* notes its use as early as the sixteenth century to denote any personal "record of events, not purporting to be a complete history, but treating of such matters as come within the personal knowledge of the writer, or are obtained from certain particular sources of information" (828). On the other hand, the word "autobiography" was first used in the early nineteenth century to describe the more individualistic narratives of the self that were beginning to grow out of the revolutionary period and the Romantic movement. While the term "memoir" has remained largely unexamined by literary critics and theorists, the term "autobiography" has taken up a central position in the history of what we now call "life writing." The lack of examination of the term "memoir" may be due in part to the identification of the form as a life-writing practice associated more with history than with literature. However, memoir does not claim to be a "complete history," but rather the testimony of a writer who has "personal knowledge" of the events, the era, or the people that are its subject. As a result, in terms of historical studies, the memoir serves as a historical resource rather than a historical discourse. Thus, memoir continues to occupy a marginal status in historical studies as well as in literary studies. Yet memoir endures as a much used form of discourse in Western culture because of its accessibility. In earlier times it was practised by a broad range of people from pilgrims to explorers and aristocratic family historians. The democratization of more recent centuries has made it an accessible format for celebrities from retired politicians to actors and ex-criminals who wish to revise the public record of their ways and days.

At the moment the memoir is proving a flexible vehicle for a great variety of people. For some it is not only an easy discourse to access, but also one that is elastic enough to bear considerable experimentation. It is becoming a discursive practice in which material realities and imaginary possibilities coexist. It can accommodate both the factual and the theoretical, and it may concern itself as much with the life of a community as with that of an individual. It uses a style that is at the same time narrative and essayistic, descriptive and imagistic, factually testimonial and anecdotally fictive. It bridges the typical strategies of historical and literary discourses in order to establish necessary connections between the private and the public, the personal and the political. The view that the personal is political has always been at the heart of all feminisms, therefore it is not surprising that memoirs have become popular with women. The memoir is increasingly used to interrogate the private individual's relationship to a history and/or a culture from which she finds her experience of her self and her life excluded. Although individual men can also find themselves in an excluded position (and do write memoirs as a result), it is women who most often take up the memoir form for the specific purpose of revising cultural contexts so that their experience is not excluded. In doing so, these women are changing the ways in which we tell our stories as human beings; they are bringing female gendering to bear on our previously male-gendered narratives of the self and culture.

Contemporary women's adoption of the personal account to interrogate and repossess the culture is part of a great increase in life-writing practices of all kinds, and in critical attention to those practices. Georg Misch, who began the critical investigation of autobiographical practices in the 1950s, observed, after surveying personal writings since ancient times, that such texts flourish when people "wish to regain the harmony and inner tranquillity" (356) of a congruent relationship with the realities of human existence. Later, Alfred Kazin identified the twentieth century as such a time, "where so many values have been overturned without our admitting it, where there is an obvious gap between the culture we profess and the dangers among which we really live" (216). Kazin, writing in 1964, found that autobiography was an important tool with which individuals could revise a culture to make it more accurately reflective of reality. I agree with Misch and Kazin, who, although primarily concerned with male-authored texts, identified the need of human beings to make a connection between their lives and their culture, especially when culture fails to represent their perceived identities. The first "autobiographer," Saint Augustine, was such a man. A scholar trained in the Greek tradition of rationalism, but living in a Christian world where faith was beginning to triumph over reason, he was well placed to write an autobiographical account that would enlighten others in adjusting old realities to new ones. Rousseau, in the eighteenth century, was also in a good position to write the story of the romantic, bourgeois individualist battling the chains of a hierarchical mindset that privileged birth and title over talent and accomplishment. But Augustine and Rousseau, while representing their own times well, do not represent ours. Bella Brodski and Celeste Schenck observed in their 1988 collection *Life / Lines: Theorizing Women's Autobiography* that "[a]t both extremes of subjectivity and publicity, the female autobiographer has lacked the sense of radical individuality, duplicitous but useful, that empowered Augustine and Henry Adams to write their representative lives large" (1). In contemporary times, when "radical individuality" is becoming more a burden than a blessing, new syntheses of group and individual identity factors are being made. Women growing up today have a particularly intense experience of the identity changes of the present and are therefore well placed to represent our era to others.

The Need for a Genre/Discourse Study

In 1976, just before life writing became critically central to literary studies, Elizabeth Bruss noted the arbitrary use of the word "autobiography." In *Autobiographical Acts: The Changing Situation of a Literary Genre* she proposed that the imposition of the word "autobiography" onto accounts whose writers would have conceived them as something else was a problem that contemporary criticism had failed to address. The issue has still not been satisfactorily explicated from a critical standpoint, since the word "autobiography" is used to describe many diverse texts, some of which are far from those the word was invented to describe. In bringing the older word "memoir" into the discussion I do not wish to make a similar imposition. As Philippe Lejeune observes, there is an "illusion of perspective" when we believe that there is a "birth of genre, after which a new genre, born all of a sudden" (145), comes into being independently of other writing practices. Lejeune quite rightly warns against an essentialist search for origins in genre study. Nevertheless, I propose that the naming of writing and reading practices is essential to understand how they are changing. When writing my memoir, I found that I had to be especially aware of the rhetorics and stylistics of the generic tradition in which I was working, since one is continually making decisions that involve generic choices. As well, I find that both readers and writers move from old namings to new namings in a process of generic evolution and devolution. In this regard my project is aligned with other efforts to complicate the traditional definitions of the word "autobiography." Susanna Egan sees many contemporary writing practices in autobiography as "genres in crisis" and asks: "How do autobiographers co-opt and adapt the genres that express this fraught moment of in-between?" (*Mirror Talk* 13). While Egan does not name specific generic locations, preferring to concentrate on the dialogue between various writing strategies, I do. This is a specifically political and feminist act. As I wrote in my own memoir, making a hyperbolic comparison of myself with the Biblical Adam, "[n]aming does give you power over creation" (xiii). I believe that to not name is to risk reappropriation into older, less useful generic definitions that may limit our practice. As Leigh Gilmore observes, we need to engage in "reexamining autobiography as discourses of self-representation rather than as a genre defined in its post-Augustinian lineage" ("The Mark of Autobiography" 10). Therefore, I wish to make my naming, my refreshment of the term "memoir," in the form of a "convenient approximation" (Lejeune 146), one that can help us think about the present moment in life writing. I do not wish to construct a "mythical independence" in which I hold fast to enduring characteristics (Lejeune 146), but rather to name provisionally so that we may more clearly identify the directions of the discourse we are in the process of making. My naming is meant to be an enabling gesture, as was Domna Stanton's naming of "autograph," or Doris Sommer's naming of "testimonio." I wish to name difference, while not making a prescription for sameness.

My decision to name "memoir" as a contemporary life-writing practice follows the lead of the books I take up, which are called "memoirs" in their titles or texts, or otherwise referred to as memoirs in the reviews and other critical literature that follow them. In highlighting this naming, I wish to call attention to a set of memoir practices within the larger field of autobiographical and biographical practices that we name "life writing." This field extends from what Marlene Kadar calls the "most fictive," such as the autobiographical novel, to the "least fictive," (10)[1] such as the bare-bones testimony to daily activity that we find in the reticent diaries of nineteenth-century farm women.

Since Bruss's challenge to us to inquire into our use of the word "autobiography," critics have been reluctant to do the naming I plan to do. The naming of genre has tended in the past to be an exclusionary process whereby men with power over language usage delineate what is and is not a part of the genre in question. This has often been an unacknowledged male-gendered act, one that unfortunately excludes the accounts of most women, whose practice is never quite the same as men's. As Leigh Gilmore remarked in *Autobiographics*: "The law of genre which defines much of traditional autobiography studies has been formulated in such a way as to exclude or make supplemental a discussion of gender" (21). This does not make generic study wrong-headed by definition; it merely means we need to nuance our tools of generic study to make them sensitive to materialist issues such as gender, class, and race. We need to make genre theory as it concerns life writing into a non-traditional practice, as many theorists of genre in other fields of literature are presently doing. In current theorization "genre" is understood as discursive practice, in which we take into account not only the rhetorical strategies and salient features of a particular writing practice, but also the functional aspects of that practice. That is, we consider the way in which a genre arises from particular social needs, such as shifting notions of gender and sexual orientation or the need to re-examine race and class assumptions, and becomes a cultural practice with the power to

---

[1] For a discussion of the broad range of documents that can be treated as "life writing" for critical purposes, see Kadar's introduction to *Essays in Life Writing: From Genre to Critical Practice*.

remake ideology.² It is my aim to use the generic term "memoir" in the spirit of this new understanding of socially located discursive practice.³

While only a handful of academics have paid any attention to the theorization of the discursive practice called "memoirs," the press has popularized the term to the extent that it has begun to displace "autobiography" to describe any narrative or essayistic life-writing practice (excluding biography). A recent full-page newspaper advertisement by a major book chain leads off with the headline-size words "Memoirs, Diaries" to catch the attention of a public that no longer automatically turns to the novel for recreational reading.⁴ A newsmagazine sums up the current popular interest in the form in an article by Emily Mitchell, playfully entitled "Thanks for the Memoirs," about the wide variety of people who write memoirs and the proliferation of "how to" books and Internet sites devoted to the craft.⁵ Such articles unselfconsciously use the word "memoir" whereas some years ago "autobiography" might have been the word of choice. The new popularity of the word "memoir" may well be a result of the difference in who writes such texts nowadays. One bookseller observed to me that autobiographies are written by famous people, while memoirs are written by the rest of us! Certainly, one does not see the word "autobiography" used as a descriptor anywhere near as often as a decade ago. For example, Jill Ker Conway's first anthology of women's life writing, *Written by Herself*, published in 1992, was subtitled *Autobiographies of American Women*, whereas her 1999 anthology *In Her Own Words* was subtitled *Women's Memoirs from Australia, New Zealand, Canada and the United States.*

Despite the welcome existence of anthologies such as Conway's and the veritable boom in the publication of memoirs by women, the genre has received little academic attention. The study of memoirs from a theoretical and critical perspective

---

2 For an example of contemporary work on genre theory, see Freedman and Medway's introduction to *Genre and the New Rhetoric*.
3 For an understanding of how "discourse" is socially located, see Paul Bové's "Discourse" in *Critical Terms for Literary Study*.
4 In *The Globe and Mail*, November 8, 1998.
5 In *Time*, April 12, 1999.

informed by scholarly research is now overdue. I find that memoir practice borrows freely from other generic practices, and many readers, unused to thinking of memoirs as different from other autobiographical practices, may need comparative touchstones. Therefore, I shall begin with a brief overview of the memoir form's connections with other life-writing practices and with related techniques in poetry, fiction, and drama as well as the essay form.

Memoir and Traditional Autobiography

In the Western tradition, autobiography as a genre begins with Rousseau's revision of the confessional form, a mainstay of Christianity since Augustine. He uses the motif of searching one's past for the various incidents of sin that have contributed to a personal crisis in the life of the soul—a crisis viewed from the retrospective position of the redeemed individual. This motif became central to the confessional practice of autobiographical writing for more than a millennium after Augustine. While Rousseau called his account *Confessions*, the title is ironic. Rousseau is right when he begins his book by saying that he has "resolved on an enterprise which has no imitator" (17) since he is the originator of "autobiography" rather than "confessions." He has had many imitators since. Rousseau's work is not a confession of sin for the purposes of subsuming his own desires and individuality into obedience to God. Rather, it is a detailing of rebellions against the prevailing ideology for which he feels no religious guilt; indeed, he insists on validating these rebellions as essential to the construction of his self as a secular being, capable of asserting his own will and way in the world. Rousseau marks the beginning of both the romantic ideal of the individual genius struggling for freedom from the constraints of traditional society, and the bourgeois ideal of the self-made man who makes his material way upward from rags to riches. In the life-writing tradition that precedes Rousseau there are religious figures such as Augustine writing confessions; following him there is a secular tradition that we have named autobiography and which includes figures as diverse as Wordsworth and Roland Barthes, Benjamin Franklin and Malcolm X.

Introduction: Memoir As a Life-Writing Discourse

The secular tradition has dominated the history and criticism of autobiography since Georg Misch began writing his history of the genre's practice in the 1950s. It has held sway from Georges Gusdorf, who tried to determine the cultural limits of the genre as a construct of Western individualism, through James Olney, who expanded the definition of what is called autobiography and placed the practice in an interdisciplinary cultural framework, to Paul Jay, who traced its development through male writers from Wordsworth to the present day. These male critics (and many others) consolidated a "founding" history of the genre. But since the 1980s a critical history that describes a female tradition has co-existed in the work of critics such as Estelle Jelinek, who summarized how women's practice is different from men's, and Mary Mason and Domna Stanton, who opened the debate on women's different subjectivity. A very intense period of theorization took place during the late 1980s and early 1990s and produced Sidonie Smith's historically and ideologically conscious work on the "poetics" of women's autobiography, Françoise Lionnet's critique of the narrow Western-based boundaries of the genre in her theory of "*métissage*," and Leigh Gilmore's theorization of an "autobiographics" of reading and writing autobiographical practices.[6] A parallel and related critical trajectory has been the consideration of women's diary literature. Beginning with Margo Culley's and Elizabeth Hampsten's ground-breaking work in the 1980s, the critical consideration of diaries has produced a plethora of articles culminating in a collection of essays edited by Suzanne Bunkers and Cynthia Huff. Indeed, the critical literature devoted to women's life writing over the last two decades is at least as rich as that devoted to men's life writing.

---

6 Gilmore's note on the publication history of theory and criticism on page 21 of *Autobiographics* is as good a summary as any of the publishing explosion of criticism on autobiography that has taken place since the 1970s. However, her overview misses some publications important to women's texts such as Liz Stanley's *The Autobiographical "I"* and Shirley Neuman's collection, *Autobiography and Questions of Gender*. Helpful publications have come out since her book, such as Jeanne Perreault's *Writing Selves* along with Smith and Watson's collections of essays, *De/Colonizing the Subject* and *Women, Autobiography, Theory: A Reader*. My own text, *Mapping Our Selves: Canadian Women's Autobiography*, is also part of this critical history that concentrates on women's texts.

However, what this critical history largely leaves out is any reference to "memoir" as an ongoing generic practice, a practice which, if examined theoretically and critically, can help locate and further explicate many of the markers that distinguish women's autobiographical production.[7] Since medieval times the memoir form has attracted women as much as, and perhaps more than, the confessional and its later offspring, secular autobiography. For example, Margery Kempe's fifteenth-century record of her search for the religious life, while imitating the confessional form in its preoccupation with the individual's soul, does not as easily fall into the Augustinian pattern of sinful past and redemptive incident, followed by a merging of the self with God's will. Indeed, Kempe is foiled again and again in her desire for a chaste life by the mundane fact that her husband insists on his earthly conjugal rights, blocking his wife's spiritual progress (to which chastity is assumed to be central) through the birth of fourteen children. Thus, to tell the story of a woman's progress toward God's grace, Kempe must resort to something other than the confessional form in which sin is thrown off in a climactic moment. Her progress is full of false starts, reversals, and renewals, and the episodic structure of her book reflects this. As well, because her story necessarily involves the obstacles put in her way by a highly gendered material world, her plot is more concerned with the detail of daily life in that world than is typical of the confessional style. Interestingly, a modern reissue of Kempe's story subtitles it *The Memoirs of a Medieval Woman*, indicating its concern not only with the trials of a soul, but also with the details of the material conditions of a life, a place, and and an era. Thus, two principal features of the contemporary memoir—its incremental, episodic structure and its preoccupation with the physicality of a materially located place in history and culture—are present as early as the fifteenth century.

---

7 Only two critics have published articles that have as their primary concern the generic location of memoir: Marcus Billson and Francis Russell Hart in the 1970s and 1980s, respectively. Although Lee Quinby takes up "memoirs" in her Foucaultian study of subjectivity in 1992, she is not especially concerned with the gender of her subject, Maxine Hong Kingston, but with how memoir aids the development of new subjectivities in general.

Another feature of the memoir highlighted by Kempe's account is its accessibility. This ordinary medieval woman, like most folk of her time, could not write. A priest had to act as amanuensis. The account would have been considered not literary product but Christian testimony that needed to be more widely available than in oral form. To this day critics have not generally considered the memoir as a specialized literary or historical form, tending to classify such texts according to their usefulness in terms of subject matter rather than genre location. Yet memoir's accessibility as a form that is associated with both literature and history is an important part of its ability to represent human subjects who are not normally represented by the central discursive forms of our culture. Since the Middle Ages, the memoir has been a staple of autobiographical expression in the English language for both men and women who may or may not have literary pretensions and who do not necessarily present themselves as professional historians. This proved to be the case for hundreds of non-literary writers. Travellers used the form for describing the changing scenes and peoples of their journeys. Merchants recording the details of business transactions also remarked on the personalities of their customers and told anecdotes about business practices in foreign places. Writers concerned with the genealogical value of the deeds of distinguished family members found the memoir form useful in glorifying their ancestors. The form became serviceable and accessible not only because of its use of plain-speaking, vernacular language, but also because of its preoccupation with the immediate scene, with the details of individual, local, and communal history. In addition, it accommodated itself well to an emphasis on a sense of the writer's self, not as a person free from dependence and community, but bound always by the necessity of community.

For women, this same material anchoring of the memoir form offered an alternative life-writing tradition to the one that emerged from the confessional and which critical history and the Rousseauian tradition of life writing has renamed "autobiography." Indeed, in the eighteenth century a phenomenon known as the "scandalous memoirs" marked English literature profoundly in helping to shape the novel form in its earliest stages.[8] But besides their influence on English literature in general, these memoirs can also be seen as the precursors of the contemporary memoirs of women. A series of accounts by women who had "fallen" by the standards of their day—who had become actresses, prostitutes, writers, or otherwise independent women—were published. These accounts play on the conventions of the "confessional" form, revealing past "sins" but in various ways undermining the "redemption." In place of the crisis and conversion to a better way, these women recount lives in which they defend themselves as more sinned against then sinning. Quite simply, no redemption was available to such women in the increasingly secular society of eighteenth-century England, where they were either the legal property of a father or husband or had no respectable place in the world. Unlike Rousseau, who found a series of havens, these women, living in an age when institutions such as the convent or the extended, rural, and land-based family were no longer available, found no safe spiritual or physical haven. They wrote to accuse the world of men and to defend their actions as having been forced upon them by public ideology and the narrow circumstances it offered women, in the hope that more benign powers would understand their plight and offer reintegration into the community. Such stories offer an alternative to those sanctioned by society, and in their continual reference to material circumstances they stand as witnesses to the details of actual lives. This building up of material evidence marks these texts as different from the typical confessional story, which is one of conflict, struggle, and resolution. In making this change, one occasioned by the actual conditions of their lives, these women move from confession to memoir.

Thus the memoir form, as practised by women, plays off the confessional form in that it has at its core a desire to reveal the hidden thing, the forbidden knowledge, the shameful and guilty secret, and to make what was formerly a private matter into

---

8 See Felicity Nussbaum's *The Autobiographical Subject: Gender and Ideology in Eighteenth-Century England.*

public knowledge. As well, it has secular interests similar to the Rousseauian revision of confession into "autobiography" in that it revises the place of the individual in the cosmos from that of a soul to a secular person. But instead of having the individual's self-realization, self-justification, and independence as its goals, women's memoirs generally strive for a reintegration of community and individual. This reintegration is neither Augustine's merging of self and God nor Rousseau's realization of the independent autonomous self. Rather, the memoir form in general, but women's accounts specifically, seeks a reintegration that leaves the self desiring both autonomy and relationship in continuing negotiation with its community.

Augustine's text begins with a very personal story, proceeds to a conversion scene, and then becomes a meditation, a hymn to God, at which point Augustine largely disappears from his own story. Rousseau's text traces the detailed development of the independent bourgeois subject from adventure to adventure. The memoir form, as practised by women, tends to be a more relational story from its beginnings, proceeding in a series of incremental scenes of realization that always involve relationships with significant others as well as efforts to achieve autonomy. Such memoirs often end not with resolution, but with a condition of continuing renegotiation with whatever material conditions and actual persons represent community for the memoirist. These are highly "relational selves" that are played out in these texts, because they spring from highly "relational lives." In his chapter "Relational Selves, Relational Lives," Paul John Eakin argues that "the criterion of relationality applies equally *if not identically* to male experience" (50). Eakin's italics are important as they allow for at least the possibility of difference between men's and women's lives. I agree with Eakin that men's lives certainly are relational, but in ways that men's autobiographies and the critical history have been unwilling to recognize. It would be exceedingly helpful to the criticism of life writing if Eakin's assertion began an investigation into how masculinity has been plagued by its refusal to acknowledge its relational underpinnings. Some contemporary men, as Eakin illustrates, are writing their stories with a new consciousness of their relational dependence, with a desire to avoid coming across as the autonomous, self-invented "Marlboro Man" (49). It is my assertion that feminist theories of relational identity as well as the practice of the memoir form by women in recent years have helped in the critical recognition of this change, just as the increasing presence of women and their texts in our culture has highlighted relational values. However, the fact that men are discovering relational selves is no reason for critics studying women's identity to assume that women's experience of their relational lives is the same as men's experience of the relational aspects of their lives. We need to insist on taking into account difference as well as similarity in our critical acts, since it is in the location of gendered difference that we can locate a difference in generic practice.

Women's memoir writing as it emerges into a life-writing practice today reminds us of both "confession" and "autobiography" (as they have been defined in our critical practice), yet it is surely a different life-writing practice because it asserts female-gendered life stories and female-gendered selfhoods. In my study of this phenomenon I will not be asserting these female-gendered selfhoods as essential and unchanging, as always necessarily different from men's. Nor will I assert that there will never come a time when men's and women's experience of the relational in their lives will be similarly important to their selves. One can only hope for such a great change in gender-based experience. What I do assert is that lives, and the stories those lives produce, are culturally mandated and historically contextualized at all times by the processes of gendering. A generic discourse such as memoir, one that is so directly a product of a life being lived in its "times," is inevitably a gendered performance of self.

Memoir, Memory, and Narrative Voice

In describing how the "reminiscence" kind of memory needed for writing memoir is different from "computer memory," Tristine Rainer says that "reminiscence is closer to the process of poetry...'emotion recollected in tranquillity'" (103). This likening of poetic process to memoir is connected to the latter's use of the first-person voice. The memoir's voice is somewhat akin to that of lyric poetry in its evocation of the intimate and the personal as well as its preoccupation with the facts and feelings of the past self brought to life in the present moment of the recollecting self. The "lyric" voice is not so common in contemporary poetry because it is viewed as being unfashionably solipsistic. However, the need for a self-referential voice satisfied by the "lyric" has not left our culture. It begins to re-emerge in the memoirs of women who find the same need as the earlier lyric poets. They too had to relocate their personal identity in terms of a world in which their old self-definitions had been swept away and new identities demanded a search through past and present realities. Key to understanding this narrative stance is in appreciating the words "emotion" and "tranquillity" as they relate to the Romantic movement's formulation of the voice of lyric poetry. Contemporary woman memoirists recollect "emotion" in the broadest sense of that word. They do not wish merely to recall past events, to write history whether personal or public. They wish to work through the varied felt realities—the sensations and resulting feelings and thoughts of the self as well as the viewpoints, opinions, actions, and reactions of significant others involved in an event. They wish to retrieve the emotions and thoughts of the past—fears and desires, angers and delights—in a therapeutic process that is much like the voice of lyric poetry, a voice that speaks neither from complete present involvement in the event nor from complete objective removal from the event. This is the voice of "tranquillity" that re-experiences the event, reprocesses it more fully than it could have been felt and understood in the first instance, and comes to an understanding of the event for the purpose of increasing the "tranquillity" of the memoirist's present self.

However, the "tranquillity" of the contemporary memoirist does not mean the kind of passive serenity that we imagine the Romantic poets sought; rather, it implies the composure, the peace of mind, the more complete understanding that comes from having done the hard work of remembering the past. Reminiscence or "recollecting in tranquillity" can be seen not as a passive, largely pleasurable activity, but as a subject position that comes as the result of a difficult, sometimes painful, sometimes pleasurable, but always intense working through of the past. This performance of recollection can make for a richer understanding of the present because of the more mature knowledge the process renders in the memoirist's reminiscence on the past.

Therefore, while the "poetic" voice needed for writing memoir may well seem to have a romantic quality that makes it hard to describe, the way it works is, in fact, very open to examination. The voice can be analyzed as tripartite in its function:

(1) that of the participant, the central protagonist in a story, the one who acts, is acted upon, who senses and feels and attempts to process the stimuli;
(2) that of the witness, who observes and records the actions of others from a particular and localized viewpoint in the past time of the action;
(3) that of the reflective/reflexive consciousness, which, working from a writing time distant from the events portrayed, supplies various contexts.[9]

These "contexts" are historical, sociological, psychological, political, literary, and cultural locations through which to rework the events in terms of the needs of the *present moment*, both the needs of the individual memoirist and the needs of the readership she addresses. But they are also "contexts" that are specific to the personal experience of the memoirist, selected intimate, familial, and personal contexts generally not taken into consideration by public histories.

If any one of the three functions of the narrative voice is neglected, the memoir's power is lessened. For example, if the recollecting process refuses the participant stance—perhaps the memoirist has not fully come to terms with her past participa-

---

[9] Marcus Billson, in 1979, first suggested the tripartite division of the narrator of memoir as "the eyewitness, the participant, and the *histor*" (271). However, I prefer the more general word "witness," since we witness with more than our eyes, and my concept of the "reflective/reflexive consciousness" more accurately describes the complexity of memoir's third narrative function than does "histor."

tion—and retreats too often to the safety of the witness, the memoir loses its impact, its immediacy, its sense of risk taking. It will seem less authentic (authenticity being not a essentialist value, but rather an effect of selection and shaping of detail). On the other hand, if the memoirist enters so fully into the emotions and actions of the experience of the past moment that the witness stance is neglected, the narration can become confusing and lose its sense of verisimilitude for the reader. The witness position is the one that supplies important information such as details of the setting, an account of other participants in the action, and the order of events. Most important, if the narrative voice has not carried out the process of "recollection in tranquillity" that is the work of the third aspect of the narrator, the reflective/reflexive consciousness, the memoir can fail in its goal of reaching the reader. The mere recitation of participant and witness recollections will be less than successful in reaching a present-day readership that has come to expect the active relationship with the reader that the reflective/reflexive voice offers.

The difference between the "reflective" and "reflexive" parts of the narrative voice is also vitally important. The "reflective" voice is, as Susan David Bernstein says in analyzing autocritical academic writing, "the product of a uncomplicated 'I' whose unveiling of 'experience' provides a shunt to a personal, which is also a political, truth." While I might not agree that the ability to be reflective is "uncomplicated" (since much can stand in the way of looking back on our lives), I do agree with Bernstein about the relative complexity of the "reflexive" voice. She sees it as "primarily a questioning mode, one that imposes self-vigilance on the process of subject positioning both in language and discourse and at a specific historical moment or a particular cultural space" (141). This "self-vigilance" with which a memoirist reassesses, reconsiders, and reconfigures her memories and subject positions while allowing for the possibility of more change in the future—at the same time allowing her reader to observe that process—is a very important aspect of the narrative voice. Without the reflective/reflexive consciousness, the memoir fails to do the work of identity making for its writer, and by implication for its reader, that is more and more a characteristic of contemporary memoirs by women. It is the attention to reflexivity and the resulting revisions of self and world that mark the contemporary memoir form as practiced by women as a life-writing practice, as a generic expression. As well, I find that the balancing of the three narrative functions is central to the *art* of the memoir; the memoirist who achieves this balance stands to produce a culturally and historically valuable document that is also an accomplished work of literature. Memoir is fast becoming one of the central discourses of the broad area of what the popular media calls "literary non-fiction," as well as a component discourse of what academics call life writing.[10]

Memoir and Research

In addition to offering a format for a literary working of language, the narrative voice of the memoir, especially in the operation of the reflective/reflexive consciousness, also engages in the work of "research" in the broadest sense of that word. Since the memoirist seeks a specificity of location in society, history, and culture, such research may involve the writer in tasks as diverse as interviewing other participants, reading other participants' testimonies, revisiting settings, and studying historical and literary accounts related to the events. "Research" is also involved in finding the right discursive mode for the memoir. This might be a language that is sociological, psychological, historical, or the figurative language of literary trope. It might be a combination of these as well as other more accessible modes of non-fiction such as journalism and reportage. Some of the activities of the memoir writer are similar to those of the scholar. However, while the memoirist may do traditional "research," she does not require the scholar's expertise or detailed specialization, but rather seeks the informing contexts that make the personal story a part of a larger cultural framework. The memoirist seeks to place her personal story in the context of its communal

---

10 In "To Fashion a Text," American writer Annie Dillard, who has written in several fictional genres as well as practising poetry, says that non-fiction is now becoming the site for the practice of "literary technique" (74).

location, and her research is limited by that need. The scholar may well feel a great personal involvement in her research; however, she need not be either witness or participant—that is the memoirist's responsibility. At the same time, memoir has become a format for academics, particularly female academics, who wish to use the skills of the researcher in a writing mode that can address their career motivations and goals in the contexts of their life experiences as professionals.

It is sometimes useful to compare memoir research to that of another life-writing form: biography. Memoirists, like biographers, are vitally concerned with the lives of others. In fact, memoirists in the late eighteenth century often used the words "memoir" and "biography" interchangeably.[11] Although the memoirist usually has the advantage of the biographer in terms of her intimate knowledge of the era and her subjects, many memoirists find that extensive research is still necessary to make their stories specific and effective.

Memoir, Dramatic Scenic Structure, and Self-Performance

To the degree that memoir writing can be defined as an active stance, a task involving research and attention to facts, the realities of others, and larger public events, the operation of memoir's narrative voice can be understood in its material construction as relating to discourses that claim referential truth to historical events. However, this does not change the fact that acts of the imagination are involved in constructing a memoir. This imaginative process can be described as "imagination" playing with the "experienced past."[12] But how does imagination play? Unlike history, with which memoir shares a factual basis, the writing of memoir is a literary enterprise and must use the devices of literature to represent itself. The use of these devices is the source of its imaginative play. Most critics compare autobiographical works to fictional genres, principally the

---

11 See my article, "Memoirs Discourse and William Godwin's Memoirs of the Author of *A Vindication of the Rights of Woman*."
12 Marcus Billson alerts us to the importance of the joining of "imagination" and "experienced past."

novel (although the episodic nature of many women's memoirs would indicate more affinity to the short story). I would like to point out the degree to which memoir is similar to, and makes use of the devices of, dramatic structure as well as those of prose narrative.

Evelyn Hinz has proposed that "aesthetic pleasure in [traditional] fiction depends upon a sense of the autonomy of the art object, whereas in drama and life writing what we delight in is a sense that the subject can never be pinned down, that what we are witnessing is a performance" (199). The sense that the memoir writer "performs" a self, one caught at a moment in time, a moment when the present self reflects—often through a scenic anecdote—upon some significant moment of the past self, has two important implications for contemporary memoirs. The first implication is that the writer desires authenticity and truthfulness in representation, but recognizes the conditional and temporal nature of representation of the self. The self that is represented is not guaranteed as factual in a strictly historical sense, because of the recognition "that the subject can never be fully pinned down," that in another performance it may shift and change, and indeed, in the episodes (acts) of the memoir itself, does shift and change. Nor is the represented self guaranteed as a fiction. Whatever fictional means may be used to perform the self, the memoirist seeks to ground that performance in her own lived life, typical modes of behaviour, personal preoccupations, embodied speech patterns and typical gestures as well as actual historical events.[13] Paul John Eakin asks us to think of the self "as less an entity and more as a kind of awareness in process" (x). Jeanne Perreault (building on Jane Flax's concept of a "core" self) would have us think of the "core" self not as a location but as an "energy" (17). I find that the term "performance," which implies both scripting and improvisation, as well as the possibilities of variations in incremental performances over time, also suggests these senses of the self as "awareness in process" and "energy," rather than self as a fixed entity. So when I use the words "self-

---

13 In chapter 3 I will take up Sidonie Smith's "Performativity, Autobiographical Practice, Resistance," which is helpful in thinking about how the self is "performed" in autobiographical practice.

hood" and "self" in my discussion I do not mean to imply that I believe in an essential self. Rather, I mean to imply that there is a kind of energy that may have certain recognizable features over time; however that energy, in performative contexts, constructs many and varied aspects of selfhood. Aware as I am of the special complexities of the acts of female gender making, I also recognize that the word "performance" suggests the nature of that gender making, in that various acts that build a female script of gender must be continuously performed to make that gender happen. I must confess to a personal fascination with concepts of self as performance, because I was constantly told as a child not to "make a spectacle" of myself. It seemed to me that the boys were always invited to make spectacles of themselves, acting out autonomy in ways forbidden to nice girls. Thus, I am very conscious of the subversive uses to which a concept of the self-performance of women might be put.

The second implication of the concept of performance for contemporary memoir is in the way "performative" language is understood by speech-act theorists.[14] Language can be understood as referential and descriptive in that it is used to denote real objects and describe actual circumstances. However, language can also be understood as "speech acts" in that the language causes the action it describes to happen, as a marriage ceremony or a legal judgment changes the status of the subjects involved through the performance of language. Indeed, drama, when it is located in the ritual practices of religion, is performative in this same sense. In many women's memoirs a desire to ritualize practices that perform the self is an important part of the memoir act.

Contemporary women memoirists are performing their selves as they write their texts; their performances are speech acts in a way similar to (yet different from) Freud's "talking cure": a therapeutic process that reshapes the self through language. Although the completed memoir with its selectively shaped text contrasts sharply with the activity of the therapeu-

---

14 In developing a theory of memoir as "speech act" I rely on critics such as Sandy Petrey and Mary Louise Pratt, but particularly useful is Victoria Myers's work on Maxine Hong Kingston.

tic session, the energy and desire for change and the reconstitution of the self and experience are common to both. It is also no accident that many who have suffered trauma—from Holocaust survivors to the victims of sexual abuse—have chosen the memoir form. The memoir form can imitate through self-performance the ways in which trauma victims process the fragmented or silenced memories, feelings, and events of a past that they were not able or permitted to process in language at the time. Nothing in public language and ideology can prepare one for the experience of sexual abuse or the concentration camp. The writer of a memoir of such an experience is "testifying to an absence" (Felman and Laub 57) in the sense that the actual events may be partly or fully suppressed. Even when they are clearly remembered, such experiences still do not have satisfactory linguistic expression, and one task of the writing process is to retrieve and recreate the experience. Until we have heard and recognized the individual stories of many sufferers, performed for us through the acts of memoir, we are not prepared as a culture to revise history and literature to include such experiences. Thus does memoir "perform" not in a trivial way, but in a serious linguistic act that involves the pain of recovering the past and the work of shaping a life in memoir so that these speech acts will reform and revise public ideology.

This idea of memoir as the site of trauma recovery may seem a long way from the lyric voice of "experience recollected in tranquillity," but the two concepts are closely related. In both cases, experience cannot be fully processed in its initial occurrence. For the trauma victim, making scenes from memory in the tranquillity of a safe place, remote in time from the original trauma, is essential to the performative process of reliving the pain to make a story. The intimate, personal, thoughtful voice of lyric poetry adapts well to the needs of the sufferers of major trauma. They require that their voice will be received by listeners who will not deny its truth value merely because its specificity is also a partial, limited, and inconclusive performance that cannot be cast in the language of objectivity.

William Zinsser says that "memoir assumes the life and ignores most of it. The writer of memoir takes us back to a corner of his or her life that was unusually vivid or intense—or that was framed by unique events. By narrowing the lens, the writer achieves a focus that isn't possible in [traditional] autobiography; memoir is a window into a life" (21). Memoir, unlike traditional autobiography, is often specifically occasional, concentrating on a small but significant period of time. The "narrowing of lens," the "focus" on the significant event, helps create the dramatic nature of memoir with its scenic quality, which de-emphasizes linear narratives that are necessary to telling a whole life. Its concentration on scenes of trauma, initiation, and radical changes in consciousness are performed through the writing, which makes real what the larger culture may not as yet recognize. Set in vivid, scenic recreations of lived experience, the memoir wishes to register as history formerly untold, but must use the devices of drama and fiction to create new realities. Fictional techniques such as constructed dialogue, metaphors, and other literary tropes, and vivid descriptions are the stock and trade of the memoirist. As Annie Dillard observes of writing creative non-fiction, "nonfiction prose can also carry meaning in its structures and, like poetry, can tolerate all sorts of figurative language, as well as alliteration and even rhyme. The range of rhythms in prose is larger and grander than it is in poetry, and it can handle discursive ideas and plain information as well as character and story. It can do everything" (74-75).

Memoir and the Personal Essay

While I do not claim that memoir can do "everything," I find it does have a tremendous reach in its ability to bring together diverse discourses, blending literary and historical narratives, psychological and sociological concepts, factual and imaginative language. A principal reason contemporary memoir can do this is that it enacts some important stylistic strategies of another very old (and also underrated) form, the personal essay. From Montaigne to Adrienne Rich, the personal essay that comments on the broad issues of human culture, that editorializes and advocates through the use of personal anecdotes, has been a part of Western culture. Certainly, for women, the central feminist mandate that the personal is the political makes the essay an ideal form, since it uses the matter of the personal life to construct arguments that have trajectories into the larger public world.

From its beginnings, the personal essay has been linked with the vernacular. Montaigne's choice to write in vernacular French rather than the Latin he knew better (and which would have given his ideas a greater authority for his contemporaries) indicates the ethic of democratization that the essay aspires to. The essay is not only an expression of ideas, but also has a broad connection to the reader's lived life which can elicit a resonance, a response, a dialogue that can lead to a change in the reader's view of the world. To do this, the essay must allow the reader to feel a measure of trust in and comfort with the writer, an identification of interests, a sense of direct person-to-person communication. This sense of personal contact is especially important to women writing memoirs since they are often attempting to bring to the reader a point of view that has not been previously sanctioned. The point of view, especially if it deals with the relational nature of life, will be more convincing if a sense of personal contact is established between reader and writer. To do this the essay form provides the memoirist with a most useful tool, the self-identification of the writer in the writing. This is what Elizabeth Mittman refers to as the essayist's "signature." She sees it as the "single most important convention that governs the essay," and notes that the reader of an essay will usually identify the "I" of an essay with the author. However, Mittman finds that the politics of the essay changes when the essayist requires that the "constructed nature of that signature be explored" (97). In the memoir, as in the essay in recent times, writers are examining the construction of their own narrative voice, often through the device of the pointed anecdote, which combines personal concerns with an illustrative scene that points to broader concerns. This is a process by which the memoirist questions and doubts the remembered past and the remembered self, investigates her own present motivations in relation to the past, presents contradictory voices, suggests alternative ways of thinking, admits her own shifting and even multiple viewpoints and self-assessments.

One of the results of this rhetoric of de-authorization is to accommodate a relational identity, in which more than one reality exists, even within the narrative "I" of the text who, as a female person, daily experiences identity as what Julia Watson calls "a connective tissue" (182).

Women's use of a "strategy of otherness" (Watson 182) has been observed from the beginnings of critiques on contemporary women's life writing. I find that the adoption of the personal essay's style of "signature" by memoir writers allows for the construction of a narrator whose intimate address to the reader performs a non-authoritative stance. Ironically, this non-authoritative narrator is often more convincing because it implies the multiplicity of a relational field, rather than the singleness of viewpoint that traditional narrative voices project. This offers the memoirist a rhetorical means by which "otherness" can be constructed, an "otherness" that is essential to contemporary women's practice of the memoir. These women's reasons for writing inevitably involve telling a story in which their identities are inextricably tied up in their relationships: they write as survivors who come to us to tell us of significant others who did not survive, but who allowed them to survive. They write to tell us of being mothers of daughters and daughters of mothers, and the complexity and importance of that primal relationship in our contemporary times. They write to tell us that even having an "I" that can write is the result of the thousand acts of the others who made them.

The practice of memoir that I have briefly described here is a complex blending of genres that borrows from the whole past of writing practice, while it seeks to write a different way of being in the world for the future. The flexibility of the memoir form is summed up by Jane Taylor McDonnell in her introduction to a book about how to write a memoir: "[O]ne of the major attractions of contemporary memoirs is that they not only 'show' and 'tell,' give scenes and summary, but they also reflect on the very process of telling itself. These books show an 'examined life' in a particular sense of the word. A flexible form of writing, memoir can combine the techniques of fiction with essay writing, the personal with the public dimensions of an experience, and the documentary account with poetic and evocative recreations of experience. A dramatic story can be told, but there is also room for reflection on memoir and the imagination and on the creation of a sense of self in the world" (14). I want to assert that part of the "dramatic story" that is happening when we read a memoir, part of the reflective act that the form encourages, part of the self-performance that is going on, is the reader's own story, her act of self-performance. As I observed in my preface, I have received communications from women who have read my memoir and who write to me of themselves in memoir-like letters and e-mails (and, on one memorable occasion, by telephone). The conflation of narrator and writer that the memoir-reading contract offers encourages this self-performance by readers. In my next chapter I would like to "perform" my own reading of a much-read woman's memoir.

2

Memoir with an Attitude

One Reader Reads *The Woman Warrior: Memoirs of a Girlhood among Ghosts*

Oh, that narrator girl....She is so coherent and intense always, throughout. There's an intensity of emotion that makes the book come together....I feel different when I write her at different ages. I like her viewpoint and her intensity so much.

—Maxine Hong Kingston, quoted in Thompson, "This Is the Story I Heard."

As I indicated in my preface, Maxine Hong Kingston is part of the tradition in which I write as a memoirist. I have read her memoir *The Woman Warrior: Memoirs of a Girlhood among Ghosts* many times and taught it often. Kingston's book could be considered the starting point for contemporary women's experimentation with the memoir form. Its influence has become pervasive in the study of contemporary women's writing, and it is the subject of numerous critical considerations. In reading through the two decades of literary and cultural analysis of *The Woman Warrior*, I am struck by the fact that every noun in its title and subtitle has been placed under intense critical examination except the word "memoirs."[1] When critics refer to the book's identification as memoir, they generally do so incidentally or parenthetically, or with the assumption that the memoir form is the same as autobiography.[2] My intention is to critically examine the book as an example of the discourse of memoir, discovering its usefulness as a women's writing genre. I will combine that examination with a theorization of my place as a feminist reader of the text in order to offer an autocritical reading practice that highlights how the active reader of memoir, the reader with "attitude," performs her own life and self as part of her reading acts.

I observed in my introduction that the current critical tendency is to put the issue of genre aside, because it so often ill serves a text. This is especially true of women's texts that work at defying generic homogeneity. Arguing for *The Woman Warrior* as "Postmodern Autobiography," Marilyn Yalom asserts that "any label affixed to Maxine Hong Kingston will invariably fail to encompass the multifaceted nature of her work" (108). By this argument any attempt at the generic location of *The Woman*

---

1 See Shirley Geok-lin Lim for an overview of the variety of critical approaches. The critical history ranges from aesthetic/feminist considerations (Suzanne Juhasz) to cultural/feminist explorations (Leslie W. Rabine). Studies of ethnic and racial considerations range from Deborah Woo's examination of "dual authenticity" to Frank Chin's treatment of Kingston as an inauthentic Chinese-American. The text seems to thrive in every critical context from socio-linguistic (April R. Komenaka) through ideological studies that efface identity politics in favour of economic politics (E. San Juan, Jr.), to speech-act theoretical inquiries (Victoria Myers).
2 One exception to this phenomenon is Timothy Dow Adams's consideration of A.O.J. Cockshut's distinction of the forms of memoir and autobiography.

Warrior should be as fluid as the kind of descriptive act offered by Shirley Geok-lin Lim: "[*Woman*] is a complex, highly inventive, historically embedded work. It is part biography, part autobiography, part history, part fantasy, part fiction, part myth and wholly multilayered, multivocal, and organic" (*Approaches* x). While I agree with Lim's description, I want to show how *The Woman Warrior* can be considered an example of the memoir form without limiting its "multilayered" effect. In fact, I find Lim's words to be a good description of what memoir does at its most experimental. By theorizing a generic position I do not wish to limit this text by Procrustean prescription, but rather to use Kingston's own naming of *The Woman Warrior* as "memoirs" as a guide to my reading. In doing so I need to consider how generic assumptions affect readership and how reading this text as memoirs empowers the reader to read her own life.

Kingston herself has sometimes sounded downright frustrated and annoyed at the way some reviewers and critics have cramped her book by their reliance on narrow approaches. In "Cultural Mis-readings by American Critics," she points out that in writing *The Woman Warrior* she was writing a "memoir" and does not feel she should be judged by narrow definitions of other generic contracts. She expresses exasperation with reviewers and critics who keep trying to fit her book into categories of history, sociology, anthropology, or mythology, and thereby fault her. Admonishing them, she says: "I do not slow down to give boring exposition, which is information that is available in encyclopedias" ("Cultural Mis-readings" 64). She is also annoyed at reviewers who try to read the book as a verification of their own stereotypes of inscrutable Orientals because they find her use of the memoir form inscrutable. Kingston briefly proposes how her book can be read more productively as memoir by quoting two reviewers who do attempt to locate it generically, one describing memoir as a form "which...can neither [be] dismiss[ed] as fiction nor quarrel[ed] with as fact," and the other describing it as a form that seeks "to illuminate the times rather than be autobiographical" (297-98).[3] These

---

[3] The two reviewers are (respectively) Diane Johnson writing in *The New York Review of Books* and Christine Cook writing in the *Hawaii Observer* (quoted in Kingston's "Cultural Mis-readings").

reviewers imply that the memoir is different from other forms, being a life-writing mode suitable for writers concerned with discourse on the boundary of fiction and fact—a discourse that neither separates itself completely from the use of the devices of fiction nor accepts being completely subsumed under the category of fiction. This mode is relevant for those concerned with the human subject in the context of her "times" rather than a construction of subjectivity that is a self-actualizing, discrete entity. Certainly, in terms of these considerations, Kingston has aptly chosen her subtitle, *Memoirs of a Girlhood among Ghosts*. In a text that consistently borders fiction and fact, using fantasy, speculation, and anecdote to interrogate traditional notions of historical and mythic truth, the insistently present narrator ties the text's discrete parts together by always reporting on what she knows from personal observation and experience. The narrator admits the particular and limited nature of her sources, while maintaining a biographical concentration on the other as the source of self-performance.

This relational performance of self also "others" the self in terms of her ethnic and gendered place in the America of her times. In fact, a single significant other that dominates the text is typical of many memoirs, and it is from the omnipresence of the mother as significant other that the biographical and memorial quality of Kingston's memoir derives its most spectacular feature. Kingston has observed that whenever she makes a public appearance people ask her about her mother, believing in the biographical reality of Brave Orchid, a fact Kingston affirms by relating her mother's reactions to her writing and career ("Personal Statement" 23). As well as merging the narrator and writer, the reader of memoirs is invited to believe in the extratextual existence of the significant other (even though that real-life person may not conform in all ways to the writer's characterization).

While women writers in our time often call their autobiographical accounts "memoirs," theorization of the memoir form is rare in current critical practice. The quotations that I use as epigrams for my chapters come largely from "how-to" books for writers of memoirs. Some are observations made parenthetically in book-length works that do not have the form of memoir as their subject, and others are from articles on memoir that are more descriptive than theoretical. However, two articles on memoir, written fifteen years apart, have helped me construct a reading practice. Marcus Billson's 1977 consideration of the memoir form calls it "the forgotten genre," its products despised by literary critics as "incomplete, superficial autobiographies" and by historians as "inaccurate, overly personal histories" (259). Certainly, Billson would seem to be right in calling the memoir the "forgotten" genre, since it received no new theorization until Lee Quinby's 1992 consideration of the form. Quinby explores it as a practice through which marginalized persons can refuse "the totalizing individuality of the modern era" and construct what she calls, in reference to Kingston's text, "an ideographic selfhood." This performance of self occurs through bringing together seemingly opposed discursive practices (e.g., myth, history, biography, fiction, autobiography) in a process whereby they clash with, inquire into, and blend into one another, in order to promote "new forms of subjectivity" (297–98).

Billson's essay is a traditional generic examination with echoes of an ideological positioning. His stand is that generic classification has marginalized memoirs (and by implication the beliefs and lives of those who practise the form). By contrast, Quinby's essay is an ideological positioning of memoirs as part of a discourse of self-making. However, since it makes reference to an actual book of memoirs to support its argument, it also echoes with generic implications. I am concerned with how generic choices influence the self that can be constructed in a text and how our assumptions about genre influence the way readers read that self. Both critics have ideas that are useful to my concerns. Billson asserts that to describe memoir we must first know "what memoir is *not* in relation to history and autobiography" (261, emphasis added). Quinby sees memoir writing as a way to achieve what Foucault suggests is "the target" of present-day discursive acts of subjectivity formation, which is "not to discover what we are but to refuse what we are" (297). Billson, in proposing the generic difference of memoir from history and autobiography, proposes the same difference in terms of the human subject as does Quinby. Memoir's ability to both use and negate current and expected practices (of genre and subjectivity, respectively) is common to both critics' analyses.

Billson, for his part, shows how memoir is unlike traditional autobiography in its emphasis on "being in the world rather than becoming in the world" (261). It is the memoirist's relationship to the events and people of her times rather than interior psychology that becomes the typical mode of constructing subjectivity. In terms of being "not" history, memoir "defamiliarizes the common [historically mandated] experience of the past, transforms it, and makes it new" (262). Billson holds that in the "best memoirs" the autobiographical act of constructing "the psychological life" may well go on, but it does so indirectly. The memoir is more directly working at "the synthesis of a confrontation between the experienced past and the imagination of the memorialist" (263). I would take Billson's point further, using Kingston's book as reference point. The ongoing "inner self" performance that occurs indirectly in memoir always has the potential—because of the memoirist's preoccupation with historicity—of "confrontation" with contemporary accepted versions of the self, whether the self is theorized as a subject of ideology or as an inner self. In *The Woman Warrior*, the narrator constantly "confronts" her own identity issues through the "experienced past" because of her preoccupation with the histories of women—figures such as the aunt who committed suicide, or the aunt driven insane by culture shock, or the speechless girl whom she abuses. Each challenges her with the need to rewrite the position of the female victim and thereby rewrite her own performance of self as it is located in gender, class, and race.

Billson points out that the very obsession with public history and its relation to the private life in the act of writing memoir (the way in which the "imagination" of the memoir writer plays with the "experienced past") is a principal characteristic of the form. It is in this regard that he notes the special tripartite role of the narrator in memoir as a combination of "three rhetorical stances—the eyewitness, the participant and the *histor*" (271), which I have reshaped as the witness, participant, and reflective/reflexive consciousness. I am concerned with the way in which memoir shapes this tripartite figure and how the memoirist, through this tripartite narrative function, constructs the figures of significant others as representations of actual people in her lived life. In this regard Kingston locates *The Woman Warrior*'s reality base in her actual family's history and testifies to the reality of the biographical subjects she constructs not only by naming the book "memoirs," but by giving news of her mother (and father) in her public appearances. She verifies the reality of Brave Orchid and her family history outside the text. Inside the text she uses each narrative function—witness, participant, reflective/reflexive consciousness—as a reality check on the other, reinforcing the reader's sense that these figures are drawn from the lived life of the writer. Each of the book's five sections contains narratives of the child/adolescent Maxine as witness to the events of family, history, and culture, as well as narratives of the child/adult Maxine as active participant in the historicity of the cultural moment. Each also contains the adult writer's comments on her life and her family members' lives in the history of American, Chinese, and Chinese-American cultures, all of which she experiences from her position as a female-gendered person. (The subtitle emphasizes the importance of gender by using the word "girlhood" rather than "childhood" in naming the early years of a female life.) We see Kingston conflating her childhood experience of her vivid mother—her witness of her mother's actions in the larger world—with her record of the histories (and family myths) of her mother's narrated past. In this way the reader receives the memoir's guarantee that although "truth" as an absolute standard cannot be attested, a truth, in the sense of a sincere personal testimony, can. This element of personal testimony makes the memoir an attractive form for those who wish to make themselves "real" in terms of a history and culture that denies or excludes their experience.

In this regard, Quinby's consideration of memoir emphasizes the form's advantages as a social practice that can perform new subjectivities. Quinby uses the memoir form's "confused" location at the intersection of other discursive practices as grounds for asserting its role in constructing a "new subjectivity [that] refuses the particular forms of selfhood, knowledge, and artistry that the systems of power of the modern era (including the discourses of autobiography) have made dominant" (298). Thus, memoir is a discursive practice situated on the borderline of genres, interfacing the discourses of history, autobiography, and prose fiction, negotiating uneasy, shifting human subjectivities.

Francis Russell Hart, in "History Talking to Itself: Public Personality in Recent Memoir," notes that "other autobiographical modes flourish at other times: confession abounds in times of soul-searching, apology in times of confrontation. But ours is a time of survival, and memoir is the autobiography of survival" (195). I would agree with Hart, but emphasize that to survive one must shape the self by allowing for "braiding", or what Francoise Lionnet calls a rhetorical and linquistic "*métissage*" of self. This braiding understands identity as a "strategy" of resistant subjects in which features of identity are brought together in combinations that are not traditionally recognized as those that constitute a human subject. Acts of survival involve neither a revolutionary break with the past nor a retrieval of the past self unchanged. Memoir's acts of survival are restoration, reformation, and reinvention. Through making the old alive in the new, we can perform acts of repossessing the self and the world.

I find that the memoir form as used by Kingston is able to assert that different reconstitution of human subjectivity by arousing the desire for, and refusing the fulfilment of, various generic expectations. For example, she offers us the story of her aunt who drowned herself in the family well in the visually dramatic language of a spectacle of violence and sexuality that we can view without risk. In doing so Kingston arouses the desire that is built into each of us in this society for the voyeuristic gaze that the genre of pornography brings upon the victim: the gaze of the perpetrator of violence, rather than that of the sufferer. But just at the moment we are drawn into that pornographic gaze, Kingston elides that genre's traps for women by co-opting the victim story into a personal essay on her own efforts to avoid being a victim. In this way the memoir arouses the generic expectations of another discourse (pornography), co-opts us into its narrative, obtains our complicity, and then refuses easy satisfaction. By moving on to other discourses, such as the personal essay, in which we are asked to identify with Kingston's "narrator girl" and through her the aunt/victim, we learn not to depend on the stereotypical subject that the exploitive discourse offered. What remains, in this shifting discursive medley, to focus our desire is the human subject negotiating the discourses of culture and history. After several such shifts we can see that repossessing her past through various rhetorical strategies allows Kingston to more fully authorize her own self-performance in "the times" of the text's present.

That self-performance is not only the playing out of the narrator's identity; because of the special way in which I am aroused (but not satisfied), the performer of memoir is also me, as reader. Because I do not receive the expected script, I must become active in making the performance of self. The memoir narrator, through the three functions of witness, participant, and reflective/reflexive consciousness, is full of reassessments, rejoinders, doubts, and reassertions. I therefore cannot reside in the predictable place of identity that a traditional generic contract offers where there is the sure sense that the narrator is in control and I will be led along. Neither am I invited into the nonpersonal place of irony, the reading position that satire offers me, where I am invited to stand apart, filing my nails in godlike objectivity. Nor am I offered the contract of traditional autobiography by which I read primarily for the self-development of the author, because in this memoir the history of others is always highlighted along with the history of the narrator. Finally, I am not offered a contract as a reader of history, because these "histories" are the taboo stories of subjects absent from traditional historical narrative. Instead, I am drawn into the narrator's world with all the power that these discourses evoke, but once inside I have a very different reading experience: I live, through the work of the tripartite narrator, the intense experience of my own life as material for a similar revision.

Francis Russell Hart comments on our late-twentieth-century "identity crisis" and the conflict of our desire for "going public" and "choosing a collective identity to which we can 'belong'" with our contrary desire for individual identity caused by the "self-alienation which 'belonging' engenders" (209). Hart brings that dilemma home by writing autobiographically at the end of his essay of his chagrin when asked at hotel desks what organization he represents: "I hadn't known I was expected to be representative, yet how else can I identify myself publicly in the intimate society?" Hart's solution to the public/private split that contemporary memoirs wrestle with is to "retreat to the 'privacy' of my anonymous, indistinguishable room where, unable to 'opt for us,' I relax with the public intimacies of television and occasionally talk to myself" (210). Hart's instinct to break the impersonal discourse of his academic article and to perform the irony of our contemporary problem autobiographically is in keeping with the memoir form he describes: he, as critic, like the memoirists he discusses, must bring together more than one discursive form to represent himself. Such critics find they need both literary criticism and a more intimate reference. I also find I need more than one discursive form, and it is this autocritical representation that I am working toward.[4]

Like Kingston, I find myself caught between systems of thought, modes of subjectivity, opposing histories. This subject position leaves me seeking modes of linguistic performance that can generate new meanings concerning self, race, class, gender, literature, and history. A reader like myself has a particular problem with closure in more traditional forms. Leslie Rabine observes that because of women's place in many origin myths, in which they rarely figure as the quester, there is no "lost paradise" to be regained by such writers, no endings that are a completion of quests for return. We should therefore expect the plots of such women subjects to be different. In their memoirs, in which every ending of an incident involves an uneasy settlement between more than one life story, there can be no easy endings. In *The Woman Warrior* the aunt's story comes out of the mother's story, then goes into the teenage girl's search for "ancestral help," and leads back into the mother's story. Each discursive solution, be it that offered by history, literary plot, or mythic symbolization, is inevitably com-

---

[4] See H. Aram Veeser's Introduction in *Confessions of the Critics* for comments on "autocritography."

plicated by the presence of other histories, other lives, so that the memoir does not end, it stops. Kingston's memoir stops, not with a solution or answer to an identity quest, but with a song that "translated well" (209), offering the narrator not a stable identity, but a contingent self, provisionally performed in the (perhaps temporary) usefulness of a particular discursive activity.

Especially useful to a provisional and contingent subjectivity unable to buy into traditional constructions of the self is the way memoir always memorializes the other. The narrator finds her own self-performance through the exploration of the biography of significant others who occupy the text as fully as she does. In fact, memoir can be a kind of intensification of narrative voice by which a narrator, who is intrusive by other generic standards, empowers herself through forbidden namings that violate the taboos that keep public discourse and private life separate. She appropriates histories in retellings into which she writes her self, and she asserts her fragile existence through interweaving herself with the other, as Kingston's "narrator girl" does in writing the lives of the immigrant Chinese family in such intimate and personal detail.

These are rude gestures that publicly flaunt taboo subjects, shamelessly borrow others' histories, and recklessly risk betraying the people one loves most by telling their stories in ways that may be offensive. And certainly women like Maxine Hong Kingston, who dare to make such stories, have been chastised for breaking the rules of women's place in their various patriarchal communities. This is exactly what happens to Kingston by way of Frank Chin's critique. He finds Kingston to be part of "the Christian autobiographical tradition" (thus using generic misreading to mount his attack) and accuses her of "faking" a Chinese identity to please the masters.[5] Readers find it hard to be neutral about narrators of memoirs. Indeed, the examination of the relationship of the reader

---

5 Ironically, the "authentic" Chinese-American identity Chin constructs—a combative, individualistic, heroic and male model—shows a derivative nostalgia for the old (white) American West and speaks to his own writing to please the masters. His motto reads: "You write alone, kid. That's the lesson. Code of the West: Writing is fighting. Life is war. If you're a soldier you have to know everything—and trust nothing" (129). Such a patriarchal credo would necessarily assign women (and women writers) to a highly limited place. Indeed, women are for Chin comparable to consumables such as food. He says to white men: "I eat your food. Love your women. And vice versa" (118).

to the narrator is central to an understanding of how memoir works, of how the "attitude" of my chapter title can be understood as something happening between reader and narrator.

Critics have noted the special opportunities and difficulties that exist for readers of *The Woman Warrior*. Students expecting the traditional narrator of fiction find that the doubts and uncertainties, the assertions and confusions of the narrative voice are a challenge to their reading.[6] David Leiwei Li has noted that producing meaning in this text of "multiple narration also encourages the reader to participate in the narrative acts creating a talk-story community in which both the speaker and listener are involved in a powerful creation of themselves" (329). The very fact that the book is identified as "memoirs," rather than as a novel or a collection of interrelated short stories, leads to a special "illocutionary" dimension that affects reading. Victoria Myers points out that we need to recognize that language has "illocutionary" power in that "communicative acts take place in a context whose conditions determine the interpretation and effect of the act. This includes the kind (or by extension, the genre) of the utterance, as well as physical, psychological, and cultural facts of which the listener must be aware" ("Speech Act Theory" 132). Myers notes that the "explicit label" of the text matters to interpretation, therefore, whether that utterance consists of a novel or an autobiography is germane to interpretation. However, she does not explore what different "illocutionary" power might adhere if the reader understands the memoir discourse as different from either traditional autobiographical or novelistic discourse.

It is my goal to find the appropriate attitude to bring to the reading of memoir, and to discover what difference that change in attitude makes. This is especially important in reading the memoirs of a writer like Kingston, who is so different from me. The figure Kingston calls her "narrator girl," a very "intense" rhetorical construction, reaches out in a very appealing way to my own intensity. I must be careful to find the source of my

---

6 See, for example, the student responses in Vicente F. Gotera's "'I've Never Read Anything Like It.'"

intensely felt identification in order not to appropriate her voice, her experience (ethnically, racially, and nationally so very different from my own), by an easy homogenization of her and me. Sau-ling C. Wong has pointed out the fondness that "white women with feminist sympathies" have for "mother/daughter stories by women of color such as Maxine Hong Kingston's *The Woman Warrior*....Based on a presumption of a sisterhood of equals, this appropriative reception is oblivious to the inverse relationship between political power and cultural visibility" (82). I do not assume an unmediated "sisterhood" relationship to Kingston, nor do I wish to read with a "white reader's penchant for deriving inspiration and little else from the struggles of the marginalized" (Wong 82). Kingston's book is a powerful political statement about cultural and racial marginalization and its effects. It is also a powerful statement about gender, particularly in its exploration of "girlhood." In that regard I think it is possible (while recognizing the cultural and racial contexts of the text as different from my own) for a white female critic to find areas of represented experience that speak to commonalties of gender experience. These are commonalties of women growing up in the same era, the same public mass culture, no matter what their ethnic and racial differences. Thus the word "attitude" in my title refers not only to the ongoing performance the writer makes of the narrating consciousness of the text, the "intense" tripartite "narrator girl," but also to my ongoing gendered construction of myself in relation to that figure. It is through recognition of my ongoing construction of my self in relation to Kingston's text that I hope to avoid appropriation of voice. Our stories remain separate although they travel side by side.

It is vital in theorizing this active response to avoid positing a kind of essentialist self, one who guarantees her critique on the basis of authenticity. Elspeth Probyn's study *Sexing the Self: Gendered Positions in Cultural Studies* is helpful in this regard. She uses Foucault's theories of the technologies of self to view the self as the result of experience *bent* on itself, in a kind of pleating of experience that constructs the sense of interior and exterior, as the hidden and visible surfaces of the self. If the self is the result of such a folding over and layering of experience, then the performance of the self can be accomplished by a use of personal anecdotes, illustrative incidents, parables (etc.), which inquire into the folding, expose the pressure lines of folds, and expose for inquiry what was hidden by the folding. A positioning of settings and actions of the personal life of the critic (the so-called interior life) can be put into play and exteriorized, much as *mise en scène* (the placement of objects and actors on the stage) operates allegorically in relation to action in drama. This exposure will show that what is perceived as interior is not different from the exterior. It is merely what the pleating of experience has hidden. In such an operation the "experience" of the critic cannot be understood simply as factual truth. Our experience is, like our selves, always in process, always being perceived from different, changing perspectives. Joan W. Scott, in "Experience," says that we need to "historicize" our experience by seeking the conditions under which we perceive our experience, understanding that our narrations are "discursive productions of knowledge of the self, not reflections of either external or internal truth" (67). This carefully acknowledged constructed self, showing the joined nature of "interior" and "exterior," and letting go of the notion that our "interior" selves are mysterious, deeper and truer and more authoritative and authentic, allows the critic to avoid the two major pitfalls of autocritical work. One of these is the drive for authenticity by which the experience of the critic takes on the authority of a romantic subjectivity whose deeply felt emotional response to data is its own guarantee (as in Rousseau's *Confessions*). The other is the position of epiphany by which the intuitively felt aesthetic unity derived from the experiential data constructs its own authority (as in Joyce's *Portrait of the Artist as a Young Man*). As Probyn states: "Instead of representing a 'truth,' or a 'unity' or a 'belongingness,' a critical use of the self may come to emphasize the 'historical conditions' involved in its speaking" (28).

The "gendered position" I am describing as appropriate for readers of memoirs begins to sound very much like my description of the position of the narrator in memoirs. The reader needs to be not only a witness to the text, but also a participant in its construction. She brings, as a reflective/reflexive consciousness, different contexts from her own life experience to the reading. Reflexivity is particularly important in this autocritical act since it registers, as Susan David Bernstein puts it, not only a "critique of power" but also "complicity with the institutions that structure representation" (140). Part of the "vigilance" that both Bernstein and Probyn recommend for autocritical writers is the investigation of our own formation in ideology and our representation of that formation in language. I must take risks that are similar to (if not as extensive as) the memoir writer's risks. I must adopt, through my self-construction in the critical text, what Probyn calls (building on Foucault once more) "limit-attitude." Probyn asserts that in constructing an anecdotal reference to the critic's own position in the critical text, a reference that performs the critic's "attitude," the critic is constructing a "limit-attitude [that] stipulates that we work at the frontiers of ourselves" (140).

This working at the frontier of my self involves performing the self on a "terrain [that] holds both myself and herself" (Probyn 140), this "her" being the textual self of the other under consideration. It is this act that could lead to an accusation of appropriation of voice. How do I, as Probyn proposes, speak in "compatible registers," but maintain a "profound recognition of the deep structure of difference" (140)? It is this risky critical act, one that recognizes the "deep structure of difference" between myself and my subjects and yet finds "compatible registers," that I wish to engage in, at strategic moments, for the rest of this book. I begin here by specifying which of my life experiences became important to me while reading *The Woman Warrior*. This involves several risks; it risks "transgressing [academic] sensibilities," committing "epistemic violence" to my subject, and "mak[ing] a fool of myself" (Probyn 145). But in taking these risks I may be able to offer readers a guide to how the act of reading memoir with an "attitude" can be different from the reading acts suitable to other genres. While doing so I must, as Probyn advises, maintain "enormous political commitment as well as a ferocious vigilance" (148) against appropriating the experience of the other. I find that reading *The Woman Warrior* with Probyn's theory of "limit-attitude" in mind has made me think more carefully about the different class, race, and gender realities of another woman. This kind of reading makes me more aware of the need to, as bell hooks puts it, "enter realms of the unknown with no will to colonize" (58).

In examining my own life in an attempt to find the source of my unanalyzed intensity of "attitude" as a reader of this text I discover that I have been made more aware, by the study of memoirs, of my life in the perspective of history. I notice that Kingston states that she was born "in the middle of World War II" (96). As I was writing my own memoirs of childhood as a war baby while rereading *The Woman Warrior*, I became aware of the particular psychic histories carried around by little girls born in the years immediately preceding the baby boom. Although we share many of our historical circumstances with little boys of our cohort, female gendering inflects identity differently than male gendering. Female gender adds a special awareness of the contradictory nature of our historical moment, as females find that what is supposed to be the focus of the moment sometimes has nothing to do with the facts of their lives.[7] Working at the edge of my own knowledge of myself and at the edge of the personal information given me by Kingston allows me to find my different and self-referential reading of *Woman*.

The embeddedness of Kingston's birth and mine in that historical moment of "the middle of World War II" allows me to interpret some of the constructions of females in the text—No Name Woman, Brave Orchid, Moon Orchid—as tactics for self-performance through the representation of victimized self-surrogates. For women of my and Kingston's cohort, these figures are one generation older than we are and their victimization is greater than that typical of women of Kingston's and my age group. Although class and race intensify or alleviate the positions of individual victim, these women's relatively greater oppression in relation to our own offers us clues to the more subtle nature of our own oppression. I recognize a similar desire

---

7 I use "cohort" in the sense that social scientists do, to describe the four- or five-year time span, much smaller than a generation, that represents persons born in the same historical context and subject to similar ideological factors, which can often traverse class, race, and gender divisions.

in Kingston and in myself to reconstruct these women's lives in order to explore the contradictory messages we received from them regarding the female condition in the years before, during, and immediately following World War II. This assertion of commonalty, rather than appropriativeness, leads me away from the tendency to locate racial and cultural difference in the exoticism Kingston complains of in "Cultural Mis-readings." Indeed, because of our cohort similarity, I can use her different experience not to colonize her story, but rather to help me to de-colonize my own past so that I can find the victimized women in my own historical, cultural, and personal story. These women in my own history were not the victims of racial prejudice, but they were certainly victimized because of their gender and sometimes their class.

An exploration of the first section of *The Woman Warrior*, "No Name Woman," while keeping in mind Kingston's and my common birth moment, will illustrate my autocritical reading. The mother's words with which the narrator begins her story— "You must not tell anyone" (3)—point to a significant detail of entrance into womanhood we both share. The onset of menstruation in my culture was not accompanied by spectacular cautionary tales of aunts who drowned themselves in wells, but rather with a conspiracy of silence that forced girls of my cultural place to piece together knowledge from highly suspect sources. We did this in the often unspoken, but well-apprehended, condition of not being allowed to tell anyone. The era in which we were born and raised did not allow us to speak and write openly of female physical life. We were not entirely certain what menstruation had to do with sexuality, birthing, or the ebb and flow of the hormones we felt, but could not perform as part of our selves. In such a conspiracy of silence the onset of physical womanhood was discursively contained to act as the experience of disempowerment. When I read Kingston's breaking of taboo by writing the story of her aunt, I am empowered to break all sorts of taboos that are part and parcel of my own upbringing, particularly the taboos on discourse concerning the female body. I understand these taboos differently through Kingston's text. My childhood ignorance of bodily functions becomes connected to the suppression of the ability to speak of them in the way in which other health issues are spoken of. I also see that this has something to do with the disenfranchisement of voice that I have felt at the level of public culture. Kingston's mother's menstruation story as reworked by her daughter becomes a series of tactics for obtaining a voice through imagining her possibilities of self-performance. And my reading of it becomes a series of tactics for realizing my own past differently.

For this set of tactics to work, Kingston cannot write a female *Bildungsroman* for her aunt, writing her through fictions out of her disempowerment. If there are no "lost paradises" in female experience, there are no paradises to be regained. Given the impossibility of the generic forms centred on the restoration of an original or true self, female subjects such as myself and Kingston are drawn toward memoirs. Kingston needs the memoir form so that she can recall in historical detail that her aunt lived and died in a society where personal freedom for anybody, least of all a woman, threatened survival. Kingston would like to write in a generic form that would romanticize her aunt into sexual freedom, but history, her own and her aunt's histories, forbids that: "Imagining her free with sex doesn't fit....I don't know any women like that, or men either. Unless I see her life branching into mine, she gives me no ancestral help" (8).

The help she needs from her aunt's story is the sense that there is some way to gain power from the female condition. Neither Kingston nor I as girl children growing up in conservative family-oriented cultures in the 1940s can pretend to the narrative of sexual liberation. Whereas the generation following us may have been able to find a public culture beginning to figure their private desires, no such subject position could be performed in the historical moment when Kingston heard her cautionary tale and I heard silence. Nor can we pretend to the ghettoized solidarity of former generations of women living in more homogeneous societies, who would have shared a private discourse of female life, one which partly compensated for the lack of public discourse. Both Kingston and I were born in the moment of rupture when mass culture, the one Kingston met in what she calls "American" school, encouraged girls to not look to their mothers' lives for authority in their own lives. Those very mothers told tales of their own momentary empowerments, while showing through the examples of their lives that they had been disempowered. As well, the late forties and the fifties represent a time before any other female role models were readily available to compensate for this limitation. The particulars of the rupture are different for each woman in our cohort. For Kingston it lay in the wrenching nature of reality as a Chinese-American woman, caught between a mother who wants to assure her daughter of the security of the old ways and the reality of the mother's own experience as one outside the old ways. As well, the two worlds of the daughter's existence, Chinese and American, offer radically different ideologies of the feminine. Maxine must find meaning in this world of double messages if she is to survive.

In my own life the double message is less spectacular, but equally real, and Kingston's memoir makes me realize it and perform it in my own writing. For middle-class girls of my place and time our rupture was highlighted by the fact that we had mothers who were of the first generation of women to be legally enfranchised. At the same time we were aware that these mothers, at least those of the middle classes, were profoundly dissatisfied. This dissatisfaction we now know was a result of being allowed an education and voting rights, but encouraged to do nothing with such benefits. These women often actively encouraged their daughters to identify with their fathers, who did seem to have full enfranchisement, while at the same time requiring that their daughters fulfil the agendas of what Kingston calls "American-feminine" (11). For me this meant performing the middle-class feminine behaviours my parents—who were upwardly mobile, but formerly rural, working-class people— thought would free me. I experienced working-class women, including my grandmother and mother, as noisily and embarrassingly garrulous, much as Kingston experienced the "villager" women of her own world. Little girls like myself, daughters of parents ambitious for middle-class status, were given elocution lessons at school to help us speak a more British-accented English. We were supposed to learn to speak in tones that could not be mistaken for the assertive, challenging voices of the fathers we so adored. Nor should they be mistaken for the loud voices with which our female relatives asserted power in the home, the same voices that revealed these women as lower class in the public world. Women such as Kingston and myself need to gain "ancestral help" from the construction of some female person as a possible rebel, and thus Kingston constructs her aunt, making her drowning a revenge suicide, imagining the possibility of private choice despite the consequences. Kingston's example encourages me, as a member of her age cohort, to break the taboos on using the public discourse to repossess my history in order to inquire into the personal and private world through the memoir act of reconstructing a female ancestor. Locating the common historicity of our lives, through the recognition offered by the historicity of the memoir form, allows this gendered, empathetic reading. In making this empathetic reading I realize, as Probyn says, that "I cannot be empathetic in a purely altruistic way. My self is selfishly involved, I have an investment in the concerns of others" (149). In having that investment, I work with our similarities, while acknowledging our differences.

However, to take up the act of literary criticism that breaks the autobiographical silence that traditional academic discourse requires I must understand how "memoir with an attitude" is constructed by Kingston. She has the ability to use certain aspects of memoir towards new performances of female subjectivity in such a way that I am able to read and write my own past differently. I must also recognize that these performances begin at the level of style and rhetoric. The construction of No Name Woman's rebellious story is made possible through a series of persuasive stylistic rebellions by the writer working at the "frontiers" of her own knowledge of herself and her culture. This story can than be read with a similar "attitude" by a reader ready to risk reading intimately through the thoughtful examination of her own cultural construction.

While the story of No Name Woman begins in the mother's voice as a cautionary tale, it signals the first generic disobedience that "memoir with an attitude" allows. By deliberately breaking a primary rule of prevalent linguistic practices that separates the private world of oral storytelling from the public world of the written account, Kingston begins her disobedience. She also breaks the rule that insists upon a linear plot line of written narrative by telling the ending first. In this way the horror of the aunt's death is not saved for the ending where it would operate as a powerful cautionary closure. The memoir form, because of the permission it gives the narrator to defamiliarize the past, allows for this. In her narrative roles as witness, participant, and reflective/reflexive consciousness, the writer disobeys the rules of the cautionary tale, making of the past something different from what the tale would allow. Kingston breaks her bond as passive witness to her mother's telling of the cautionary tale and acts as a participant, who tells how the tale operated in her own life to confuse rather than teach. Also, in her role as reflective/reflexive consciousness she is able to generalize the condition to her wider culture: "Chinese-Americans, when you try to understand what things in you are Chinese, how do you separate what is peculiar to childhood, to poverty, insanities, one family, your mother who marked your growing with stories, from what is Chinese? What is Chinese tradition and what is the movies?" (5–6). At such rhetorical and editorializing moments of the reflective/reflexive narrator, the reader with attitude can enter the text without possessing it in a colonizing gesture. I do this by asking questions of my own past. What part of me results from being raised in the insular, very class-conscious society of colonial Newfoundland? What is a result of the upward class mobility that arrived just a few years earlier (and perhaps more fully because of our eurocentric heritage) for working-class people in my part of the world than for the Chinese-Americans of California? How can I separate the neurotic features peculiar to the family I lived in as a child from the greater insanities of war that dislocated my family and culture? How can I work with the stories that informed my childhood to locate a cultural inheritance formerly undervalued by those who owned it and those who sought to destroy it in me? How can I find a supportive tradition useful in an academic world that often tells me that a tradition only shackles? These are the kinds of questions that reading Kingston's memoir with "attitude" evokes in me. They are questions that not only made my reading more active, but also helped engender my own memoir writing.

Working at the edge of the forbidden, at the edge of her known self, using her intense "narrator girl," Kingston disobeys the rules of history to imagine a life for her aunt. Although in doing so she uses the devices of fiction, she does not make a text that is fiction in the generic sense, because at each moment of generic disobedience she warns me of her deliberate transgressions. Rhetorical qualifiers (which I have set in italics, below) flash like red lights telling me to enter without expecting history or fiction, but to expect a discourse that lives on the edge of both to create a new memoir reality. "*Perhaps* she had encountered him in the fields" (6) Kingston guesses, trying to deepen the cautionary tale into support for her own self-construction. "It *could very well have* been" (8), she imagines, seeking an empowered aunt. "She *may have* been unusually loved" (10), she proposes, seeking the parental approval of girl children despite the societal prescription that girls are "maggots." "He *may have* been somebody in her own household" (11), she suggests, as she breaks the taboo on discussing incest. And at each moment of imagination she weaves the reality of her own life with that of the immigrants' lives. She reports the fears, the cautions, the requirements that the older generation makes of the younger, combining them with the possibilities she is imagining and the material conditions of the aunt's history and her own life. These imaginings allow her to reflect on her own life: "I used to add 'brother' silently to boys' names. It hexed the boys, who would or would not ask me to dance, and made them less scary and as familiar and deserving of benevolence as girls." In the sudden flashes of humour that occasionally lighten the dark seriousness of this text, she reveals the double bind of every precautionary action in female life: "But, of course, I hexed myself also—no dates. I should have stood up, both arms waving, and shouted out across libraries, 'Hey, you! Love me back.' I had no idea how to make attraction selective, how to control its direction and magnitude" (12).

In breaking into the construction of her aunt's story in her role as participant and reflective/reflexive consciousness, as well as witness to the times she grew up in, her intense tripartite narrative act is able to call up in this reader with attitude the dilemmas of my own girlhood. In my world, sexual assertiveness and sexual arousal made you a bad girl and threatened your future. Arousing desires that you would not, could not satisfy condemned you to the category of tease. Refusing sexuality and treating all boys as brothers guaranteed your status as an old maid.

By the time Kingston has constructed her aunt as a vengeful suicide, this reader with attitude is ready to perform her own memoir acts through the stories that follow. Witnessing the construction of the aunt as rebel—she strikes out at her oppressors in the only way she can, literally poisoning their lives by poisoning their well with her victimized body—encourages me to shape the rebels of my own past. In my case I seek the aunt that disregarded her own health, lied to family and doctors in the name of gaining personal freedom (and probably hastened her own death as a result). I ponder the aunt who went off to war in a time when youngest daughters were supposed to stay at home, and who was censured by her own mother when the adventure turned frightening. I recall as well the aunt who worked in the world rather than accept her place as wife, gaining economic advantage, but incurring a societal disapproval that expressed itself even at the heart of her family. The realization, intensified in me by reading No Name Woman's fate, that such rebel aunts are always punished in spectacular or subtle ways, helps me understand my own aunts' lives while preparing me as reader for the chapters that follow "No Name Woman." These explore the various possibilities and traps waiting for women by using the generic forms of myth, legend, realistic narrative, and history.

In each titled section of *The Woman Warrior* particular generic forms are used in non-traditional ways to construct the possibility of a female tradition that will help free female identity construction from past oppressions. At the same time the writer uses her own life as participant, her testimony as witness, and her powerful observations as reflective/reflexive consciousness to reveal how difficult this positive gesture is, given the way plots appropriate female life into the patriarchy. For example, in "White Tigers," the attention to detail in the mythic rewriting of the male martial arts tradition is for the purpose of showing female strength. Yet it also refuses the plot trap of glamorizing violence as a solution to female victimization. This is done through the narrator's eyewitness of the actual history of violence in her own world. She speaks of the fights in junior high school that were "confusing as to who has won." She witnesses the "slum grubby" world where "corpses I've seen had been rolled and dumped, sad little dirty bodies covered with a police khaki blanket" (51). The device of using personal history to inquire into mythic construction encourages me as reader to question the myths of romanticized violence in my own life experience. I inquire into the assumption of my childhood culture that all adult males in the familial/neighbourhood context were benign, non-sexual "daddies," when indeed they were not. I question the way my culture sanitized or censored public violence, from the stories of war to the sexual abuse of children.

In the worldwide popular culture in which both Kingston and I were raised, through school and the media, the most misrepresented figure has always been that of the mother. In "Shaman" and "At the Western Palace," Kingston takes on her most difficult task, the encounter with the figure of her mother in all her negative and positive possibilities. This is the most dangerous territory for women memoir writers (as I will discuss more fully in chapter 4), since the mother (or her surrogate), while being the primary source of the female child's subjectivity, is also (in patriarchy) the policing agent of her daughter's training as a patriarchal woman. Colleen Kennedy locates what she considers to be the betrayal implicit in this double bind in the very discourse of traditional narrative that Kingston must enter to tell her mother's story:

> Her mastery of any public discourse threatens to place her, in turn, in the role of oppressor....*The Woman Warrior*'s narrator, speaking in the discourse of narrative, by necessity exposes her mother, her aunts, her sisters to a critical Western gaze....[M]any critics of *The Woman Warrior* cover up, forget, her self-accusation in the interest of celebrating her song, in order to preserve narrative as a safe (because powerful) mode of female expression....If

one voice emerges at the end of *The Woman Warrior* (and Western constructions of artistry, as well as critical constructions of *The Woman Warrior*, stress the unity of the narrative voice), it is certainly not Brave Orchid's. In fact, her voice becomes the discourse to be resisted. (123-24)

The double bind for women writers that Kennedy's critique identifies is similar to the sexual double binds of women of my and Kingston's generational cohort. Narrative (like sex) must be entered into by women to become full adults and to recreate life, but entering narrative (sex), except in the highly prescribed scripts offered women, always endangers the self. As well, it betrays the mother whose cautions of "don't tell" forbid discourse. I assert the proposition that such postmodern/feminist critiques as Kennedy's can construct new "don't tell" cages for women writers and their readers. What Kennedy's critique of the use of narrative does not take into consideration is how the construction of several narratives—through the memoir form's complex narrative voice—deconstructs the oppressiveness of one narrative thread. And because this narrative method offers the contract of memoir—the individual life constituted in its specific history—it does not have to repeat the reifying and stereotypifying tendencies of traditional narratives; rather, it can mandate contingency and conditionality as part of its very nature. It does this by being a discourse located in a narrator who admits partiality, incompleteness, and personal bias.

Put simply, Brave Orchid is not rendered a negative female stereotype by one narrative script told by an authoritative narrator. The tripartite narrator situates herself in a number of ways in relation to Brave Orchid, as her young child, as her adult daughter, as her biographer, and as a conduit through which Brave Orchid makes "talk story." Also, she constantly reflects on the social and historical contexts of Brave Orchid's life and makes no secret of the fact that she is herself involved in a reflexive act of self-performance through the detailed portrayal of the other in her text. Through the memoir act of detailed reference to the life of the other, Brave Orchid is positioned by the narrator as several things at once: not only daughter, wife, mother, emigrant, and sister, but also scholar, midwife, doctor, honoured villager, and powerful moral arbiter. By telling this fuller history of Brave Orchid in both its positive and negative expressions, Kingston is able to reveal her mother's hard-won accomplishments. Brave Orchid becomes the tough woman who returns to school in mid-life after the death of two children and achieves a prominence that her younger student companions cannot. Kingston is also able to show how immigration to the United States, her mother's racial status as Chinese, and her gendered status as wife mean a loss of power for Brave Orchid the doctor. In this way Kingston can revise the culturally dominant narrative of immigration portrayed as opportunity and the romantic narrative of reunited husband and wife as happy ending. The achievement of birthing six babies past age forty is not sufficient compensation for the loss of status in going from honoured doctor to laundry worker. In these roles Brave Orchid is caught once more in the web of ethnicity and family, from which her role as doctor had allowed her some escape. Brave Orchid possesses a powerful drive to shape and mend the lives of others, but she is able to express it only through her often resented interventions in the lives of her children and the tragic attempt to manipulate the life of her sister Moon Orchid.

In fact, the complicated narrative pattern of these two sections of the book, far from "expos[ing] the mother" as Kennedy claims, gives voice to the oppression of the women of Kingston's and my mother's generation, shows how patriarchy reinscribes their achievements to its own purposes, and twists talent, accomplishment, and best intentions into negative expressions because of the limited field of action such training and ability are allowed. Women like Brave Orchid and my mother, although living in different racial cultures with different effects, were similarly made to function by ideology in subject positions in which they had to be guardians of ethnic traditions that inculcated their daughters in patriarchal values. However, women of that generation had also experienced temporary and partial escapes from their traditional roles by getting an education and holding jobs, in my mother's case as the result of the women's suffrage movement. They had sometimes been allowed leadership roles in wartime economies starved for labour and skills in the civilian work force. In Brave Orchid's case the desire of a colonized China to quickly and cheaply incorporate Western science and medicine into an older tradition played a part in her education as a doctor. Such an experience of public and professional competency, taken away from that generation forever by the gender conservatism of post-war culture or the experience of emigration, emerges in the unconscious double messages such women give their daughters. These messages tell the younger generation to be obedient daughters and accomplished women at the same time. Such conflicting agendas construct the rebellious daughters of my and Kingston's time.

But to see Kingston's complex history of her mother in this light, it is necessary for the reader to avoid entering the text seeking to deconstruct the writer's narrative for the purpose of showing her inevitable betrayal of other females. Rather, it is necessary to enter the text believing that a new discourse of memoirs is being performed, and the reader can participate in that construction by risking her own life story in her reading. Kingston teaches me how I can understand my own relationship with my mother, my daughter, my sister as an entanglement of interrelated stories. In this entanglement we reach out to the female other with loving arms, but arms that have been twisted to the purposes of our own oppression and that of the women we love. Kingston's memoirs, read with attitude, can also show us routes out of our double bind.

Ironically, for Kingston, the route out of the double bind lies in borrowing that oldest of autobiographical forms, the confession, as she does in a portion of the last section of her memoirs, "A Song for a Barbarian Reed Pipe." Confession, as Irene Gammel points out in *Confessional Politics*, is a dangerous modality for women, one in which their stories are open to "appropriation and recolonization" (2) and which feminizes those stories into positions of powerlessness and exploitation. Therefore, to make a new discourse of female subjectivity it must be confession with a difference, with an attitude, a difference made by the memoir form's mandate to narrate the confession in the specifics of history and culture, not as merely a personal failure.

Kingston's confession of her oppression of another female is not just a recitation of sin through recognized formulae, performed for the masterful priestly reader who can then give or withhold absolution. In the fullness of its detail (eight pages of detail), the attack on the little girl in the school washroom (whose victim position mirrors her own) once more finds Kingston risking the generic gaze of pornography as she did the first story of the text. But what forbids the pornographic reading in this instance is that the silent little victim and her narrating persecutor are twinned: "Her sobs and my sobs were bouncing wildly off the tile, sometimes together, sometimes alternating" (181). Every detail of physical abuse is portrayed, but not for our enjoyment as masters of the gaze, nor for its disciplining power over us as victims. The account escapes the appropriation of the other's story as well as the exploitation of the pain of the other and the self by twinning the victim who is silenced with the persecutor's painful and failed attempt to liberate herself by making another responsible for breaking their mutual silence.

This twinning works fully only when the reader, working at the "frontiers" of her own experience as victim and persecutor, enters the story ready to meld both positions. When I am willing to do this, I own up to my own complicity in patriarchy. The most important gesture of solidarity with the mother in this text, as it is in actual life, is the recognition that we are guilty of the same betrayals of which we accuse her. As the narrator reveals the full extent of her bullying, I recognize my own gestures of self-hatred acted out against other women. As she details the physicality of the humiliation, the cheek pinching, the hair pulling, the name calling—those humble, but very real and frightening, gestures of female childhood—I join the terror of the little victim's silence, giving up my bodily integrity to the persecutor. I weep my tears as surely as I did in my own childhood and as surely as I have made others do. In the dramatic re-enactment of the ways the mother's oppression becomes the vehicle for the daughter's oppression—who in turn learns to oppress others—I find a vivid image of my sobs and tears before a mother who blames me for the limitations of her life. I find, as well, the sobs and tears of my daughter hearing once again the old blaming script from her mother's mouth. We learn to blame our mothers and our daughters because we have learned that being female means being blameworthy. As the Chinese ideograph for the female "I"—which is also the ideograph for slave—tells us, we are slaves and the daughters of slaves.

To bring psycho-social cycles of abuse of any kind to an end they must be discursively performed in a carefully selective specificity. We must enact the narrative to see how it enslaves us, so that we may narrate our way out of our enslavement and repossess our own stories and the culture of which they are a part. This can be done through the actions of the intensification of narrative voice that the memoir form allows, an intensification that is the result of enacting the history of the mother, the narrator's witness of her life, and the daughter's participation in that life's effect. We must bring those stories out of the forbidden private world and into the discourse of our creative and critical feminist texts. One of the ways in which such accounts can escape women's discursive double binds is through the memoir form's ability (when it is read with attitude) to enact a discourse that risks changing the self through narration. It risks the selves of the writer who signs her book "memoirs," and the reader who brings her own life—lived in the specifics of place and time—to the reading act. Since to read with attitude inevitably involves the reader in the risks that comes with any performance of the self, it becomes necessary to theorize what kind of female self is needed to take on such risks. That practice of self is the subject of my next chapter.

Identity As a Balancing Act

Memoirs' Practice of Non-Sacrificial Rituals of Self-Performance

> Central to self-identity...is the capacity to sustain and in some sense reconcile multiple and often conflicting identities....The experience of lack of self is the familiar dark side of a culture characterized by increasing pressure for self-identity under conditions of increasing fragmentation....The development of self-identity requires the cognitive capacity to reflect on who I am and what matters to me, and to organize diverse identities, and identity-attributes, into some sort of meaningful narrative or constellation.
>
> —Allison Weir, *Sacrificial Logics*

IN TAKING up basic issues of identity that impact on the reading and writing of memoir, I would like to begin by returning briefly to the bullying incident in Kingston's memoirs, referred to in the last chapter. I take it up as a kind of cautionary tale in order to identify the way in which the very real issues of identity making facing women in contemporary times can lead to a denial of identity. It can also lead to the choice of no identity, in order to avoid an oppressive or oppressed identity. Such a decision leads to silence and self-effacement. In "A Song for a Barbarian Reed Pipe" Kingston is performing an identity out of silence and into words. She tells us that she spent "three years" in silence while in primary school, where she "flunked kindergarten" (165) and "covered my school paintings with black paint" (165). She connects her silence at this point in time "with being a Chinese girl" in white America, since she has no problem speaking at home and does talk "to one or two of the Chinese kids in class" (166). It is only self-possession in the public white world that eludes her. At first, Maxine actually enjoys being silent, communicating with others by gestures and motions. It is only when "I found out I had to talk that school became a misery, that the silence became a misery. I did not speak and felt bad each time that I did not speak. I read aloud in first grade, though, and heard the barest whisper with little squeaks come out of my throat" (166). Maxine pushes herself to talk as the grades go by, but there is another Chinese girl in her class who represents the extreme form of the disability she herself suffered from: "She would whisper-read but not talk. Her whisper was as soft as if she had no muscles" (173). Acting out her self-hatred, building her own assertive self on the sacrifice of another to victimization, Maxine eventually attacks the girl in the school washroom. Hating her softness, her pliancy, her "skin...like squid out of which the glassy blades of bones had been pulled" (176), Maxine becomes a bully, poking, prodding, and lecturing the child, trying to make her speak: "Sounds did come from her mouth, sobs, chokes, noises that were almost words. Snot ran down her nose" (178). Her harassment yields "quarts of tears but no words" (179). Treating the little girl as if she is her double, Maxine demands that she perform the very acts of self-assertion that Maxine herself is trying to practise: "'Get tough. Come on. Throw fists.' I pushed at her hands; they swung limply at her sides" (179). She tells her that "[n]obody's going to notice you. And you have to talk for interviews, speak right up in front of the boss. Don't you know that? You're so dumb" (181).

The incident ends with the sudden appearance of the girl's older sister and Kingston tells us of the dramatic change that follows, not in the little victim, but in herself:

> The world is sometimes just, and I spent the next eighteen months sick in bed with a mysterious illness. There was no pain and no symptoms, though the middle line in my left palm broke in two. Instead of starting junior high school, I lived like the Victorian recluses I read about. I had a rented hospital bed in the living room, where I watched soap operas on t.v., and my family cranked me up and down. I saw no one but my family, who took good care of me. I could have no visitors, no other relatives, no villagers. My bed was against the west window, and I watched the seasons change the peach tree. I had a bell to ring for help. I used a bedpan. It was the best year and a half of my life. Nothing happened. (181-82)

Kingston does not take up a psychological analysis of this almost complete negation of self through passivity, a mode in diametric opposition to her aggressive effort to possess the public world. Rather, she leaves the reader to read the incident with the other acts of identity performed in "A Song for a Barbarian Reed Pipe," and with the identity performed throughout the text. The reader can also read it in relation to the reader's own life.

Her story of going silent at puberty, of giving up on any public self-possession, resonates with many women's lives. The authors of *Women's Ways of Knowing* (Belenky et al.) acknowledge women's adoption of silence as a refusal of the aggressiveness of words. In the view of many of the interview subjects in this study, "[w]ords were perceived as weapons. Words were used to separate and diminish people, not to connect and empower them" (24). Going silent can also be a reaction to feeling out of place in an alien environment, as public life, even school life, can be for some. From my own mid-teens, I remember this same fear of words and their power not only to separate me from others, but also to reveal an unwanted difference. When I moved to the Prairies in grade nine, after a vocal childhood in Newfoundland, my St. John's accent—made from broad vowels and a fast-moving verbosity with a bit of an Irish cadence—caused everyone around me in my new school considerable amusement. The minute I spoke there were coos of "Oh, I love your accent!" and "Say that again, you sound so Irish." Some simply laughed at every sound out of my mouth. Even the benevolent commentary shocked me. I suddenly heard my own voice as loud, assertive, and harsh, like those of the mothers of my own class and place. My voice did not resemble the gentle Prairie voices around me, especially those of the girls, who spoke in more modulated tones than the boys and with polite, if limited, vocabularies. There seemed to be no place for adjectives or the colourful idiosyncratic phrases of my childhood. What I now realize is that a richness of language suddenly seemed to me, confronted by my schoolmates' language, to be a disgusting showiness. My silence, although more selective than Kingston's, lasted in one form or another for a couple of years until I could imitate the accents around me, limit my rich verbosity, and make my vocal cords as calm and economical as my peers.

The experience of going silent in young girls or women can be associated with a fear of self-assertion as unfeminine, a fear that can be intensified by racial and ethnic factors. I believe it is a learned gender fear that perceives self-assertion as an act of aggression, a sacrifice of femaleness. I find that it illustrates theorist Allison Weir's ideas about the "sacrificial logic" of identity making in our culture. In her critique of contemporary concepts of identity, Weir outlines the identity issues that have plagued feminism since Simone de Beauvoir's *The Second Sex*. Identity, in the West, is traditionally associated with autonomy, a maturation process that requires separation of the self and the repression of fragmentation and multiplicity. Feminism, in Weir's formulation, asks, "Is it possible to affirm some sort of self-identity which does *not* repress the differences within the self, or the connectedness of the self to others, and to do so without making false claims about authority and authorship?" (1). In other words, can we have an identity that does not demand the repression of the multiple facets of the self's potential? Must we be satisfied with a definition of maturity that encourages a sense of a separate self at the sacrifice of connectedness? Can we assert identity in ways that do not impinge on the sense others have of themselves as we do when we use them as sacrificial mirrors or projections for our own needs? Such questions bring up a subsidiary, but equally important, question: "Is there any way of affirming any kind of women's identity without repressing differences of race, class, culture, sexual orientation, and so on which divide women, without reinscribing the oppressive institutions through which gender identity has been constituted, and without denying the wide historical and cultural variation of what the concept of women means?" (Weir 1). In short, can women repossess a world beyond the confines of the home without colonizing it in imitation of traditional male identity patterns? Weir does not favour throwing out the whole concept of gendered identity, as some theorists do, nor does she wish to avoid using the category "women." I agree with her and feel that if we do not use concepts around femaleness as a positive value, we may be in danger, in the absence of such values, of imitating male identity patterns since they are still dominant in our society. Weir's concern is with women's ability to perform identities that establish non-oppressive forms of female identification as norms for our culture. My concern is with identifying ways in which the memoir form facilitates this activity. Both concerns are attempts to counter the silence that girls and women resort to when faced with dichotomous identity choices.

As Weir outlines this impasse, feminist theory, having tended to implicitly accept traditional philosophic values "that identity is *necessarily* a product of the repression of difference" (7), tends to lead feminists subscribing to such views inevitably toward negative critiques of the category "women." Weir uses Judith Butler as her example of this negativity. In Weir's reading, Butler "rejects both self-identity and women's identity on the grounds that any identity is repressive" and to even name such a category as "women" will "repress the fluidity of difference" (Weir 11).[1] Such

---

1. See *Gender Trouble* and *Bodies that Matter* by Judith Butler.

an argument leaves women in a double bind. To seek identity—a coherent social self and the consequent ability to act in the world in deliberate manner—is to seek masculine patterns of autonomy and separation. To remain "fluid"—and thus avoid suppressing one's own multiplicity and the differences of others—is to accept the position of the "second sex" that de Beauvoir described at the beginning of the contemporary feminist debate. The condition Kingston describes as happening to her at puberty, turning from bully to invalid, is an extreme example of this dichotomous identity situation. Weir would call such a situation a "sacrificial" one (and thus her book's title, *Sacrificial Logics*) in which something must always be sacrificed to make identity. She argues that feminists need a fuller concept of identity that embraces "concepts of the self which could include difference, connection and heterogeneity." She asserts that while "individuals must be understood as embedded, embodied, localized, constituted, fragmented, and subject to systems of power, oppression, and exploitation" (184), at the same time they must be understood to have "[t]he capacity, and the responsibility, to problematize and define [their] own meaning" (185).

This last statement concerning our "capacity" to "problematize and define" our selves is very important to my study of contemporary women's memoirs. It is through this capacity to "problematize and define" our selves as women that we repossess what the private/public division of culture has taken away from us. I find that the memoir form as used by contemporary women is an important ground for working through these feminist identity questions. Such memoirs have as their central motif exactly the identity crisis that Weir has described, characterized by the dichotomy of self as a separate entity from others and self as what Julia Watson calls a "connective tissue" in which relationships with others replaces the sense of the self as separate. Other features of such a crisis include the problem of self-assertion leading to the repression of multiplicity and difference and the challenge of finding a way of being in the world that harmoniously accommodates both the world's multiplicity and our own difference. Shirley Neuman calls this concept a "poetics of difference" and says that "such a poetics cannot be systematized; it can only be accumulated from the ongoing writing and reading of many autobiographies, many readers, occupying many simultaneous and sequential subject-positions" ("Different Poetics" 226). By making reference to a sampling of memoir texts, I hope to illustrate but not systematize this "poetics of difference." Further, I want to show that the formal arrangements of memoirs generate and work through the very identity issues Weir describes, and make possible through their "balancing acts" the solutions individuals perform to avoid the dichotomies of traditional identity patterns. Weir asserts that to make such identities "requires the learning of social and linguistic norms, through which the expression or realization of one's specificity, and the development of the critique of norms, becomes possible" (187).

Part of the development of different norms is through their performance as narrations of various kinds. The memoir form, as practised by contemporary women, is exactly the kind of "linguistic" space that allows for both narrating activities: it allows for "specificity" of person in the complex and necessary deployment of the narrator's tasks as witness and participant. It also allows for a "critique of norms" through the ongoing activity of what I have called the "reflective/reflexive consciousness" function of the tripartite figure of the narrator. Through its continuous weaving of self and world, self and history, self and significant others, the memoir sets up the "meaningful narrative" that Weir says can make complex identities capable of both freedom and responsibility.

Many contemporary women's memoirs, on first reading, seem not to assert the traditional "I" of autobiography, the self that defines its maturation through a process of increasing separation and distinctiveness. Women's memoirs often seem to be about fitting in, finding a community, and suppressing any separate, distinctive identity. Yet, in such texts, an "I" is at work through the writer's emphasis on the specificity of the quotidian, reiterative, and ritualistic details of lived life. To further explain what I mean by the way memoir works with the "specificity" of "lived life," I turn to Sidonie Smith, who in "Performativity, Autobiographical Practice, Resistance" views self as in a constant process of performance: "Everyday, in disparate venues, in response to sundry occasions, in front of precise audiences (even if an audience of one), people assemble, if only temporarily, a 'life' to which they assign narrative coherence and meaning and through which they position themselves in historically specific identities. Whatever that occasion or that audience, the autobiographical speaker becomes a performative subject" (17).

Smith does not see the subject thus performed as an "essence" or an "inner self," but in fact believes that "there is no essential, original, coherent autobiographical self before the moment of self-narration" (18). The self is an "effect" of our own performance, our own self-narration. This self changes over time. We forget parts of the self that are not regularly performed and we gain new identity features through the reiteration of performance. Smith takes the idea of reiteration from Judith Butler's work (which she views in a more positive manner than does Weir) and sees these acts of reiteration as necessary to the performance of the self. The translation of these acts into narratives, into "autobiographical" practices, is the foundation of self-empowerment. Smith demonstrates how the reiterative performance of self in various autobiographies leads not to the automatic repetition of societal norms but to a resistance that establishes difference. I would go further and say that we often weave these reiterations into rituals, sometimes rejuvenated rituals, which become dependable repeatable acts that perform the self. This concept of our ability to resist and by implication revise norms is based on Butler's idea that, especially in regards to gender, the societal injunction to be a certain kind of subject "produces necessary failures, a variety of incoherent configurations that in their multiplicity exceed and defy the injunction by which they are generated" (*Gender* 145). Smith extends this idea to show how autobiographical practice performs these acts that "exceed and defy" norms and thus perform new subjects. The idea that the very acts of obediently performing accepted gender roles may not result in always performing them successfully has particular interest for my purposes. In performing not quite as we are required to by our ideas of what is normal, we may find other possibilities for identity, ones which once performed—as if by accident—can be reiterated in a more deliberate manner. I suggest that in memoir women make those more deliberate performances. In this way we can resist, experiment and change our performance of self by acts of deliberate reiteration that can then act incrementally to establish identity. Obviously, deliberateness will depend on the degree to which we have developed what Weir calls "the capacity, and the responsibility, to problematize and define [our] own meaning" (185). Intriguingly, in Butler's and Smith's estimations, the development of this capacity depends on some degree of failure in reiterating societal norms. Thus, in memoir we can expect to see the kind of failures of femininity that Kingston elaborates with such humour and pain.

As one concerned with the forms that may best accomplish this incremental kind of reiteration—forms that do not take up a sacrificial logic of identity—I look to how memoir may enable such a process. For example, Kingston's memoir is a series of episodes, each performing identity through different kinds of otherings, otherings that are brought back continually to the problem of how Maxine is to become a woman. In "No Name Woman" the doubly othered story of the tragic death of an aunt told by Maxine's mother results in a daughter reworking her mother's cautionary tale. In "White Tigers" myth is used as the significant other of self, to build in fantasy what does not exist in life, but which rehearses the qualities that are needed to make a life. In "Shaman" the mother's life story as a figure of authority and importance becomes the material for self-making. And so on. Each section seems different, but in terms of the othering process—going out from the self, bringing back, in a non-appropriative way, some quality learned from the other in order to remake the self—they each reiterate a process. There is a gradual performance of a self moving out of silence into language through the reiteration and reshaping of figures who represent femaleness, and the "necessary failures" that are produced by the performance of old norms in new situations.

Kingston's self-performance demonstrates how reiterative story-telling can bring a child or youth to an adult selfhood. Other memoirs demonstrate that the silencing of non-identity, what Weir calls the "lack of self," can happen to a woman even in the midst of a successful adult life. I would like to take up a contemporary memoir in which this reiterative performance is more obvious, perhaps because it takes as its reiterative central focus for self-performance a very ordinary, materially located ritual of daily life: the preparation of food. In choosing such a domestically centred activity, I wish to make the point that we can seek a more effective performance of our identities without sacrificing the "ways of knowing" we have gained in women's traditional places. We can do this by bringing old ways of knowing that are allied with the domestic into whatever public worlds—spiritual, social, or political—that we wish to repossess. Elizabeth Ehrlich's *Miriam's Kitchen: A Memoir* is a demonstration of how important such a process is to non-sacrificial identity. Ehrlich describes the subject position she attains as the adult child of "left wing, bookish, hypersensitive, white, Jewish, anti-middle class" parents who while having "few institutional ties to The Faith...selected from and approximated the traditions they took for granted" (xi). At a stage of her adulthood in which she and her more traditionally Jewish husband have children, she finds her performance of the usual secularized activities of identity, which are her norms, to be insufficient to her new situation. Like many young women in the late twentieth century, Ehrlich was able to extend the period of male-style independence through late marriage and postponement of children. She now finds that the liberal, secular, highly individual, non-communal self she has built up through the years of her young womanhood, when she worked as a journalist, has meant a sacrifice of values that she now feels she needs for family life. She sets out to find a set of repeatable domestic rituals that will build those parts of her identity.

Interestingly, Ehrlich's sense of needing to perform another kind of self starts with the realization of what she has forgotten from her childhood: "I forgot the childhood appetites that could only be satisfied in my grandmothers' kosher kitchens. I forgot the practical, mystical teachings, spiraling back through time, that the grandmothers had once dished out with their soup. I forgot the dignity my immigrants had, that comes with the connection to something larger than everyday life, even when you are doing nothing more than stirring soup. I had the bequest of my grandmothers' details, but I devalued all this for many years as one does" (xii). This description of how she felt about her need to rediscover the preparation of food as a way to establish her communal and relational identity as Jewish woman, wife, and mother sounds startlingly similar to Smith's theoretical description of how our tendency to forget is a factor in identity making: "The very sense of a self as identity derives paradoxically from the loss of consciousness of fragments of experiential history. Benedict Anderson suggests that this 'estrangement' from our experiential history necessitates 'a conception of personhood, *identity*...which, because it cannot be 'remembered' must be narrated'" (quoted in "Performitivity" 18). Ehrlich's use of the phrase "as one does" in speaking of how she forgot the practices of her ancestors indicates that she sees the process her own identity's maturation as a common one, and that it might be quite typical of youth to require separation and of maturity to require community. Certainly this desire is made more dramatic by women's lives in contemporary times, where one can, like Ehrlich, live like an independent man for quite a long time without serious censorship from society, until one chooses the (typically late) motherhood stage of life. As she observes, the desire to honour the old traditions "came back to me when I became a mother" (xii). Ehrlich finds that she wants to develop a more healthy diet for her family than she practised as a busy journalist. Since her mother-in-law Miriam (whose only daughter died young) yearns to pass on her recipes, Ehrlich decides to learn from her the cooking skills and management of a kosher kitchen. "For me," she observes, "it is a voyage of discontinuity and connection" (xii), indicating that her secularized, liberal identity as an individual making "free" choices makes her feel a profound lack of continuity and certainly affects her ability to perform in her new situation as mother. She seeks the "connection" that a more communally located identity will give her.

At the same time she feels the ambiguity of her identity situation. As much as she wants to rehearse old traditions to find community connection, she is cautious of the ways in which strict adherence to kosher law might limit her choices in terms of time and personal freedom. She does not intend to move from one end of the identity continuum to the other, from honorary male subject position to woman entirely in service to others. She refuses a sacrificial logic of identity. But her desire to develop a "sinkside, stoveside, personal perspective, not a rabbinical one," makes her resolve to keep the dichotomies in mind, to "turn over the old stories in my mind and collect new ones. I choose my own history, deciding which snapshots, decades, recipes, versions of arguments and events are to be discarded, and which will stand for the whole. That history is my own little temple where I measure my life against a reliable standard. I find meaning there....I consider the law, the restrictions, the presumptions of holiness, the doubt. I inventory layers of translucent recollections evoking food, love, home, apocrypha, anger, ritual, laughter, conflict, and regret. The result is a collage, but also a way of life. That collage is my religion, and it is what I am passing on" (xxii–xxiii). In repossessing a domestic world Ehrlich has every intention of repossessing a public world as well, the world of "the Faith." And she intends to do so on her own terms. At the same time as she wishes her collage to contain her choices from all the inheritance of the past, she knows that it must not leave out the oppression of women: "We will try for a Sabbath more often, think about holidays in advance. But I remain cautious. I long drew from observant households a metaphor never written in the Book: the symbolic sacrifice not of Isaac but the Mother. The mother who bends the course of life to have everything ready for that Friday night, who brings in the Sabbath but never rests. And always, I have feared my own obsessions. I fear losing myself and then discovering my location is a point of no return" (24).

Collage, expressed as a formal choice in the episodic, genre-blending style of memoir, is a good word to describe the aesthetic practice of women seeking, as Weir puts it, a "self which could include difference, connection and heterogeneity." Such a self is also constructed on the recognition that "individuals must be understood as embedded, embodied, localized, constituted, [and] fragmented." Collage can address multiplicity, but because collage allows such multiplicity, it can also allow room to explore the hold of "systems of power, oppression, and exploitation." Thus there is a necessarily cautious quality for women such as Ehrlich in writing their memoirs. As narrators they are continually stepping back from the participant and witness roles to reflect on the patterns of the collage they are performing. They reflexively comment on their fears of going too far in one direction or another, correcting, deprecating their own ego inflations, inquiring into their own othering, as they rescue, reassess, repattern, repossess.

Collage is the ordering principle of Ehrlich's memoir. She names her chapters after the months of the year, but each month represents a number of cycles of that month, starting with "September" and Yom Kippur and rolling through the seasons of holy days and ordinary days to a final chapter entitled "September" at the end of the book (subtitled "continuity"). This book repeats in its interconnected episodes wide-ranging but discernible patterns at the same time as it builds its narrator's identity through her discovery of her tradition's rituals. Each chapter contains several subsections that outline, in anecdotal narrative form, Ehrlich's learning process, but each stage of the learning process brings up memories of past family events and practices, and the women who knew the recipes before her. Ehrlich builds her memoir's incremental seasons into an identity interwoven with her familial community past and present. Each stage also involves hearing Miriam's story of her family's deaths and survivals in the Holocaust, and thus the inheritance of a personal history that individuates the collective history is also part of the ritual building up of Ehrlich's chosen identity in an old culture.

As Ehrlich moves through her first season of collaging her identity through memory, rituals, and practice, she feels the fear of difference that I have referred to. The chapter "November" begins, as does each chapter, with the narrator acting in her capacity as reflective/reflexive consciousness of the text. These sections are always in italics, as if to indicate their difference from the participatory acts of learning to cook and care, and the witnessing acts of hearing and remembering the stories of others. Three months into her cycle of seasons, Ehrlich admits her ambivalence about the dichotomies of female identity: "I am not sure that I want this. I always have wanted the world. So I teeter, I worry, but I don't turn away....I am trying to balance the claims of the mind and the soul with the belly's blind indulgent appetites. I am trying to respect the life of the calf that I eat. I will imbibe of its mother's milk, but at some other meal. Still I do not say I can possibly meet the detail evolved by generations of rabbis. I don't know if I can truly scour myself and begin afresh. I don't know if I really wish to. Purge the ambivalence, the daring U turns, and what is left after all?" (53–54). Part of the sacrificial risks of contemporary female identity is that whatever parts of the cultural inheritance women select for their identity formation, they must face the fact that all of it has been shaped by patriarchal hands. There is no pure women's culture; any culture we make must come from acts of repossession of materials that have been long possessed by others' values.

For example, Weir illustrates her discussion of women's identity dilemma through the history of the Roman Catholic Church's appropriation of the figure of the mother. Working through Julia Kristeva's writings on this subject, Weir shows how the church adapted ancient beliefs in the "archaic mother" to create the Virgin Mary. She cites Kristeva, who "argues that by taking up the myth of the mother goddess, thereby preserving the maternal order within the jurisdiction of the paternal one" (175) the church made an accommodation that worked for a very long time. In Weir's view the loss of this accommodation for many Christian women in contemporary times does not liberate us in the modern world; it "has given way not to a freedom of difference, an open identity process, but to a new trap of emptiness" (178).

It is emptiness that Ehrlich feared as a secular person, yet she is all too aware of the "generations of rabbis" who have accommodated the female world while appropriating authority over it. Ehrlich takes what I find to be a creative approach to the problem. She turns the dilemma on its head by deciding to put aside, for the moment of her learning, the question of the rabbis' authority. She treats the female tradition rather than rabbinical authority as paramount and as open to an improvisational collage approach through which she can perform her own identity in her variations on tradition: "Keeping kosher has this value: I daily reaffirm identity, purpose, and rhythm" (54). Yet, like other women, she fears exhibiting difference (ironically, in contemporary secular culture, traditional practices are "difference"). She knows that Kosher practice means "separation from the world outside as well as within the meal. Yet I do not enjoy setting myself apart. I fear a statement of difference in a world that needs to see itself as one" (54). Moving between ambiguities, negating nothing (except blind allegiance to rabbinical teaching), she begins to perform her collage of selfhood.

After beginning the chapter "November" with reflection on her ambivalence towards difference, the subsection "Old Neighborhood" moves her back into her memories of her childhood in Detroit. There her family stayed on in a neighbourhood that was becoming home for black people, after other Jews had moved to the suburbs. This experience has many positive benefits, since she and her family, as liberals of a socialist bent, perceive themselves as part of a larger workers' solidarity and generally get along well in their changing community. At the same time she is inevitably made constantly aware of her white and Jewish difference. At camp one summer she learns that areas of Detroit near her neighbourhood are in flames in the race riots of 1967, and she fears for her family's safety. As she witnesses to this childhood memory, she also remembers how she stayed on an even keel in the confusing years of college by learning to cook "Stuffed Cabbage" (as the next subsection is entitled). Opposed to the fear of difference and its consequences is a sense of continuity that she develops out of cooking. The inheritance of her grandmother's pots and pans connects her past and present into the future as she recounts in this section how, many years later, she shows her four-year-old daughter how to wrap the stuffing in the cabbage. She also narrates how a black family prepared a dinner for her family on the day they finally began packing up to move away from the neighbourhood. Her father insisted that they eat it, even though it contained food that the family was unused to, food that broke even their lax kosher practices. This section sets a collage pattern: an act of food preparation and religious practice leads to an incremental review of child, adult, and maternal memories, which leads back to cooking and a renewed appreciation of its significance for non-sacrificial self-performance.

The Detroit memory would seem to assert the discord and danger of living in a community that is not made up of one's own kind. Cooking and honouring one's ongoing sense of belonging in a community mark the comforting world of tradition. These would seem to be two dichotomies. Yet the three-part collage that is "November" continues into the section called "Apple Cake," in which Ehrlich describes how her very traditional mother-in-law Miriam brings her Kosher world together with the secular holiday of American Thanksgiving. As Miriam teaches Ehrlich a recipe for apple cake she inherited from her mother, she also tells her of how, after the war, the surviving family members (her mother, herself, her husband Jacob) emigrated from Poland to Israel. They then once again left the "Promised Land" to come to America for the opportunities it would offer their children. In America Miriam memorializes her mother by cleaving to her recipes, developed long ago in the restaurant her mother ran in Poland, before the Holocaust. But she also makes her mother's recipe for apple cake each year in celebration of Thanksgiving for the prosperity of America. As well, she bakes cookies in the shape of pilgrims and turkeys and pumpkins. Ehrlich observes: "It is Miriam's American statement: If apple cake had made Thanksgiving Jewish, these cookies, something new, represent a late, sugary embrace of the New World. Maybe having grandchildren allowed that to be" (70). Stories, history, the daily improvisations of cooking and its rituals bring old and new worlds, past and present, together, and allow difference to survive and inform the identity within the larger world of American culture. The chapter ends, as do many, with the recipes for the food that has informed this section of Ehrlich's building collage of non-sacrificial self.

The recipes, strategically placed throughout this book, have the effect of encouraging that active reader "attitude" that I advocated in the last chapter, one produced as a consequence of the memoir form as used by contemporary women. The recipes are the writer's (and Miriam's) practical gift to the reader, an invitation to interact with their world by using their recipes, an encouragement to seek out the recipes of the reader's own tradition. As well, the presence of the recipes symbolically imitates the ritual of shared meals, the breaking of bread together, a ritualistic and practical part of many religions. It reminds us that we celebrate and renew the things we most believe in by developing rituals of sharing and embodiment that food preparation and communal eating imply.

My own unconscious reaction to this text surprises me regularly. I now clean out the gloss of white inside an eggshell, wasting no part of the food, as Miriam taught her daughter-in-law to do. I now warm chopped onions in the pan until they begin to "sweat" (to bring out the desired flavour) before adding oil. Ehrlich's "December" chapter, the month she decides to give kosher a "trial run," is also the chapter in which she explores the years she spent being assimilated (as the result of her aunt's marriage to a Christian) into her aunt's deliciously prepared Christmas dinners. I learn tips on cabbage salad and Christmas goose that remind me that despite my alienation from my Christian heritage, I have held on to some of the Christmas foods that were prepared in my mother's kitchen (and her mother's kitchen) in my childhood. I become the active reader with attitude who uses the text to learn a new respect for the domestic skills that are an often unacknowledged part of my own identity. I contemplate performing domestic identity rituals of my own. At the end of this chapter, after expounding on "Christmas Goose" and "Hanukkah" goose, Ehrlich, with egalitarian élan, calls her recipe "Winter Holiday Goose." This memoir asks me to think seriously about the saying "You are what you eat" (or you are what you cook and eat) by conflating issues of food and issues of identity.

Miriam's Kitchen performs a series of balancing acts as a solution to identity dichotomies: balancing the strictures of the kosher law with the demands of a modern household. Ehrlich balances the demanding preparations for the celebrations of the many Jewish holidays with her own and her family's schedules. She balances her commitment to a kosher kitchen with her often less-than-enthusiastic endorsement of temple rituals, and even decides to accept some of those very temple-sanctioned acts when she sees that they facilitate some of the family life she is trying to build.

Perhaps the most telling balancing act she performs is in her portraits of her own mother and her mother-in-law, Jewish women with two very different backgrounds and philosophies of life. Feminists have long recognized the tendency of our culture to dichotomize femaleness: virgin/whore, witch/saint, good mother/bad mother. This memoir, along with many I write of in this study, works toward breaking down this dichotomy. It would be an easy and conventional act of obeying patriarchal norms for Ehrlich to dichotomize her own mother as the one who let the tradition lapse and Miriam as the mother who restored her to that tradition. Since her own mother returned to school to get an education while her children were still at home, it would be an easy binary for Ehrlich to imitate in a popular culture that has become once more hostile to non-traditional mothers. Ehrlich takes pains to avoid this. She speaks of her mother as living "with a problematic legacy. On one side, her mother's fears and generosity and confidence in her....On the other, her father's esteem for learning, his frustrations, his dashing of her dreams. Nothing was going to be easy" (147). To see one's mother's life not just in terms of her function as mother, but also in terms of her positive differences from her daughter, is no easy task, and one I will write more of in the next chapter. But in understanding why her mother returned to school, why she simplified kosher traditions, why she needed other investments beside her children, Ehrlich honours the part of herself that is not like her mother-in-law, for whom dislocation and personal tragedy have made family the whole of her life. She not only sympathizes with both of these mother figures, but she allows them to emerge as positive, yet different, presences in her text and as important significant others of her self-performance process.

In the "February" chapter, in which Ehrlich begins to get very serious about issues of "observance" of the kosher household that she is learning from her mother-in-law, she also tells the story of her mother. Raised in America, Ehrlich's mother did not attempt such an elaborate practice because of her desire to have a life outside the kitchen. Ehrlich observes that despite being denied an education by her own immigrant father, her mother "forgave her father. More than this: she honored him" (148). The lesson her mother's life teaches her is "that a mother could have a determined, separate life" (148), could even honour a parent hostile to that separate life. She recognizes that in a home where a mother has such a life the children learn early that "all of us [were] essential to the economics of the family life" (149). One of the ways Ehrlich honours her two mother figures is by dramatizing their responses, and by giving them the last word in a number of instances. For example, after describing her own mother's attempts to keep some of the rituals of Sabbath by "reciting a prayer in English I am not sure she did not believe" (150), Ehrlich writes a brief subchapter, in a scripted scenic style, entitled "Revision":

> "I'm writing about the way you kept the flame alive," I say to my mother.
> "I wasn't trying to keep a flame alive," she says to me.
> I look at the page in my hand, and wonder.
> "You children had to eat something, and I did what I knew how to do." (151)

In staging responses such as this one, Ehrlich allows the significant other's point of view to stand, and if the reader wishes it, to be used as a deconstructive device for the author's own versions of her mother and her mother-in-law. The inconsistent, the oppositional, the diverse in the identity-making process is enacted on the pages of the memoir. In the same way, Ehrlich honours Miriam's stories of the Holocaust by placing them in italics, to indicate they are her mother-in-law's direct account, rather than the daughter-in-law's use of them in her own story.

The final chapter of *Miriam's Kitchen* does not work toward a resolution of identity issues, but rather toward the creative balance Ehrlich has maintained throughout. She knows that she is "drawn to ritual" in the hope that she "may perhaps draw nearer to meaning" (351), emphasizing for me how ritual acts can be, for many, a way to perform the self. The other side of that performance is letting go of what fails to give meaning to the self, and understanding that the process is never a sure one but is always full of doubt and questioning. Ehrlich realizes: "I can relinquish, perhaps, the physical things of the past, if I believe that their essence continues through time. I can go on with everyday life in the company of ancient values, insights, questions, and doubts." She adds: "After all the millennia, I give my doubts another year" (351). "Values" and "insights" are necessarily joined to "questions, and doubts" in her identity performance. She has come to the realization that one can live in a both/and rather that an either/or world; one need not resolve every question on the spot with a sacrificial gesture of eliminating possibilities in order to have no doubts. Some things can wait for another year, when the effects of incremental reiteration may make doubt into belief, or may show that some element fails to cohere in the incremental performance of the self.

The formal arrangement of the last chapter confirms this. Its first and longer section is entitled "Sabbath," which begins, as is Ehrlich's practice throughout the text, with a reflective/reflexive contemplation of the holy day of the week. "Is Sabbath objective reality?" (354), Ehrlich asks, "Or is Sabbath more kin to the artist's paradox" (355). Ehrlich compares the practices of the Sabbath to the painter's use of perspective, the technique that deceives the human eye into seeing relative distance and nearness in objects in a painting. She finds that "spirituality, like vision, is flawed and emotional, shaped by experience." In a sense she both defies rabbinical tradition and yet cleaves to the faith when she writes: "Shabbas feeling cannot be attained from a color-by-number kit" (355). She dwells on the ambiguity of words such as "welcome" and "make." A woman is said to "welcome" Sabbath by lighting candles, a woman is said to "make" Sabbath when you "wash your floor, dust, cook, and set the table on Friday" (355). Then, with that dissenting difference that always slyly asserts itself at such meditative moments, she asks "So, what exactly is it that women do?" and answers her own question with another: "Are women God?" Thus, a radical feminism is contained within, but not restricted by, the traditional meditation on the value of Sabbath.

The "Sabbath" section ends with Ehrlich describing how her family, after a year of correct Friday Sabbaths at home, decides to go out to a Chinese restaurant for dinner. They walk to the restaurant to observe the rule forbidding the use of transportation on the Sabbath and they order vegetarian food. Despite the feeling of un-Sabbathlike occasion (especially since the restaurant kitchen is not kosher), at the end of the meal some young Jewish men at another table put down their chopsticks and sing *Birkhat ha-Mazon*, the after-meal grace. As the family walks the eight blocks home, her daughter repeats the singing and Ehrlich feels that they have kept the Sabbath well. Thus the feminist reshaping of the role of women in Sabbath is followed by the creative compromise of an actual (if unconventional) Sabbath, spent in a Chinese restaurant, where the mother does not cook. But it is not with this sense of the easy reinvention of the Sabbath that the book ends. Rather, the ease of the contemporary restaurant compromise is balanced by the anecdote called "Sponges," which ends the memoir and emphasizes the constant compromises, difficulties, and humorous adjustments that make up the kind of balancing act that Ehrlich has chosen.

Ehrlich relates her experience of coming home late one night, tired, hungry, and cold, with a terrific yearning for leftover chicken soup that she knows is in a glass bowl in the refrigerator. She finds that the kitchen, where the babysitter and children have feasted on cheese pizza, is in a terrible mess, with "leathery pizza crusts, rancid glasses half-filled with tepid milk, an empty ice cream carton." The mess speaks loudly to the fact that she has a "dairy" kitchen, "a dirty, *miikhdike* kitchen." She has beside her sink, as any kosher kitchen should, four sponges: "blue for dairy, pink for meat, green for *pareve*, and yellow to clean the kitchen" (161). The sacrificial dichotomies of the situation would dictate that she either ignore her children's mess and break kosher rules and have her soup or clean up: "I should wash the dishes with the blue sponge, stack the dishwasher and run it. I should wash the blue rack, dry it with the blue dish towel, and set it aside. I bag the trash, sweep the floor, use the yellow sponge to wash the counter and scour the kitchen sink. I should rinse the sink with boiling water, and lay down the white sink rack. Then, yes then, I could prepare my *fleyshik* meal, gently reheating soup in a saucepan, sitting down to soup in a white soup plate, and later wash it all and dry it—saucepan, black ladle, soup plate, meat spoon, cranberry glass storage bowl—with pink sponge and pink towel." Ehrlich's specificity concerning the demands of a kosher kitchen dramatically illustrates the problems for contemporary women of holding onto tradition, when a busy life outside the home means they cannot stay confined in their kitchens in order to control their operation. But Ehrlich's solution is not to throw up her hands and resort to the other half of the dichotomy, that is, to give up on kosher. Instead, she humorously recounts her final balancing act of obedience to tradition through creative improvisation:

> I know what I will do. I will put the whole glass bowl in the microwave and zap it. I will rummage about for a meat spoon. I will dim the lights, and when the timer beeps, I will peel the plastic lid from the glass bowl, lean against the counter, and eat the soup standing up, hoping that my husband will call from Ohio, where he is away on a business trip. Then I will leave the unwashed bowl and spoon on the furthest corner of the counter to deal with tomorrow.
> It is as good as any soup I ever have had. (361)

Ehrlich's domestic compromise drolly illustrates Weir's serious philosophical observation of current identity issues for contemporary women. Weir says that "[t]he development of self-identity requires the cognitive capacity to reflect on who I am and what matters to me, and to organize diverse identities, and identity-attributes, into some sort of meaningful narrative or constellation" (187). This is what *Miriam's Kitchen* succeeds in doing.

In concluding this chapter on the balancing acts women perform, the rituals they construct to have an identity they can live with, I fear that the reader, caught up in my detailed analysis of Ehrlich's memoir, may mistake my purpose and think that I am advising a neo-domestic retreat for women seeking a fuller identity. This is not the case. My choice of Ehrlich's memoir as my principal illustration is mandated by my interest in how self-performance is both quotidian and ritualistic. The irony of a contemporary career woman going back to the kitchen to find herself is one that Ehrlich herself contends with through her whole text. Like Ehrlich, I feel cautious, fearful of courting an unwanted dichotomy. Ehrlich, throughout her chapters, cannot resist adding one more incident, anecdote, or short narration—building the Chinese restaurant Sabbath on top of the home Sabbath and the night of the lone chicken soup in the kosher kitchen on top of that—so as to avoid any impression that clear choices are available. In the same way, I wish to add references to other memoirs, just to counter any easy reading for domestic prescription.

In many ways, Alix Kates Shulman could be considered as occupying very similar subject positions to Elizabeth Ehrlich: Jewish, urban, east-coast American, second-wave feminist, memoir writer. However, she is at the other end of the domestic/career identity complex that Ehrlich writes from as a mother of young children. When she began writing her memoir *Drinking the Rain*, Shulman was a married woman in her fifties and well-known author of the much read *Memoirs of an Ex Prom Queen*. When she finishes she is a grandmother past sixty living the life of a single, self-employed creative writer. Shulman performs the identity-making balancing acts of a woman past the middle decades of life. I feel an intimate connection with Shulman's position. I find old age rushing at me in what seems not so very long a time after I performed the teenage loss of self described by Maxine Hong Kingston, a disturbingly short time after enacting the young woman's dilemma of multiple role demands enacted by Ehrlich. When I began to feel the demand for more freedom that Shulman's subject postion manifests, I wrote a novel about a woman who took to living alone in a lakeside cottage.[2] Shulman's memoir has a broader reach in that she describes the occasion of her loss of identity after the middle years as an experience of dispossession that has public, professional, and per-

---

2 See my novel *The Cutting Season*.

sonal dimensions. At a public level, she finds that "the very word *feminist*, which we had rescued from the dungeon of ridicule where it had languished for decades, had been recaptured, bound, and gagged" (4). Professionally, as a writer, she discovers "in the bookstores I was shocked to find the newest books written by authors whose names I didn't recognize on subjects I'd failed to consider" (5). On a personal level, not only did "the decline of the women's movement [become] a personal loss, for my own work had grown in its nourishing soil" (5), but Shulman finds herself being interviewed by young historians in "tailored suits" as if she were "a relic" of some distant past.

The course of action that Shulman takes, while different from the "Victorian recluse" behaviours that Kingston describes and the kitchen rituals that answer Ehrlich's needs, has some interesting similarities. All three have the same need to regroup and recover, to confront old issues, old practices, to work through them and perform the new self inside and outside the old forms as a way of repossessing the public world through first restructuring the private life. In Shulman's case, finding her children grown, her long-distance marriage less and less central, her writing suffering, she leaves New York to spend many months alone at a small cabin she and her husband own on Long Island, Maine. Here, without the distractions of city life, she hopes to return to her writing. Like Kingston's withdrawal from her school world into non-identity, Shulman's withdrawal would at first seem to be an effacement. Now that she is alone, she finds she has extraordinary fears of "lack of self" that Weir identifies as the "familiar dark side of culture" (187) that a busy life, marriage, and children have kept at bay. Having previously come to her "nubble," her small peninsula of land, only on high summer vacations with lots of company, she now fears sounds in the night, the prospect of days without company, hours of time unorganized by specific commitments. She also endures every woman's deep-seated fear of falling prey to the predatory male, the anonymous "hacker" (a male stalker/slasher figure) that she imagines hiding under her cabin, behind rocks, along trails. She is "afraid not only of assault but afraid that hidden away [she] would be effaced, forgotten" (8). Shulman has little sense of possessing the small piece of land that is the "nubble," just as she has little sense of possessing the world of her own self-performance. This identity crisis strikes despite the activist, feminist writer's life that, in the past, has given her a sense of effective identity in the larger culture. It strikes despite the assurance that comes to a woman as the result of having successfully mothered children.

The powerful feeling of effacement, what Weir calls the "the familiar dark side of a culture characterized by increasing pressure for self-identity under conditions of increasing fragmentation" (187), can hit hard for a contemporary woman past fifty. Such a woman finds all the public, professional, and personal fragments that she has stitched together to make her identity as a young woman have fallen apart, as the others that made that identity possible (career, marriage, children) are lost or move on into their own separate futures. Yet, like many woman in the same identity crisis, Shulman finds a fearful freedom in this reflection on her condition: "I allow myself the reckless thought that it may not matter if I write or not: with no one here to judge me, discovering what exactly I will do may be a more interesting project than writing a book" (17). For Shulman, ironically, the remedy for her loss of identity lies in practising, in a new way, old mundane rituals, beginning with the preparation of food. However, this is not a return to a past in which she learned sophisticated French recipes out of love of the art of cooking and to entertain her many friends. Nor is it a repetition of the excesses of the vacation weekends when she and her husband churned out pancakes breakfasts, hamburger and hot dog lunches, and great slabs of barbecue meat to feed friends and family at seaside dinners. At times she fears that turning to cooking has the "taint of the female" and that "when a man cooks, when a man is domestic, in place of the taint there's honor" (28). Her new concern with food, building on but not replicating the past, helps her to conquer her fear of being a woman alone in an isolated place. For here she discovers she can gather her own food and find comfort in an isolated environment, while learning about every available product of nature from mussels to wild salad greens. Shulman uses the natural world as a ground to practise her identity as a woman of some self-sufficiency, realizing her connection to the natural world.

Yet this is not a memoir that pretends to an unmediated eco-feminist connection between world and woman. The larger world where she buys vinegar and flour and pasta is as essential as the "nubble" world where she practises identifying pigweed and strawberry goosefoot. The books that the larger world produces to teach her independence, *Stalking the Wild Asparagus* and *Stalking the Blue-Eyed Scallop*, are as important as her adventures in tide pools and along beaches and footpaths. The text has a tripartite division into "The Island," "The Mainland," and "The World." This format indicates that the retreat to the natural world is about learning to practise rituals of self-sufficiency and economy of living that will be re-enacted in the larger world to which the writer will eventually return and repossess through a refreshed identity.

For the active reader that performs her own changes, in part through her reading of other women's experiences, there are many contemporary memoirs that allow the experience of others' rituals of self-performance. I will conclude by referring briefly to a few of these. Memoir, which Marcus Billson maintains has always had a "moral vision," has, in the hands of women like Sharon Butala, taken on the form of the spiritual journey. In *The Perfection of the Morning: An Apprenticeship in Nature*, Butala records the self-invented ceremonies of intimacy that she learns to perform in reaction to a complex "anomie," or loss of self, which she experiences in losing her city identity as a result of marriage and moving to a Saskatchewan ranch. Her growing spirituality comes in large part from the very daily and humble activity of walking in nature, which, incremented by study, contemplation, reminiscence, and the chores of life on a working ranch, teaches her through reiteration a woman's spirituality. Her use of "apprenticeship" in her subtitle signals the practical and practice-based nature of her new identity as a spiritual person and a creative writer.

Anne Herrman's *Menopausal Memoir: Letters from Another Climate* recounts the female "change of life" in a series of letters to significant others. The letters perform cycles of intimacy and alienation, circling around the fact of a surgically induced menopause, each reiteration of a past relationship with another performing necessary realizations, which while sometimes quite negative, also make life livable. The form of the letter softens and balances the often difficult realizations the memoir writer faces. Carolyn G. Heilbrun, who has written of the difficulties women face in auto/biographical practice in *Writing a Woman's Life*, performs her own entry into old age in *The Last Gift of Time: Life Beyond Sixty*. The topical approach taken by the episodes of this text may at first disguise its incremental nature, each topic, from "e-mail" through "England" to "On Not Wearing Dresses," seeming to take up entirely different directions. Yet, with each meditation and its accompanying informing anecdotes, Heilbrun goes another round with old age, incrementally performing an identity that lets go only what it has to in growing older. In doing so she finds new ways to make a full non-sacrificial life, from substituting e-mail discussions for face-to-face meetings, to learning that yearning and desire are not inevitably linked with sex and youth.

Of the many texts I have read in which women perform balancing acts in their desire to sacrifice nothing needful in making identity, Adele Crockett Robertson's *The Orchard: A Memoir* holds a special place for me. Perhaps I like it so much because the manuscript was rescued from oblivion by her daughter, perhaps also because it makes a gripping, fast-paced narrative out of the simple repetitive acts of the seasonal round of activities involved in keeping a fruit orchard. The story of the devastations and renewals of that work, and of one woman's performance of her strength and independence through the rituals of hard labour during the personal and societal crisis of the Great Depression makes inspiring reading. Contemporary women have a lost heritage of memoir writing from their foremothers waiting to be rediscovered and repossessed. The acts of that repossession can be, in themselves, self-performing activities that can counter one of the most pernicious and consistent sacrifices that women are asked to make to participate in mainstream culture: the sacrifice of the possibility of an ongoing women's culture and history.

4

Dancing with Our Mothers

Reading and Writing Memoirs As a Mother and a Daughter

Female children are quite literally starved for matrimony; not for marriage, but for a legacy of power and humanity from adults of their own sex (mothers).

—Phyllis Chesler, *Women and Madness*

There is no easy equivalent of patrimony, since matrimony leads away from the mother and since it's always less clear what, under patriarchy, a daughter can inherit from her mother, let alone pass on or return.

—Nancy Miller, *Bequest and Betrayal*

By ending my last chapter with the assertion that memoirs can help repossess a sacrificed women's culture, the loss of our foremothers' world, I call attention to a concern that runs through my entire experience of reading memoirs. I find that the mother is the primary significant other in many women's accounts. This is an important feature, given that the larger culture has no place for the mother's story except in platitudes about the extremities of mothering, that is, mother as saint or victim, mother as monster or ineffective non-entity. When I wrote my own memoir of growing up, I was particularly anxious that the chapter about my early years not be a "blaming" of my mother for conditions beyond her control. We are encouraged, in our culture, to hold our personal mothers to blame for conditions of the wider culture that too many critics of motherhood forget are not of their mothers' making. In beginning this chapter with two statements about matrimony made a generation apart, I want to signal my own continuing ambivalence towards mothers and memoirs about mother/daughter relationships. A part of me wants to assert, as did Phyllis Chesler in 1972 when second-wave feminism was on the rise, that we must name "matrimony," as patrimony is named. By understanding matrimony as an exchange of power between mother and daughter in the same way that patrimony is understood as an exchange of power between father and son, we may begin to repossess it. Naming it will make it real, and we can then begin to know what it is, begin to repossess the word "matrimony" as a maternal concept. We can begin to conjecture what kind of power we want mothers to have, and what kind of power we want to have as mothers, not only in the personal relationships of mothering, but in the ethical and aesthetic contexts of our culture. Adrienne Rich highlighted the two-sided nature of repossessing maternality in the subtitle of her book *Of Woman Born: Motherhood as Experience and Institution*. Motherhood is both "experience" and "institution," and in our attempts to take on the power that lies latent in a feminist concept of matrimony, we must not leave out either its private or public significance.

In the early 1980s I was able to make the kind of positive assertion that renaming matrimony implies. I did that by using

Phyllis Chesler's words concerning matrimony to begin my M.A. thesis on Margaret Laurence, which was later published as *Mother and Daughter Relationships in the Manawaka Works of Margaret Laurence.* This book traces the development of the mother/daughter motif in Laurence's several novels about women. As the most celebrated novelist of the post-World War II renaissance in Canadian literature, Laurence's "Manawaka" books created an imaginative world centred on the Canadian prairie landscape, one as textured and specifically located as is Faulkner's Yoknapatawpha County in the American South. Laurence's world centres on female figures that I felt were bereft of positive maternal influences. Since most of the plethora of criticism devoted to Laurence's work concentrated on everything but the maternal, I wanted to show how a subtext of maternality shaped Laurence's novels. I was younger then, second-wave feminism was young too, and both it and I were full of optimism. Now, in the late 1990s, I find I must allow Nancy Miller's doubts about the existence of "matrimony" to qualify my earlier positivism. I have found, as a daughter and as a mother of a daughter, that there is no easy claiming of "matrimony," no matter how great may be my desire for it. In the years since my assertions about "matrimony" in my work on Laurence I have read dozens of women's memoirs of their mothers. The very number of these works would seem to constitute a subgenre of memoir itself. Yet, after so many readings, I can still pick up almost any one of these books and have a reading experience quite different from the last. I want to explore the phenomenon of my different readings over time in order to better understand the effects of the alliance that a reader like myself makes with the tripartite narrator of memoirs and how that alliance changes over time and rereading. This performance of my acts as reader is my construction of "limit attitude," the process that Probyn describes as the critic's "enunciative position" (31) whereby she constructs her historically specific subject position. My "enunciative position" includes the specificity of my place in mother/daughter relationships.

In my book about Canadian women's autobiography, I offered the concept of a woman's ongoing relationship with her mother as a "re-e-merging" process. I suggested that women make their selves "not in a continuing act of defining the separate self, as has been suggested by Freudians for male development, but in a continuing act of separation/merging" (*Mapping* 17). In retrospect, I often think that my readings of other women's memoirs depend on where I am performing, at any given reading moment, in terms of the separation/merging continuum of my own relationship with my mother and/or my daughter. Thus, reading mother/daughter memoirs is much more intensely an act of personal participation than other reading acts I make. In the late 1980s I was in a very intense "separation" stage. I was breaking the rules of long-term motherhood by taking my first university appointment away from the city where my husband stayed to tend to his job, raise our fifteen-year-old son, and keep the home fires burning for our college-aged daughter and married son. My mother had serious doubts about the wisdom of my course of action. It wasn't that she was not proud of me, even a little envious, but it was clear that she knew of no narratives of women like me that came to any good end. Although my relationship with sons, daughter, and husband seem to have survived my separation mode, I was unsure, at times, that my always defensive relationship with my mother would. At such a stage I welcomed the daughters' separation narratives that affirmed me. Now, almost thirteen years later, my own mother is declining in measurable stages that arrive before I am prepared for them. She has long forgotten that I am the daughter who rebels, who needs to be worried about. For her, I am a visitor she loves to see, a replacement for her long-dead and beloved sister, Helen. I now merge in her mind with that wonderful aunt whom she named me after, and I bask, as if it were sunshine after a storm, in the look of unconditional delight and love that comes to her eyes when she sees me. At the same time I am preparing to spend time with my now mature adult daughter, who is long past her own teenage rebellions against a sometimes interfering mother, and who has invited me to share with her and her partner the experience of birthing my grandchild. I have another grandchild as well, whose very existence during these last four years has taught me the deep pleasure of the continuation of the generations, and made my own childhood and parenting years suddenly vividly alive again. Yes, I am not in separation mode now. I am in a merging stage of "re-e-merging," as I await the new performance of self that will emerge from the experience of grandparenting and my new position in relation to my mother.

I would like to illustrate, by reference to a contemporary memoirlike text, the difference those two moments in my personal history can make to reading. I call Carolyn Steedman's *Landscape for a Good Woman* "memoirlike" since it was not called a memoir by its author at the time of publication (1986), but rather was described as "partly autobiographical." Perhaps the more correct description for it is "autocritography," a designation coined by Aram Veeser in *Confessions of the Critics* in 1996. Steedman writes memoirlike anecdotes of her relationship with her mother, which she analyzes from the position of cultural critic and historian. As an academic trained in the discourses of cultural studies, Steedman uses the insights of history, politics, psychoanalysis, and feminism to inquire into "a story of two lives" (her subtitle), her mother's and her own. Her purpose is to show how certain stories, those not privileged by dominant gender and class positions, are simply not told in our culture. She intends, as she says early in her text, to take up "the narrative form of case-study [which] shows what went into its writing, shows the bits and pieces from which it is made up, in the way that history refuses to do and that fiction can't" (21). When I first read *Landscape*, back in the late 1980s, I was fascinated by it. The fact that a scholar was discovering a way to bring her professional training and her personal life into a joined discourse was a great encouragement to me in my similar quest. And I admired her openness about her alienation from her mother. I realized that the book performed an extreme dissension, fuelled by recrimination and finally silence, which survives in the daughter after her mother's death. However, I admired the honesty and the lack of hypocrisy that Steedman exhibited in not underestimating the degree of alienation that can grow between mothers and daughters when changing class and gender roles come between them. I admired how Steedman found formal ways to handle the negative material and the class difference between her mother and herself. She does this by placing the class system in which her mother lived, and in which she herself was raised, in the context of the theories she has learned as a cultural critic. *Landscape*, a combination of memoir and academic study, was for me in 1988 a cogent condemnation of the class system in England as well as a vivid illustration of the oppression under which Steedman's mother (and many mothers) lived. It was also a dramatic portrayal of the pain and anger the daughter still carries as a result of their underprivileged and divisive world. I knew from my studies and my own experience that mothers and their daughters—given the immense changes that have happened in recent years in women's career and work patterns, in their access to economic power and the technologies of reproduction—were dispossessed of the common ties that the shared experience of oppression in a more traditional patriarchal world had provided. Women of two generations often find they live in different, even hostile worlds as far as their class and gender experience is concerned.

When I recently reread Steedman's book at a different stage of my own life in preparation for this study, I found myself protesting not so much the portrayal of the mother—a canny reader can read between the lines and against the grain of the daughter's negativity—as the daughter's blaming of the mother and her need to separate herself from any identification with her. These features dominate the book for me now, despite its careful analysis of class. The extreme form of the text's agenda of sacrificial separation now seems obvious to me, after having read many daughters' accounts and after working with Weir's theory of "sacrificial logics" of identity. One of the events posited as an originating formative moment for Steedman is the childhood visit of a health worker to her mother, who is pregnant with Steedman's younger sister. The health worker observes haughtily, without offering any solution, that "[t]his house isn't fit for a baby." Steedman is witness to her mother's tears and her characteristic picking-herself-up-and-going-on phrase: "Hard lines, eh, Kay" (2). But the narrator, after witnessing these reactions to the insult, does not pause to participate in the mother's situation. Neither does she express any sympathy for her mother's unfair degradation. There is no account of how the child may have felt her mother's pain, no positive solidarity in the face of a class insult, not even admiration for a feisty mother. Instead, there is this: "I will do everything and anything until the end of my days to stop anyone ever talking to me like that woman talked to my mother. It is in this place, this bare, curtainless bedroom that lies my secret and shameful defiance. I read a woman's book, meet such a woman at a party (a woman, now, like me) and think quite deliberately as we talk: we are divided: a hundred years ago I'd have been cleaning your shoes. I know this and you don't" (2). The effect of the insult is to make Steedman disassociate herself from her mother's condition, to make sure it never happens to her, and to carry the insult like a badge to alienate her from other women in the future. This disassociation from the mother seems to me now to also be tied up with the formal composition of the text. If the text performs the self, then the formal elements will aid or hinder that self-performance. Being more aware of the complex and necessary interplay of witness, participant, and reflective/reflexive consciousness in the narrative function of memoir, I find that Steedman's text is marked by a failure of the participant function. There is a tendency to leap too quickly to the reflective function, as well as a tendency to elevate reflectivity over its twin, reflexivity. I think this is the result of writing autocritical work that has too little "auto" in its autocriticism.

As I move through Steedman's text this time, continuing evidence of her failure to understand her mother's position jumps out at me. If Steedman had performed herself as a person too traumatized to contemplate a more tender stand toward her childhood situation I would accept her subjectivity as regrettable but necessary. However, she finds no problem in reflecting on her relationship with her father with an intelligent reflexivity that allows her to forgive him, although he left the family when she and her sister were quite young. She introduces him to her college friends as a kind of working-class hero, in the same years in which she refuses to see her mother. Even her father cannot understand why she rejects her mother. He is continually referred to in jocular or sympathetic terms. He has become "quite vulnerable in memory" (50) for her as an adult. She even apologizes to him: "I feel a great regret for the father of my first four years, who took me out and who probably loved me, irresponsibly...and I wish I could tell him now, even though he really was a sod, that I'm sorry for the years of rejection and dislike" (36). My ellipses, in this last quotation, omit Steedman's repetition of her mother's words in parentheses, her judgment that "[i]t's alright for him; he doesn't have to look after you." At the very moment of forgiving the father, she blames the mother. Steedman's judgment is that her mother forced her to choose between parents because of her own unhappiness. Fair enough; any child who lives with the experience of a bitter, deserted mother who blames the father and hates the way he gets credit for little moments of fun while she does the hard work of rearing knows what it is like to be divided in half.

However, Steedman's performance of her mother's negativity does not rest in the ambiguity of division. She chooses a sacrificial logic of identity and turns her justified distress into a condemnation. She learns as an adult that her father had never married her mother because of a previous marriage (he had deserted a wife and child in the north of England to live with Steedman's mother in London). Steedman, surprisingly, does not moderate her attitude toward her mother because of any understanding she might have gained, as a cultural critic and historian, of the seriousness of this unmarried state for women in that time. In fact, any awareness she has of how this explains her mother's secretiveness, her bitterness, is dismissed in favour of this judgment of her mother's actions: "He and my mother had been together for ten years when I was born, and we [she and her sister] think now that I was her hostage to fortune, the factor that might persuade him to get a divorce and marry her. But the *ploy* failed" (39; emphasis mine). Although I might have once been predisposed to see this as a cool analysis of a desperate mother's attempt to legitimize her relationship, the choice of the word "ploy" now signals for me the daughter's contempt for the mother's assumed motivations. Her use of the word "ploy" dismisses any idea that the mother might be justified, after ten years, to simply want to have children. It also dismisses the mother's seemingly reasonable desire to have her children born inside a marriage contract. As well, there is no consideration of the possibility that when she was conceived, Steedman might have been a wanted child for reasons other than to force a marriage. In assessing her mother's second occasion of pregnancy, Steedman calls it "my father's second seduction. She'd tried with having me, and it hadn't worked. Now, a second and final attempt" (53). The assumption is that the mother "seduced" the father, who by implication was the innocent victim with no choice or control.

    Reading this book in the present moment, a moment when I more fully realize my position as mother, rather than as daughter, and having read many daughters' accounts since my first reading, I come smack up against two disturbing questions, questions that would not have disturbed me in the days when I lived out the script of a rebel daughter: What is it that makes daughters assume that they can know, so certainly, their mothers' motivations? What makes daughters assume that their mothers' motivations are of such a negative, manipulative quality? I think the first question is answered in Nancy Miller's observation about the "founding confusion of boundaries" between mothers and daughters, the sense that daughters identify so strongly with their mothers that to separate themselves requires a negative act of denial. Part of that "confusion of boundaries" is the assumption of total knowledge of the other. Despite Steedman's attempts to disassociate herself from her mother, in some profound and negative way she feels she is psychologically joined to her mother, and she therefore knows exactly what her mother thought and felt. Even though she separated herself so completely that she did not see her mother for nine years as a young adult, she still feels this uncanny, negative merging. The irony of her choice of a separation mode is that she cannot separate herself psychologically from her negative view of her mother. The second question is answered by understanding why the feeling of being your mother could be as negative as is Steedman's experience of it. It is in the performances of patriarchally defined identity in women that the image of the mother as either saint or monster emerges. Steedman says that because she didn't have a father who "dictated each day's existence....I don't quite believe in male power; somehow the iron of patriarchy didn't enter my soul." In her nightmares "it is a woman who holds the knife, and only a woman can kill" (19).

While refusing the patriarchal definitions of father for her own father, she accepts patriarchy's definitions of her mother, a mother who is a monster holding a knife. Because her father was not powerful in the world or present in the household, she ignores the power he does have: to withhold legitimacy from the woman he lived with and the children she has by him. She ignores the power her father has to leave with the full confidence that someone else will be responsible for his children. In my recent reading of Steedman's book I came to the conclusion that a very powerful form of the "iron of patriarchy" had possessed her in the writing of her mother's life. I find the book performs a particularly pernicious brand of misogyny that, while not an active woman-hating activity, holds women and men to different standards of behaviour, which leads to a greater condemnation of women than men for similar acts.

This is a harsh judgment, and one I perform for you now with some reticence, since by exposing it I perform parts of my self that I do not always like to acknowledge. A person like myself is supposed to have a certain academic moderation in her reading acts. Yet, I am often angry, sometimes hostile, and even hurt when I read. I also expose the fact that a woman like me, who so believes in solidarity with other women that I work hard to find the positive value in any woman's text I read, can find some women's texts offensive. These emotional reactions often happen in texts about mothers and daughters, in which what I read is that either mother or daughter has gone over to the other side, so to speak, by demanding a higher standard of behaviour from women than from men. Such a woman judges other women more harshly and lets men off easier. I think these women's books disturb me so much because I have sometimes been that kind of woman. I am sometimes a woman who feels the burden of the mother/daughter relationship. Despite all my performative efforts to see my mother in the frame of history—opportunities aroused in and then denied to that generation of mothers growing up in an earlier part of the century—it has been difficult to forgive the consequences of being raised in the mother's bitterness. Steedman describes the effect of growing up while hearing constantly of all the unfairness forced on the mother: "In this way you come to know that you are not quite yourself but someone else: someone else has paid the price for you, and you have to pay it back. You grow small and quiet and take up very little room. You take on the burden of being good, which is the burden of the capacity to know exactly how someone else is feeling" (105). I note that here Steedman merges her childhood identity with her mother's and assumes she knows "exactly" how the mother feels. If a girl raised in this way grows up to become a wife and mother she has the capacity to serve exactly the role that the patriarchy desires of her, to never be quite a person. She will tend to gain existence through someone else, the husband if he allows it, or the children for as long as they will allow it. Some mothers rebel against this role, but because there was, in the era of Steedman's mother, only opportunities for partial rebellion, usually in the form of complaints and anger, children often suffered the fallout of their mothers' discontent. There is one benefit to becoming a mother in patriarchy: you can learn to better appreciate your own mother's anger, an anger that, with no opportunity to be transposed in to positive action, tends to be performed as bitterness. Such daughters are also in danger of performing another role that awaits women in patriarchy: that of the unforgiving critic of women who have not mothered well. I have performed some aspects of all of these subject positions in my time, and *Landscape* disturbs me by reminding me of my own inconsistencies, my own cruelties. It reminds me also of my own dispossession in terms of "matrimony," that "legacy of power and humanity" from the older generation of women that so often eludes women of my generation. *Landscape* becomes a difficult, but necessary, rereading practice for me, one that in its reiteration helps me assess my own self-performance.

 Steedman herself has felt some discontent with *Landscape*, and it is interesting for my purposes that this discontent expresses itself in a discussion of genre. In "Autobiography and History" she admits that *Landscape* "is a book that is designed to hurt, to tell them...that they have not experienced...that which places you on the outside, and makes you bitter and envious enough to want to hurt in this way" (43). I would point out that she does not see the book as "designed to hurt" family members (her parents are dead and her sister is apparently in agreement with her), but to hurt people of the dominant class. She sees her book as an expression of a working-class consciousness that has always been misrepresented by those in charge of various discourses of history and literature because of their upper-class "notions of cheerful decency, poor-honest-but-happiness" the class she comes from (43). It is in the context of this class discussion that she brings up genre, saying that, "autobiography is to be distinguished from such *genre* as memoir and reminiscence by the status and function of experience within it. In the form of memoir for instance, it is a series of external factors that is presented as dictating the narrative course. These factors or events may be translated into inner experience, but that inner experience—lived and felt experience—is not its focus, as it is in autobiography" (43–44). Steedman understands memoir as a different practice because of the way it can make an alliance with history in using "external factors" like class to direct plot. Thus, if enough of us write our lives, history's broad assumptions about what is important and how reality is constructed will change. Steedman says she wanted readers to begin the book thinking they were not reading history, but reach a different conclusion by its end: "I want those readers to say that what I have produced *is* history" (45). I know exactly what she means by this ambitious desire to repossess history for the purpose of performing a female-identified account of the past. Those of us who have discovered the use of memoir know that it has the potential to act as a powerful agent for change because of the way external "factors or events may be translated into inner experience" and gain power from that personalization, yet emerge finally not just as personal, but as intimately bound up with some condition of more societal, and therefore historical, importance. In this way women's memoirs can repossess the world.

Yet for women writing about their personal mothers, in the service of changing the whole history of ignorance or misconstruction of the subject of women's lives, some degree of failure and misunderstanding seems inevitable. Steedman's failure lies in the fact that by frankly representing her mother's bitter unhappiness, she may be making a stand for her class while profoundly betraying her mother as a female person. As she herself says: "One of my organizing principles in *Landscape for a Good Woman* is the pitching of class against gender, and class is allowed to win, as the more interesting, important, and relevatory interpretive device" ("History" 43). In allowing class to "win," her discourse performs an insensitivity to her mother's gendered place.

My argument is now in the ironic place of accusing Steedman of exactly the same betrayal of the mother of which Colleen Kennedy accused Maxine Hong Kingston (50–51, this text). I argued that Kingston had not betrayed her mother, because by representing the broad spectrum of her mother's performance of self she gives readers a whole woman. Many readers' testimonies seem to confirm this judgment. I think Kingston's success in this regard results from constantly maintaining a balancing act between elements of class, race, and gender in her narrative functions in the text. In her witness to her mother's life, her performance of her own shortcomings, and her reflections on the ways in which she uses her mother's talk-story talent to perform her own place in the world, Kingston balances her portrait of her mother. I find that because in Steedman's book "class [alone] is allowed to win" the portrayal of a whole woman does not happen. The portrayal of the mother becomes the betrayal of the mother. Ironically, while I do not find Kennedy's analysis of Kingston to be valid, I do find it has considerable applicability for Steedman's text. Kennedy's analysis of the problem of women attempting to speak in discourses developed by male needs is a set-up for failure: "These artists' voices in the women's tradition do rebel, but the patriarchal values they rebel against have already determined the form of their rebellion—as a self that will exclude anything threatening its autonomy" (128). I believe that many contemporary uses of the memoir form overcome this seeming inevitability, because they do not accept "autonomy" as the only ground of self-performance.

I find that Steedman's *Landscape* does seek autonomy, and that autonomy is gained at the cost of the portrayal/betrayal of the mother. I think the book is such a disappointment and yet of continuing fascination for me because the memoir aspects of her text point up the terrible sacrifice of autonomy. Every time Steedman gets personal about herself and her mother she enters a discourse whose formal elements, especially the narrative functions, require a performance of reassessment, reconciliation, and reconstitution that will lead to a "re-e-mergence" of self whereby the self can grow to understand the past more perceptively. In this case it might lead us to understand the inheritance of bitterness as a societal phenomenon resulting from class and gender, and to realize it in a way that does not place blame on an individual who was as much a victim as the memoirist. Each time Steedman short-circuits that discourse by refusing its full identity-performance capabilities, she fails to repossess the world of motherhood from a non-patriarchal position. Observing the points of entry and refusal teaches me a great deal about the act of memoir writing.

I often learn as much from memoirs that seem to have failed as I do from those that seem, at least in an artistic sense, to succeed. What I learn from my two readings of *Landscape* is that it is indeed "history" as Steedman wants it to be, if not quite in the way she wants it to be (as an analysis of class). My own emotional involvement with the book teaches me the conflicted history of the mother/daughter relationship, and how that history has helped keep many of us psychologically enslaved. That sense of a self still chained comes even while opportunities for economic advancement and individual freedom open up for women because of the efforts of other women in the past.

In an early version of this chapter I virtually excluded my tangle with *Landscape*, because I wanted this chapter on mother/daughter memoirs to have a more positive agenda, one showing the multitude of rich cultural artifacts that this art is producing. But I needed to converse again with Steedman's account to more fully discover what is successful in other accounts. Almost inevitably what I find are certain formal choices that act as facilitators for the texts and for the identity-performance that the writer is making. In this regard I want to talk about my experience of reading Margaret Laurence's *Dance on the Earth: A Memoir.*

When I wrote my M.A. thesis on Laurence I felt that she had not fully finished with the motif of mother and daughter. She had not written a novel in years, and I, full of hubris, sent her a copy of my mother/daughter study when it was published in 1985, with a secret desire that my scholarship might influence her to take up the motif once again. A few months later I received a one-line letter thanking me for my gift. I felt a little disappointed that Laurence had not commented on my work, and written a few lines to me rather than just one. Perhaps I was the kind of daughter who wants to think her mother can learn from her. I was, certainly, a daughter "starved for matrimony," a legacy of "power and humanity" from my chosen surrogate literary mother. Of course, our chosen surrogate mothers do not always know they have been given this honour and burden because in our culture mother/daughter relational activity is embedded and essential, but often dismissed or considered unremarkable. What I did not know was that Laurence was coming to the end of her life when she received my gift, but was also coming to the apotheosis of her work on the mother/daughter relationship.

When I sat down to read *Dance* four years later, after learning of the health difficulties—the vision problems, the cancer—Laurence had suffered from in those last few years of life, I had already become very grateful for the one-line thank you I had received from her. I was not prepared, however, for my reaction to her final book, edited and published posthumously by her daughter. I recall very clearly that during my first reading I sat in one position for four hours, unable to pull my eyes from her text, hardly able to reach for tissues to wipe away my tears. The tears began to fall during the first page of the "Verna" chapter, dedicated to Laurence's mother, who died when she was four. The tears did not stop through the "Margaret" and "Elsie" chapters (devoted to her stepmother and mother-in-law) as I experienced Laurence's lifting of the great weight of the subtextual mother/daughter motif of her other works up to the surface of her art. I cried for Laurence and I cried for myself. The words I kept repeating as I read and wept were "She did it. She did it. She did it." It is the first time in my life I cried not from being moved by the content of something touching, but rather out of admiration and gratitude for an accomplishment of form. I cried in pleasure at her achievement of structuring her chapters around four mothers, including herself. I cried because I suddenly understood my own search for form in my creative work, my need to break from linear narration, not with the aim of a deconstructive critique of form, but rather with the aim of creating new, more commodious forms in which I could repossess my culture. Those hours of tears have affected my own professional and writing life ever since. They made me realize how generic choices and formal arrangements are at the heart of making art, whether it is the art of fiction, of memoir, or of theoretical and critical texts. As a result of that experience with Laurence's *Dance* two important changes have happened in my own work: I have moved away from writing fiction (perhaps temporarily) to experiments in memoir, and I have worked to develop a form of autocritical discourse in my academic writing. These two efforts have required many carefully orchestrated moves, many occasions when I have stepped on the wrong toes as I construct my practice through trial and error. Most of all it has required learning to dance with my mothers as I choreograph my discourse, both my personal mother and all the surrogate mothers that have nurtured me, including Laurence.

In my enthusiasm for *Dance* I rushed it onto the syllabus of a course I was teaching in Canadian autobiography, then waited for the seminar participants (all senior undergraduates, all women) to weep their own tears. Such reactions were not to come from my clever young deconstructors. "Don't you think she appropriates the mother figures?" they tentatively asked. "Don't you find she essentializes mothers?" I was devastated. Into the silence of my devastation my canny students leapt. "Look here when she comes to the climactic moment in her step-mom's story. The poor woman seems kept alive just to read Laurence's first novel. Isn't she as much the phallic mother as any son would wish, dispensing her life and intelligence in aid of the son? Only here Laurence gets to be the son." Finding me barely able to speak, my students hurried on. "Isn't she really writing about the mother-in-law because she dare not write about her marriage? She is not the rebel that Maynard Bruser is. Laurence obeys the patriarchal law of silence on the personal world." They had read Fredelle Maynard Bruser's brave exploration of her marriage as well as her place as mother and daughter in *The Tree of Life*, and admired the way she had broken the unwritten taboos, and they were giving no quarter to Laurence. We got through the class somehow, and on to other texts, but I was perturbed enough not to put *Dance* on a course outline since then, preferring to illustrate Laurence's autobiographical art with her post-colonial travel memoir, *The Prophet's Camel Bell.*

What I have done instead is embark on a reiterative reading performance, reading dozens of women's memoirs that take up the mother/daughter relationship in some substantive way. What I am searching for is a way of validating my own first reactions, while not denying the validity of my students' critiques. I want a critical genealogy that can contain both myself and my students. In doing this I am engaged in analyzing the way narrative has traditionally worked, as Marianne Hirsch describes it in *The Mother/Daughter Plot:* "the very continuity of narrative, its potential to make sense, from syntax to plot structure, seems to depend on a relation of paternity." Hirsch, quoting Edward Said, continues: "'The narrative represents the generative process—literally in its mimetic representation of men and women in time, metaphorically in that by itself it generates succession and multiplication of events after the manner of human procreation'" (51). Hirsch points out that in Said's theory of narrative procreation the engendering of narrative takes place "without the help of the mother," and she goes on to examine the repression of the mother/daughter plot in the history of fiction.

I agree with Hirsch that the history of fiction up to very recent times is a history of maternal absence or at least repression, but I do not agree that we lack a tradition of the mother/daughter plot. Women have been trying to write about that plot in autobiography for a number of centuries, even though every pressure of culture and art teaches them to absent their mothers from the narratives of their lives. We are still working at it, now in our fiction as well as in our memoir work. It is a dance fraught with cultural traps, a dance carried on in a minefield of negativity awaiting every woman who writes of mothering and being mothered.

In a book entitled *In Her Image: The Unhealed Daughter's Search for Her Mother*, Kathie Carlson states that "the primary relationship between women is the relationship between mother and daughter. This relationship is the birthplace of woman's ego identity, her sense of security in the world, her feelings about herself, her body, and other women. From her mother a woman receives her first impression of how to be a woman and what being a woman means" (xi). Carlson goes on to observe that "as a therapist, teacher, mother and daughter myself, I have been most concerned with the amount of woundedness so many women feel vis-à-vis their mothers, how much 'unfinished business' seems to permeate this relationship." She has "also been deeply impressed both in [her]self and in others by the ferocious tenacity of longing for 'something more'" (xi).

When I read these words I nod my head in agreement. I certainly have felt a great sense of "unfinished business" between my own mother and myself and yet have also found contentment in the new pleasure my mother finds in my visits, a contentment that gives me "something more." But then I read the next line of Carlson's text: "We long for a mother who can give us all that we need from her and receive all that we want to give her" (xi). These words make the scholar in me begin to get nervous. I'm nervous because my own reading and research teaches me that "all that we need from her...all we want to give her" are sweet words for a bitter quandary that we live with in our culture. We have a tendency to blame and vilify mothers, holding them responsible for every fault in their offspring, and a contrary tendency to idealize mothers, imagining them capable of fulfilling all the needs and wants of their children. As a mother I am even more nervous, because I am aware that I never have been able to give my children all that they might have thought they needed from me, and certainly am not capable of accepting without reservation what they might want to give. With each passing year I am more aware that my mothering abilities have always had their limitations, just as my abilities in every other part of my life face limitations. I am also uncomfortably aware that many people may hear such a statement as a confessional acknowledgement of personal failure, rather than what it is meant to perform. Such "confessional" statements are not a plea for redemption but are part of my "balancing act," an attempt to avoid the sacrificial binaries of idealization and blame.

Part of the problem of this dichotomy of our concepts of the mother comes to us through a whole history of patriarchal religion, literature, and culture, in which women are idealized as the sacred vessels of male godhead, or vilified as the fleshy sewers of carnal sin. This is a large and lengthy history of maternal dispossession that I do not propose to rehearse here, but some references to recent history may illuminate the effect of this binary on my life and the lives of women like me.[1] Shari Thurer points out in *The Myths of Motherhood* that by the 1940s the couches of analysts were becoming crowded with confessions of people who had "neglectful moms." At the same moment, the military was explaining why they had to reject so many men called up in the draft who were "emotionally unstable" because of "maternal overprotection." Indeed, *Maternal Overprotection* was the title of book by psychoanalyst David Levy, published in 1942 (Thurer 272).

My own introduction to this virulent anti-mom stance came in the form of Philip Wylie's *Generation of Vipers*, which I read in 1958, when I was seventeen. I didn't know at that tender age the meaning of the word "misogynist," indeed had no concept of the phenomenon of woman hating. I swallowed every line of Wylie's poison-pen letter to the moms of America, living out through his words my own teenage rebellion against a mother who made unreasonable demands of me. (She kept insisting that I clean my own room, that I keep a civil tongue in my head, at least when her friends were visiting, and that I consider the benefits of wearing snowboots in Prairie winters.) I did not know

---

[1] An informative chapter regarding this history and its effect on autobiographical practices is Sidonie Smith's "Renaissance Humanism and the Misbegotten Man: A Tension of Discourses in the Emergence of Autobiography," in *A Poetics of Women's Autobiography*.

then of any alternative cultural models to the mother-blaming model. Wylie's book was representative of the negative side of what my white middle-class culture was doing with the figure of the personal mother in the forties and fifties. The other side was represented by those perfect television moms, such as the mom on *Father Knows Best*. What I also did not know then was that within four years of exulting in Wylie's mother bashing, I would myself become a mother.

I have spent the years of my life since that time trying, in various ways, to find a more positive view of my own maternal condition than my culture has provided me. This has not been easy. My lived life during the sixties, seventies, and early eighties was a history of mothering while working outside the home, which by the contemporary wisdom made me a "bad mom." As I became more and more a feminist as a result of my experience as a woman (as well as my intellectual pursuits as a lifetime student), I discovered, to my chagrin, that feminists didn't have much that was positive to say about mothers either, and especially mothers and their relationships with their daughters.

For the most part, feminists avoided the subject of the mother, but when we did take up the issue, in the seventies and eighties, we had some real problems. These problems are summarized by Nancy Chodorow and Susan Contratto in an article entitled "The Fantasy of the Perfect Mother." They point out that feminists, being products of their culture like everyone else, also tend to idealize motherhood and blame individual mothers, although we do not do it in the same way as misogynists. We have a tendency to accept uncritically our culture's truism that the "child's felt desires are absolute needs" (195), thus implying that it really is the job of the mother to fulfil all those "needs." To do this we would have to become the kind of mothers that Adrienne Rich imagines when she speaks of a more utopian time. In such a time, freed from the negative cultural burdens attached to living in a female body, "every woman [would be] the presiding genius of her own body" (qt. in Chodorow 196). While I mark my reading of Rich's *Of Woman Born* in the mid-eighties as an important turning point in my thinking about maternality, I have come reluctantly to agree with Chodorow and Contratto.

They point out that the problem with Rich's idea—that once we learn to live more comfortably inside our own bodies we will be better mothers—is that it implies that under the right conditions, mothering really could be the ideal state that the old patriarchal religions and philosophies teach us. We really could become the source of all things for our babies and be the kind of self-contained healthy persons who could allow our children to walk out of our lives the minute their own desires dictate it. This idealism is a dangerous condition for the reputations of ordinary women who raise children. I believe that shifting the blame from the individual mother to the conditions of patriarchy, as feminists like myself have tended to do, may be a step in the right direction, but it is nowhere near a solution. What results when we shift blame, but don't inquire into the underlying causes, is that whereas "antifeminists have tended to blame the mother, feminists tend to blame the...having of children" (200). As Chodorow and Contratto observe, as long as "mother and child are seen as both physically and psychologically apart from the world, existing within a magic or cursed circle," our thinking about mothers and their children will remain essentially what they call "extremist fantasies." This is Chodorow and Contratto's term for a condition in which I have found myself and many feminists caught: "[A]s long as we do not work our way out of these fantasies of a perfected maternal condition we deny [mothers] their place in a two-way relationship with their children, manifold relationships with the rest of the world; and we deny ourselves as mothers....Insofar as mothers are women, this involves a denial of all women as active subjects and a denial and split in our self identities as children/daughters and people as well" (206). There is no justice or even good sense in seeking to repossess the world for ourselves through our memoirs of our mothers, if by the same act we deny a place in the world to those mothers. As Weir observes, summarizing the significance of Kristeva's work, "the fantasy of complete gratification in the 'archaic mother' is itself a central fantasy of patriarchy. Thus, its adoption by women as a basis of emancipation, as an alternative to a patriarchal order, will always backfire" (148).

This is the kind of conflicted tradition that I bring to my reading of women's memoirs. What I find in my readings is that despite the many negativities they need to express, despite the silences and taboos that they nervously work at breaking, despite the failures of expression resulting from the lack of literary models, it is in the formal solutions they construct that these women memoirists find their solutions to the lack of discursive matrimony. Memoirs, by definition, are about the self in relation to others, the self in relation to the culture one lives in. Being a negotiation of self and other, self and culture, self and language, the memoir offers interesting possibilities for contemporary women concerned with mother/daughter relationships.

Negotiating binaries is tricky work. Mary Catherine Bateson, in her memoir *With a Daughter's Eye*, explores her life as the child of the famous anthropologists Margaret Mead and Gregory Bateson. She says of her memoir: "I have tried to weave my own ambivalence into this book, letting love and grief, longing and anger, lie close to the surface, and making it clear that there is no perfection to enshrine and no orthodoxy to defend but much to use and much to value" (288). One of Bateson's challenges, particularly in telling her story as the daughter of Margaret Mead, is to decide how to feel about her own unusual upbringing. She was perhaps the most recorded child in history, her mother combining mothering with anthropological observation, weaving her child's life into the tapestry of her varied scholarship. In doing so, Mead broke a basic rule of our culture, that the home is the place of private life, separate and not integrated with our public existence. Mary Bateson tries to estimate her feelings about the various ways in which her mother violated cultural assumptions.

While vitally involved in every stage of her child's development, Mead was not averse to sharing her maternal duties with mother surrogates. Indeed, sharing her mother with a multitude of others becomes one of the ironies that constructs Bateson's memoirs: Mead's exciting circle of influence both took her mother from her and provided the child Mary with an incredibly rich childhood. Margaret Mead broke all the rules that her era dictated for the proper mom, and she broke them brilliantly and with élan. Her daughter both admires and resents this cultural disobedience, both regrets the distance it sometimes induced between her and her mother and appreciates the advantages she feels her upbringing has given her. This negotiation of binaries is successfully carried out because Bateson takes up an important feature of memoir writing: the full tripartite responsibility of the narrator of memoir. She establishes a relationship with the reader that involves the writer in an intimate (albeit selective) sharing of her doubts and reservations, constructing anecdotes of the past that are constantly intertwined with the reflective/reflexive performance of the narrator in the present.

An important part of the reflexive feature of this process is facilitated by finding herself in a maternal subject position: "Only when I began trying to combine motherhood and housekeeping with professional work myself did I begin to get some sense of the complex infrastructure of my mother's life, the number of people involved in looking after me in the afternoons, getting me home, coming over to cook dinner, and of the way in which my life has been enriched by the diversity of these arrangements and the different kinds of people with whom my life was linked" (74). Ironically, part of the performance of the mother figure as positive, despite her unconventionality, lies in the equal performance of the relationship with the father. Obviously, Bateson's situation as a child of two famous parents makes it necessary to include the father in detail. The subtitle of *With a Daughter's Eye* is *A Memoir of Margaret Mead and Gregory Bateson*. This necessity also becomes a virtue. In studying both her parents with an anthropologist's as well as a daughter's eye, she is able to produce a richer portrait of each and avoid the sense of the mother and child as "existing within a magic or cursed circle." She is able to avoid the "the cultural truism" that the "child's felt desires are absolute needs."

She begins her memoir with the creation of tropes of the "two worlds" represented by her parents—the mother's by trays of miniature play worlds Mead encouraged her daughter to construct, the father's by various aquaria he and his daughter set up together. In this way Bateson makes it clear that each world was a product of the welcome difference of the two individuals' parenting. Certainly, despite her parents' divorce when she was very young, Bateson's life was one of privilege, but it is not its privilege that makes her text a model of evenhanded representation of others. She could easily complain of a mother who often put her profession first, or a father who was rarely with her because of his second family. It is her approach to memoir as a genre different from others that avoids a portrayal that is unfair to either parent. She describes it this way:

> This is not a book about Margaret Mead or Gregory Bateson that strives for completeness and objectivity and attempts to define the place of one or the other in the wider world; rather, it concerns the moments and the modalities of my relationship with each and occasionally, because these informed the relationships, my sense of each with others or of wider historical and professional contexts that converged in me. Others have other stories to tell. My father, after his divorce from my mother, had other children; my mother had no other children but many godchildren; both had students who knew them as teachers. As an adult I became an anthropologist myself and a colleague to each in their scientific work, both like and unlike other colleagues. There will be biographers aplenty who will attempt to synthesize multiple views and wade through the published and unpublished documents that illuminate lives, tracing the names and dates, evaluating and categorizing, but I have not wanted or dared to undertake these tasks. The wholeness of this book comes only from my experience and the effort to understand the first chapters of my own lifetime, incomplete, ambivalent, only partly conscious, involved as well in other worlds and relationships, a continuing odyssey through spheres of love and learning. (6-7)

By establishing that it is not memoir's task to offer "completeness and objectivity," by honouring its dependence on "relationship" and the connection of that feature to "wider historical and professional contexts," Bateson describes the special way memoir discourse works. She also understands that part of the memoirist's task is to understand that those contexts are not separate from the "I" of the memoir, but that they "converge[] in me." In this way she acknowledges her responsibility as witness, participant, and reflective/reflexive consciousness of her own text.

She does not claim that memoir is the same as biography, a related, but different genre. However, she claims a "wholeness" for her text that other genres do not offer, a process of self-performance that "comes only from my experience," which despite its necessary incompleteness is "whole" because of its "continuing odyssey through spheres of love and learning."

While Margaret Mead's daughter finds a wealth of personal and public evidence of her mother's existence available to her, other mothers' lives are lived out in anonymity. For example, Drusilla Modjeska, in writing her book *Poppy*, finds that her late mother—having spent a significant length of time in the seclusion of a hospice for the emotionally damaged mothers of the post–World War II era—leaves her no legacy of "evidence" with which to reconstruct her life. Given the lack of hard evidence (even her mother's psychiatrist refuses to discuss Modjeska's mother for fear of invading the privacy of the family), she is thrown back on her own memories and her family's, at least those members who are willing to break taboos and talk. Family memories yield many points of view, but they cannot perform a voice for Modjeska's mother. So, using the family stories, the dates, places, events, and the public history she does know about, she invents a diary for her mother, a way of allowing a fictional voice to speak for the silence that was her mother. This is a risky move for a memoir writer, undertaken out of desperation perhaps. It is a move that is suspect by traditional standards since it blends fiction, biography, and autobiography. However, it is the kind of radical move that women are forced to take in an effort to have some kind of conversation with mothers they have felt alienated from and now cannot speak to because of their mothers' deaths. The self-declared fantasy of the invented mother's diary, like Kingston's invention of herself as a woman warrior and my fantasy of myself as an incarnation of Virginia Woolf's anger, are ways that women use fantasy to repossess a world that has not been kept for them by public discourse. It is the intimate dialogic voice obtained through the daughter's alternating arrangement of imagined diary and her own experience of her mother that breaks silences for the daughter and allows her to repossess a maternal world.

On the one hand, many mothers remain inaccessible because of our culture's mistaken sense that keeping their unhappiness a private matter will somehow make the world a more comfortable place. On the other hand, some mothers are found to be surprisingly accessible if a daughter is lucky enough to find her letters. Mary Meigs, in writing *The Box Closet*, seeks a way to overcome the sadness and bitterness she experienced as a result of her inability to tell her mother that she was a lesbian, fearing her mother's negative judgment. Meigs' mother, although living a very private life, wrote a diary and kept every letter she received, and her husband and relatives seem to have kept every letter she wrote to them. The advantage of such a record allows Meigs to renegotiate her idea of her mother, learning through her discussion of the letters—which she reprints in generous detail—a loving closeness she could not share during her mother's life. She empowers herself, late in the book, to write imaginary letters to her mother in which she can speak more understandingly of her own and her mother's predicaments, and recognize their commonalties, despite a lifetime of difference:

> Mea culpa, Mother—my impatience when we went to Europe together. You were seventy-two; I was thirty-six. How slowly you moved, with little steps, holding my arm for support. How dreamily you thought aloud, gathered thoughts like straying sheep, careful not to frighten them into a stampede. As we drove along, I liked to get you started on set memory pieces, the Kings of France, for instance, which you could reel off without faltering. Now I'm familiar with the state in which the mind is full of a soft darkness like a summer night without moon or stars, when the slightest pressure drives memories deeper into their starless night. And now that I've begun to do things with great deliberation I see my impatience with you in other people's eyes. (222-23)

Meig's resolution, achieved through her formal arrangement of letters and text, is not every daughter's experience. Vivian Gornick's memoir *Fierce Attachments* performs a mother/daughter relationship that seems never to improve:

> My relationship with my mother is not good, and as our lives accumulate it often seems to worsen. We are locked into a narrow

channel of acquaintance, intense and binding. For years at a time there is an exhaustion, a kind of softening, between us. Then the rage comes up again, hot and clear, erotic in its power to compel attention. These days it is bad between us. My mother's way of "dealing" with the bad times is to accuse me loudly and publicly of the truth. Whenever she sees me she says, "You hate me. I know you hate me." I'll be visiting her and she'll say to anyone who happens to be in the room—a neighbor, a friend, my brother, one of her nieces—"She hates me. What she has against me I don't know, but she hates me." She is equally capable of stopping a stranger on the street when we're out walking and saying, "This is my daughter. She hates me." Then she'll turn to me and plead, "What did I do to you, you should hate me so?" I never answer. I know she's burning and I'm glad to let her burn. Why not? I'm burning, too. (6)

This may seem to be a pretty terrible mother/daughter relationship. However, compared with the acres of silence I have observed in other accounts, the mothers that cannot be dealt with until they are dead, the daughters who have dismissed the importance of their mothers in their lives, the mothers who cannot write about themselves as mothers for fear of invading the privacy of their daughters, I find *Fierce Attachments* refreshingly hopeful. This mother and daughter are at least talking to one another. In fact, conversations, undertaken during the long walks around New York (the one activity both women enjoy), conversations which often flash into raging diatribes, are the formal dramatic strategy on which this text is constructed. The strategy works positively, rather than negatively, I think, because Gornick's mother has already gone public, broken the privacy taboo that so often constructs that destructive silence, a silence often covered by pretty niceties between many mothers and daughters. This mother will even tell strangers on the street the painful truth as she perceives it: "my daughter hates me." In a way, her public gestures make her daughter's book more permissible.

Gornick's text brings up the problem of writing about mothers who are difficult subjects because their behaviours and histories have had negative effects on their daughters, sometimes even putting their daughters' lives in danger. How does a memoirist write about such a mother without taking up sacrificial, separation-oriented identity tactics that have the result of freeing the daughter from any negative identification with the mother, while leaving her bereft of "matrimony" in Chesler's use of that word? Mary Karr's *The Liar's Club* illustrates how the formal arrangements of a memoir text allow the writer and reader to negotiate these problems. Karr begins her memoir with a paragraph that dramatically describes a night when she was seven years old and the family doctor was sitting with her—obviously called in an emergency that also involves the police—and asking her to show him the marks of some injury on her body. The emergency is not identified; we know only that the whole household and neighbourhood has been upset and that, although the doctor is wrong in assuming the child is injured, the mother is taken away that night "for being nervous" (6). The easy way to tell this story would be the conventional way the larger world might tell it. It might be told as a sensationalistic newspaper article about a hysterical woman gone rampant, creating disorder and endangering her children. It could be told as a psychiatric case history detailing the symptoms of a disease that has no reference outside of the body that apparently suffers from it. It might become a social work report that estimates the potential for harm that such a mother holds for her children. These kinds of tellings teach us to separate ourselves from the mother, denying her a place in our community by the very inexplicability of her conduct or the pathologizing of her behaviours. These are not the plots that Karr wants to engage. She wants the "matrimony" that comes from understanding a mother who was once an artist before she became an East Texas housewife.

It is one hundred and fifty pages later that Karr comes back to the traumatic night that opens the memoir, and she reveals that her mother went on a rampage and started burning their household possessions in a giant bonfire in the front yard. One of the purposes of those intervening pages is to imitate Karr's own childhood method of dealing with the event: "Because it took so long for me to paste together what happened, I will leave that part of the story missing for a while" (9). But leaving out part of the story has another effect as well. It takes the mother out of the traditional separation narrative of the madwoman whom we "take away" so we do not have to come close to her pain. Instead, we are asked to place her into our own lives, as Karr does by writing her into a life story that eventually shows how logical, if dangerous, was that final bonfire. Karr begins that process of repossessing her mother's life by humorously observing: "I should explain here that in East Texas parlance the term Nervous applied with equal accuracy to anything from chronic nail-biting to full-blown psychosis"(6). Such a remark defuses the authority of the public institutions (police, doctors, etc.) that come to manage the hysterical woman, and allows us, with Karr's help, to begin entering her mother's world. Karr's memoir, the product of a poetic imagination that works with image and narrative with equal competency, has taught me to read for the power of the literary trope to perform identities that are not sacrificial of the mother.

Such texts are what make me a reader of women's memoirs who can return to my experience in reading Laurence's *Dance*, bringing a wider and more complex knowledge of how the memoir form can work to mediate between the binaries of my own first tearful reading and my students' negative readings. Indeed, I can admit that all the negative possibilities my students have pointed out are cultural imperatives that await any woman writing of mother/daughter relationships. Given that public discourse has offered only negative or extremist forms to contain this relationship, productive readings are ones that trace the ways in which women negotiate these cultural traditions, marking both their successes and, yes, their inevitable failures in performing this new dance.

Laurence is not exempt from these failures. My students' critiques point out the dangerous edge of essentialism in memoirs concerned with maternality. However, in her study *Essentially Speaking,* Diana Fuss writes autocritically about a confrontation similar to mine with students who dismiss a book she has assigned with the deconstructive tag "essentialist" and therefore invalid. Fuss's response is to argue that "essentialism is neither good nor bad, progressive nor reactionary, beneficial nor dangerous. The question we should be asking is not 'is this text essentialist' (and therefore 'bad'), but rather, 'if this text is essentialist, what motivates its deployment?'" (xi). In other words, essentialism can be read as a strategy for possessing or colonizing others or as a liberating means of repossessing what has been taken away, depending on who uses it and for what purpose. In returning to Laurence's *Dance* several years after my first reading, I seek the grounds of Laurence's essentialism, the reasons for its deployment, and the part that the memoir form plays in that process. As Fuss asserts, we must read an argument for essence by discovering "*who* is utilizing it, *how* it is deployed and *where* its effects are concentrated" (20). In rereading Laurence's memoir I find her engaged in an artful dance in this regard. She makes a performance that utilizes a discourse of the essence of maternality in order to establish the importance in her life of her own maternality and that of her three mothers. She deploys this discourse through the special capacity of the memoir form to negotiate the sacrificial binary that our culture makes between the private and public worlds. She constructs maternality as essence in order to produce an effect that revises her cultural inheritance to a significant degree.

In observing the performance in other women's memoirs of this "dancing with our mothers," I find women experimenting with a complex narrative voice and the genre-blending of fiction and memoir, and memoir and academic essay. I also find women reaching out to diary, epistolary, and dramatic forms in an effort to construct a dialogic mother/daughter discourse. This not only allows me to place Laurence in a growing tradition of women's memoir writing but also to note her special contribution to this form. The formal element that strikes one on first reading *Dance* is the overt use of the maternal lineage to construct the chapters: each chapter is named after a mother. This is an important part of repossessing maternality as an aspect of the plot of women's lives, even women who become well-known novelists. Yet, I find that Laurence's most important contribution is in the joining of the very personal to the very public and political in a text about people who have not led particularly public lives. This intimate bonding of the personal and the political, a basic feminist act, has all sorts of ramifications for women's practice of the memoir form.

Laurence's daughter Jocelyn says of her introduction to *Dance* that Laurence "conceived of a new structure, one in which she could not only incorporate the facts of her own life but also touch upon the lives of her three mothers....This new approach allowed her momentary digressions, too, into the issues that most concerned her: nuclear disarmament, pollution and the environment, pro-choice legislation" (xi). I would disagree with Jocelyn Laurence's description of form in only one detail: I think the discussion of issues is neither "digressive" nor "momentary." Rather, I find this aspect of the text both integral and continuous. The memoir consciously performs the connections between private lives (ones lived by ordinary people who are not direct actors in large events) and the public ideologies that they are both shaped by and resistant to.

It is this fact of private persons being shaped by and resistant to historical conditions and public ideologies that Laurence uses as the bonding element between private and public. Her purpose in bonding the private and public worlds is very political in the profound sense that Laurence herself believed art to be. Her purpose is to establish maternality at what she perceives as the neglected centre of our culture, the spiritual aspect of our lives. To establish maternality as central she must construct it as essence, as the one element without which we cannot exist. Although the text is filled with this rhetorical approach of bonding private and public, perhaps its most spectacular example is in the image of the crucified women early in the text. The working of this image into a symbol to establish a maternal essence as central to spirituality begins indirectly with a memory of the quilt that her grandmother made for the child Margaret's bed, and which, as she grew up, the girl Margaret grew tired of as old-fashioned. Laurence regrets her rejection of the art that no one taught her to value as such, and she hopes that her grandmother is now in a place that appreciates women's art. She imagines her "chatting with the generation of women who grew gardens and made quilts and told stories and sang songs and wove baskets and did all the other unrecognized and unsung work. I would like to reach back and back into time gone, and embrace these women as a mother embraces her grown children, with loving respect, as a grown child embraces a mother" (13).

Laurence uses this fantasy moment to bond private life with public ideology for a profoundly political purpose. This passage could be dismissed as a good and estimable wish (yet sentimental and essentialist) on a woman's part to praise her devoted grandmother. To honour her grandmother's quilt-making art is a motherhood statement that even the most conservative of narratologists would not find objectionable. But neither might they find it theoretically important. However, Laurence does not end her narrative of her grandmother with motherhood statements of the sentimental variety. She follows this harmless "motherhood" statement with these words: "These women are an integral part of the Holy Spirit" (13). This statement not only moves the personal acts of quilt-making women into public artistic activity, but it also moves the narrative force of the discussion into the public religious, philosophical, and political arenas.

Laurence then goes on to tie her statement about women and the Holy Spirit directly to a very public representation of a female crucifixion—a sculpture by artist Almuth Lutkenhaus that was once displayed in Bloor Street United Church in Toronto. It is an image that has upset many Christians because it insists on a female principle at the powerful numinous centre of Christianity. Laurence goes further by bringing the symbol of female crucifixion home to the lives of the ordinary women who are being written of in this memoir: "To me she [the crucified woman] represents the anguish of the ages, the repression, the injustice, the pain that has been inflicted upon women, both physically and emotionally. 'Crucified Woman' also speaks to me of the comfort and help I have known from my mothers and the unconditional love I feel for my own children" (16). She then goes on to link her overarching dance metaphor to this highly charged political statement. She does this by showing that the dance she has in mind in this text is not some pretty, decorative feminine activity, but another more powerful definition of dance, a life dance of "pain and love," which she grounds in her mothers' lives. This narrative move could be seen to posit the maternal roots of all art in the way, for instance, that Romanticism does. However, I find it goes further in not proposing the ultimate separation of artists from their maternal roots, but rather demonstrating the way the artistic life, for women at least, is always, in all of its acts, a reiterative incremental return to the maternal. Women's art needs not only the maternal as its procreative force, but also maternality's lifetime nurturing activities, from mothers both real and surrogate. Laurence risks (or dares) essentialism in order to deconstruct the masculine gendering of fatherly love that has dominated the Christian religion through most of its history. If Christianity is the public world that a memoirist wishes to repossess, such acts are essential rather than essentialist.

This narrative strategy continues in each of the portraits and is not only subtextually present as symbol, but also has continuing material reference at the level of plot, as Laurence works her way through the portraits of individual mother figures. The strategy performs the always unfinished life of her first mother, whose "baby book" of Laurence's first four years becomes the text for Laurence's meditations on subjects as diverse as Agent Orange and abortion rights. This narrative strategy also enacts the oppressed intellectual brilliance of the aunt/stepmother who is denied the full benefit of her education and demonstrates the way her intellectual interests reassert themselves in the mentoring that makes Laurence into a writer. Laurence does not sanction the world that forced her stepmother to choose between home and work, but she is nevertheless the grateful beneficiary of her second mother's expertise as a teacher.

There is no suggestion that Laurence takes up the sacrificial equation of separation with maturation in this memoir. Laurence acknowledges an identity pattern that is filled with both the desire to separate and the need to always return to that mentorship that shapes her female life narrative. Recognizing the ways in which material conditions shaped both her and the women who raised her, and shaped their differences, she is able to honour the differences of women struggling in conditions that contrast with her own. This is an important feminist maturation that is based on the personal experience of first acknowledging the different circumstances of our personal mothers. Her chapter on her mother-in-law performs her personal link to a tradition of women writing. Her emphasis on her and her mother-in-law's equal acceptance of each other as writers extends their relationship beyond historical differences in terms of the choices they were able to make, indeed beyond the very material difference that divorce often makes in this relationship. The reconstruction of Laurence's relationship with her mother-in-law leads Laurence to meditate on her own life as a writer and the way it feeds on and is subject to her life as a mother. The degree to which Laurence has broken the mould of what writers' memoirs are supposed to be like is indicated by the fact that towards the end of her life, Laurence was a central figure in the Canadian literary establishment. She makes nothing of this in her memoir (and in doing so has probably offended some of her associates). She chose the personal and political ground of maternality over the public ground of celebrity in making her memoir. In this way she redefines the use of the memoir.

By taking this pro-active stand vis-à-vis maternality as essence, Laurence constructs what I have called a complex "re-e-merging" pattern of female identity. Women memoir writers concerned with mother/daughter relationships show how this patterning of the private life works itself out in the cultural and historical intricacies of the public world, as each of us encounters history in a different body and in a different societal and personal space. Earlier in this century, one of our literary foremothers expressed this private/public place of the memoir very well. Virginia Woolf, in taking up the way in which her long-dead mother was nevertheless an "invisible presence" in her life, muses in "A Sketch of the Past": "Consider what immense forces society brings to play upon each of us, how that society changes from decade to decade; and also from class to class; well, if we can't analyse these invisible presences, we know very little of the subject of memoir; and...how futile life writing becomes" (93). Laurence's memoir of her self and her mothers performs an intricate narrative/analytical dance in a narrative voice that witnesses to her mothers' different experiences. It is a memoir that then performs its narrator's participatory role with a chapter of her own experience of mothering. It also continually reflects on how their experiences and hers are joined to those of other mothers, taking up the challenge of society's "immense forces," and what impact these experiences have on the lives of mothers and daughters. In making "invisible presences" part of our matrimony, the "legacy of power and humanity" that comes from mothers, such memoirs change the conditions of women's performance of their selves.

5

"Scenes of Language"

Trauma and the Search for Form in Women's Memoirs

> If the Greeks invented tragedy, the Romans the epistle and the Renaissance the sonnet...our generation has [also] invented a new literature, that of testimony.
>
> —Elie Wiesel, quoted in Felman and Laub's *Testimony: Crises of Witnessing in Literature, Psychoanalysis, and History*

IN THEIR book on testimony, Shoshana Felman and Dori Laub suggest how the subtle and often competing agendas of witnesses play themselves out in the acts of witnessing. To become a public witness through one's writing or public speaking requires a leap of authority outside the private life and into a public responsibility, where one must "speak for others and to others" (3). Complicating this assumption of authority to use the private experience to make public history is the fact that personal testimony to large-scale trauma involves a psychoanalytic dimension in that the witness, as survivor, is often going through an experience of suffering (and, if a positive result is achieved, healing). A testimony that may be first conceived by the witness as "a simple medium of historical transmission" can also become "the unsuspected medium of healing" (9). Acts of effective testimony therefore require the melding of historical and therapeutic discourses. Needless to say, our culture views these as separate modes of telling. A testimony can lose its veracity if it results from a "talking cure," as the therapeutic source is often assumed to be historically invalid. Yet in foregrounding the historical value of a testimony it is not always possible to work through the necessary personal revision. Ironically, the witness who insists on only the historical value of the testimony may not even remember all the relevant information.

When I think of how "testimony" is related to but different from "witnessing," I remember my father's descriptions of the habit of "giving witness" to faith in God that was part of the lives of my Puritan and Methodist ancestors. In my father's descriptions the phenomenon of standing up, seemingly spontaneously, in church and speaking of one's faith was "giving witness." But when my father would speak comparatively of individuals who were good, very good, or excellent at the act of witnessing he would remark on the nature and characteristics of their "testimony" as if, like the preacher's sermon, testimony was an art. Some of my ancestors, according to my father, gave superb "testimony." We are all, at one time or another, on diverse occasions, called on to write or speak of something we have witnessed. To make that witnessing into a testimony, one that, like a sonnet or an epic, builds through deliberate formal arrangements as much as through the sincere honesty of its content, is an artful activity. Therefore, writing such a testimony as a memoir is a delicate search for a form that can contain both the personal narrative and the cultural and historical contexts that make personal witnessing into public testimony. Such a testimony can repossess some vital part of the world for the memoirist and her reader.

A text that has made me very aware of this search for form is Eva Brewster's memoir of her life as a Jewish girl in Nazi Germany, first published in 1986 as *Vanished in Darkness: An Auschwitz Memoir.* Reading her book at that time I found it possessed the accessibility and narrative strength that I thought necessary for introducing young undergraduate students to how memoir could be used to help document major historical events. Although such events are of great magnitude and almost seem to dwarf the personal, memoirs can help us understand them. The book "worked" in class, as we like to say in my trade; it was very "teachable." My students identified closely with Brewster's recreation of herself as Daniella Raphael, the name by which the resistance movement in Germany knew her. Perhaps what appealed to my students was the daring of a young woman separated from her husband, child, and family. Daniella, only twenty years old, demonstrates the intelligence, courage, and luck that made her a survivor. Perhaps of equal appeal was the introduction, later in the book, of the mother/daughter relationship that sustains Daniella in the camps. There, after the deaths of her husband, Freddy, and child, Reha, she and her mother amazingly survive to help each other and eventually escape during the forced transports that occurred at the end of the war. Despite the success of the book in the classroom, for me a doubt lingered as to its effectiveness as an instrument of history. In class, when I tried to direct attention away from Daniella's autonomy, her adventures, her canniness as a survivor, there was a falling off of discussion. When I moved from the relational devotion of the mother and daughter to the wider communal history of the Holocaust and the war, there was a lessening of enthusiasm, a hesitancy to connect the personal story with the larger history.

I had the opportunity to speak with someone who had read *Vanished*, and who knew a great deal more than I do about the Holocaust. This critic affirmed that Brewster's memoir was certainly a well-paced, readable account, with an appealing central character, but wondered if its very adventurous quality sometimes outshone its more serious purpose as a memoir of Auschwitz. We talked for a while, and I began to realize that the delicate act of balancing personal story and history was sometimes a problem in both the writing and reading of memoirs. I could not fault Brewster as a writer, since her recreation of the camps is vivid and detailed. Brewster had dramatically represented a place where lives were constantly at risk, in camps where prisoner was set against prisoner in the "capo" system. Her detailed account of the rigid division of prisoners into utilitarian categories showed how unity was made virtually impossible, while her account of medical experimentation, prostitution, and random as well as selective daily killings showed how inmates were kept in a state of terror. Brewster's recreation does not glamorize the camps, and I and my students felt the impact of her factual descriptions. Yet, Daniella is so appealing in her youth and intelligence and courage that students tended to separate the character they admired from the fate that awaited her friends and relatives. In some ways, Daniella's story read like a novel, suspenseful, eventful, and concentrated on the survival of the main characters. Such texts, at least partly because of the desire of their readers for happy endings, may succeed in personalizing history, but they often do not fully carry out memoir's other difficult task, that of historicizing the personal. In our concern for the survival of the protagonist over all other values we may not read the text for its account of the larger event, but rather see those larger events as background. Such texts risk failing in the public mandate of the personal memoir, which is the fuller realization of the large-scale consequences of such international traumatic events.

In 1994 Eva Brewster published a new version of her successful memoir, this time under the title *Progeny of Light/ Vanished in Darkness*. Ironically, although the word "memoir" has been dropped from the new title, the book has become much more effective in terms of the mandate of memoir to personalize history while historicizing the personal. By the time I read and taught the second version I had a greater understanding of how memoir can be taught in the classroom. At the same time, the major changes that the book had undergone helped both me and my students read differently. What Brewster has done is add two new sections of text, a substantial eighty-two-page section at the start of the memoir entitled "Gathering Shadows" and a shorter twenty-one-page section at the close of the book entitled "Progeny of Light." The effect of these additions illustrates some important points about the memoir form. It highlights memoir's ability to bring history and individual life together, its typical mode of performing the self through performing the stories of others, and the reflective/reflexive consciousness of the narrator as the melding mechanism that makes the past relevant in terms of the present. A comparison of the first and second versions of the memoir is instructive in this regard.

The first version of *Vanished* begins with "Daniella Raphael" being told by a prison warden at a detention centre that she is free to go. Daniella knows that she has been a lucky girl, an exception, since "nobody in my position had ever been released from jail once the Nazis had them in their clutches" (1). This opening chapter is only two pages long and takes us in detail through her sudden unexpected release into the "warm sun and the sweet scent and promise of spring in the air" (2). Its scenic brevity calls up our cultural training in a thousand film and print fictions of the lone resistance fighter who beats the odds. This plot expectation activates all of our identification mechanisms that will, we expect, take us through the adventure of danger and escape. Chapter 2 keeps our attention focused on Daniella by giving us only necessary family background. In a brief five pages Brewster tells of her efforts to save her child by divorcing her husband and sending the child into the country with a Christian nurse while both parents take up separate and underground existences. Neither child nor husband becomes well known to us as entities important to the story. This brevity tends to keep our hearts and minds focused on Daniella and her individual sorrow and fear. We learn little of what preceded the dramatic moment of the imprisonment; then in chapter 3 we are quickly back to the world of the solitary Daniella, "on the run, always in contact with the Resistance movement" (8).

I do not think this emphasis on the individual's adventure in dangerous times is necessarily a deliberate choice on Brewster's part. Indeed, the two chapters continually hint at a more communal and relational story underlying Daniella's. However, because her purpose, in the first book, was to witness the events inside Auschwitz, the narrative begins close in time to this experience. Nevertheless, by beginning at the moment of separation from family connections and at a moment of great personal danger, the book makes it easier for readers raised on contemporary popular fiction to ignore that underlying story of the traumatic rending of family and community life that Jewish people suffered under the Nazis. It is not until we arrive at the chapters of the camps that we retrieve that sense of a community under a death sentence. By then the people characterized are often in such a condition of oppression that it is difficult to associate them with anything we ourselves have experienced. My students and I, in our less-than-intense discussion of the history of those times, did not feel as personally invested as we should have, except, of course, in the fate of Daniella.

In the enlarged 1994 *Progeny*, the eighty-four pages of "Gathering Shadows" that now precede the Daniella story have the effect of taking us out of our reader's habit of simple identification with a fictionalized protagonist. These pages bring us face to face with the effects of Nazi policies on many lives. Brewster does this by re-enacting her family's life in Berlin in the thirties, before she became "Daniella." Whereas *Vanishing* begins with her assumption of a new name in her solitary adventure, *Progeny* begins with a complex personal, familial, communal, and historical scene: "On December 28, 1933, I was eleven years old. My parents, Albert and Elisabeth Levy, my ten year old brother Stefan, and I lived in the spacious apartment on Nikolsburger Platz 3 in West-Berlin where I was born. Adolph Hitler first came to my attention as a disembodied voice over the radio, then called 'wireless.' His voice was hoarse, bawling, and aggressive and he spoke in a dialect we could barely understand.

It sent my little brother into fits of giggles ending in hiccups and he was dispatched to the care of Christian, our old seamstress who could always calm him" (7). As readers we are set very firmly not only in an individual's life, but also in the context of a family, living a good life in a actual place, and in a real historical moment, one that is already impinging on the personal life through the voice of Hitler on the radio. In this section history is personalized, but the personal is also historicized as Brewster manages to convey the mood of the historical moment of Berlin's prosperous Jewish population. She allows us to only gradually become aware of the degree of denial that her family had concerning the import of Hitler's words, a denial that was so pervasive at the time. It begins with the laughter of the little boy at what he perceives as a joke. But throughout the first section Brewster enacts scenes that illustrate how difficult it is for happy, decent people, who have lived comfortable lives among other decent people, to accept that anyone can mean them the kind of harm that was to happen over the next decade.

When I taught the second version of Brewster's book in a memoir course in the fall of 1999, my students and I became very aware of the ways in which this memoir teaches us about how people living their lives are, as one student put it, like frogs in water that is gradually heating up. You don't know you're in hot water until you start to boil. Another student, a history major, used to the special sense of all-knowing hindsight that characterizes historical narrative, talked about how he had never understood until reading Brewster's memoir why more Jews didn't try to flee (at least who could afford to), why so many seemed not to see the dangers. Brewster's story weaves together her seemingly safe and insulated upper-middle-class daily world with the seemingly incidental and controllable prejudice of her school experience, an experience that was increasingly permeated with the prejudice of anti-Semitism. She locates us in the everyday world in such a way that we can imagine that we, too, under similar conditions, might well behave as her family did. Then, through the personal experience of her relatives—a half sister forbidden to participate in the 1936 Olympics, her brother being bullied at school—she allows the reader to participate in the sense of the very gradual realization of danger. We do see that escape is an option; relatives get out to South America or Palestine. However, we also see how expensive, difficult, and uncertain such a solution is. Brewster's recreation of the pre-war experience of her extended family and friends allows historical hindsight to be suspended.

We are taught to live in the moment, rather than view it from outside and with hindsight, by her enactment of the incidental nature of daily life. In such a quotidian world, falling in love or sailing can seem more important than events in the distant public world, even when the violence of that world is all around. In the pages of "Gathering Shadows" we live with the family, understand why they laugh at Hitler's accent, why they feel victory over ignorance when they can ignore, or achieve momentary respite from, the prejudice of those who do not yet seem powerful enough to truly threaten them. We see how reasonable it must have seemed, at first, as the small intrusions of the public danger into the private life began, how logical, considering the Christians they knew, to assume that decent Germans would not swallow this evil man's philosophy. Brewster puts not just one human face to the history of Germany in the thirties, but the faces of a family and a community. For every schoolteacher who preached Aryan superiority, there was a decent school principal who "could still overrule the lone Nazi" (13). For every withdrawal of personal freedom there are sweet moments of love and happiness in the context of teenage life in a loving family, falling in love, marrying, and having a baby.

In historical narratives, only public events happen. In traditional fiction, such public events act as a background for the personal story. In memoir, real lives happen in all their daily richness in parallel and in connection with public life. We are allowed into that richness so that we can better feel the effect when private lives are crushed by public policies. Importantly, Brewster as narrator reflects on how life went on during the times she describes. She works at her own understanding of her involvement in the denial, telling us how she refused to go abroad to school when her father tried to send her and her brother away right after Kristallnacht. She describes her relief when the damage was cleaned up so that "there were no signs of [the] vandalism that had swept through Germany and her capital." She tells us that at school "teachers and students were even kinder than before" and her father "returned to his business as usual" (26). Moving through these events, not with history's hindsight, but with Brewster's reflective/reflexive narration, it is possible to believe that the evil has passed. Brewster, as narrator, can then bring hindsight back into the narrative mode: "My father had managed to surround us with a sense of security that had made this anti-Semitism appear insignificant and no more than a passing shadow. It was not a shadow" (31).

To a much greater degree in her second text than in her first, Brewster takes on the authority of the witness who not only testifies to her own story, but also "speaks for others and to others." In doing so she turns witnessing to testimony. A witness to a historical event can limit herself to the scenes to which she has first-hand knowledge and restrict the story to those incidents and people that are considered of historical importance by pre-established historical norms. However, such a witnessing is only part of memoir. Making a true testimony involves the pain of revisiting not only an era, but also one's relationships with the loved ones of that era, revisiting complex desires, decisions, and destinies. Brewster works through her own psycho-social position, her relationship with her parents, and her worship of her father, which makes her refuse to leave him when he insists he must stay. She recounts her sense of distance from her mother after her father's sudden death (from a heart attack after his business is confiscated), as her mother's grief and economic circumstances drive emotional and practical wedges between the two of them. We get a sense of the growing interaction of public and private, as the sixteen-year-old girl decides, despite advice to the contrary, that a speedy marriage to her sweetheart is the solution to her personal and social predicament. We see the rationalizations that dangerous times make possible. Marriage to her sweetheart will give her back the loving familial closeness she has lost, while increasing her chances to get out of the country. In such times parents lose their authority and young people take steps that they cannot know will bring them closer to being caught in the "mousetrap." The discourse of the personal psychological exploration is at work here alongside the recall of the historical framework.

Brewster's working through of these scenes of family life for the second version of the book must have been a painful process, but it is one that offers a more complex view of the era. By re-enacting her family's life during the thirties—including what must have been the especially painful recollection of her relationships with a husband and child who did not survive—Brewster allows us a wider identification with her and her community than the singular story of Daniella can provide. She is not just Daniella; she is also a daughter, a wife, a mother, and a worker, and in each of these roles she is involved in surviving an increasingly oppressive public world. A passage two-thirds of the way through "Gathering Shadows" makes it obvious that her intention is to have us make that broader imaginative identification, to put aside the consciousness of hindsight that might make us wonder at why she did not flee when her father had given her the chance:

> The only comparison I can think of is that of people now living in a known earthquake belt or in war-torn areas of the world. They all know that their lives are in mortal danger, but can't bring themselves to move away from all they have ever known and loved. Young people today have to live with the constant threat of nuclear accidents, environmental pollution, the depletion of the ozone layer, diseases like cancer and AIDS. But they still marry and have children though they can't be sure that their babies will have a chance to live out a normal lifespan. Perhaps it is human nature that forces us to pretend normality and to hope for miracles under the most horrible and hopeless of circumstances. (62)

This moment of reflection allows the self-reflexive narrator to carry out one of the most important tasks of the memoir: understanding the past for the purpose of changing the present. In this way she takes up the authority "to speak for others and to others" by grounding the reason for telling the story in the wish to affect the future. That is exactly the function performed by

"Progeny of Light," the section that Brewster adds to the end of her memoir.

The first version of *Vanished* ended with Brewster's mother asking her to make it her "mission in life" to "see to it that young people will not ever again be persecuted for their race, color or beliefs." Brewster tells us that "I promised my mother, my murdered little family, our six million dead, and myself that, never again, as long as I lived, would a dictatorship rob our children of their birthright, their freedom and their happiness" (163). Although such words make for an idealistic and even heroic ending, reinforcing the emphasis on the individual as a fighter for justice, this is a large promise to ask (and an even larger one to make good on), and we have to assume that the memoir is Brewster's contribution to the fulfilment of this promise. In adding "Progeny of Light" to the new edition, Brewster details the difficulty of living in a world seemingly determined to learn nothing from the Holocaust, one where the best efforts of individuals can have ambiguous success. The chapter recounts Brewster's and, later, her children's personal experience with prejudice. She sees the continuation of prejudice even as the war is ending. She observes that the British Control Commission in Germany (for whom she works) "seem to have felt more sympathy for their defeated enemies, the German officer corps and aristocracy, than for the ragtag flotsam from all parts of Europe now crowded in to refugee camps" (247). Her British superiors hire many "former members of the German police and of Nazi organizations who continued to terrorize the refugees" (248). She also finds it almost impossible to get the British officers to act on (or even read) her "meticulous" reports on the very conditions of persecution and property confiscation that she had been hired to research and write. At the point when she is in danger of losing her job for her "impudence," Ross Brewster, a young British Special Branch Intelligence officer, "came to my rescue" (249). She wins a small victory when Ross Brewster proves that her list of confiscated properties is correct. She eventually marries him and later in life they immigrate to Canada. It is not until she has had children and spent many years in a very private life that the promise to her mother begins to take her back into public life.

In 1971 she complained in a letter to her local paper about having to listen to musical numbers by a German band at the Calgary Stampede, tunes that had been Nazi favourites. These were tunes that many survivors heard in the death camps as accompaniment to their enslavement and the deaths of their loved ones. Her small complaint "raised an unprecedented storm of protest from the large German community" (257) in Alberta, and Brewster found herself a spokesperson for survivors. This led her to a journalistic career. As well as her own experience with the ethnic German backlash, she finds that both her children met with incidents that show that Canada it not as free of prejudice as Canadians would like to believe. As the seventies and eighties bring more virulent neo-Nazi activists to the fore, Brewster herself becomes more willing to battle them in public forums such as her newspaper columns. The effect of the added closing chapter is to indict the "apathy and indifference" (6) of the present.

This chapter also brings home, through the reader's new ability to compare "Gathering Shadows" and "Progeny of Light," how what happened in Germany in terms of the "final solution" dramatically portrayed in Daniella's story—now the middle section of the new book—could happen again. All it would need is a government that encourages and legislates the prejudices that are already there. The reader is not permitted an easy identification with the adventures of Daniella in a far-off, hardly recognizable European past, but must move with the adult Brewster to the peaceful and prosperous Canadian Prairies of the present to find that anti-Semitism still exists. This section seems directly addressed to the very young people who would most easily identify with the youthful Daniella, and ends with these words: "my Auschwitz Memoirs are now included in many schools' Social Studies curriculum" (267). Among the photographs from the past in this edition there appears one of Eva Brewster talking to schoolchildren in her home province of Alberta in 1994. The same province was home to a teacher, Jim Keegstra, who for years was allowed to teach children that the Holocaust never happened before the provincial government finally prosecuted him. This photograph, Brewster's statement about her book being taught in schools, and the information given in the introduction about Brewster's work in school broadcasting and as a public speaker struck my Albertan students with the importance of memoir as a tool for the writer's empowerment in direct political action. Indeed, the new, larger, more substantially bound paperback edition that the publishers have produced indicates that the schools are where the publisher expects to place this book.

I realized when I read the second version of Eva Brewster's memoir that she has accomplished a difficult transition from witnessing to testifying. In expanding her narrative backward and forward in time—and by necessity moving to a larger familial and communal story—she makes her story more pointedly political. By shaping it more deliberately through the reflective/reflexive narrative voice of memoir, she has taken on a new authority to "speak for others and to others," an authority that her public work as spokesperson and educator reinforces. By moving from witnessing to testifying, she has repossessed the world in an important way: she can not only "speak to" others as a witness and participant, she can speak "for others" who have not been able, or permitted, to speak for themselves. She does this by developing her own ability to reflect on history reflexively, infusing the authorized public modes of telling our world with the authority of her own experience.

What I did not realize, until my students (who had read only the second version) taught me, was the ways in which the Daniella character of the middle section of the text is informed and deepened by the addition of "Gathering Shadows" and "Progeny of Life." My students' identification with her was now informed by their knowledge of her as a mother and wife in the past and as a political activist in the present moment. They saw her amazing capacity for quick thinking and adaptive behaviours not as heroic hyperbole, but as a quality formed in the quick maturity that her tragic teenage years forced on her. They saw her survival as not just tied to her personal achievement, but also very much tied to the courage her mother had always shown in the past. They noted how practical conditions, such as the nursing training her mother had dearly won (at the expense of leaving Eva alone and often lonely after her father's death), can have unexpected consequences for later survival. The death of Eva's child and husband in Auschwitz was more shocking to my students because of the real presence of these people as significant others in the "Gathering Shadows" section. As one student said in telling us how it made her appreciate the degree of the tragedy of the Holocaust, "Children are not supposed to die in stories. It's hard to think of all the children that died." The new text encourages readers to invest themselves in those who did not survive.

I have no doubt that it must have cost Brewster emotional pain to write the new sections. She observes in acknowledgements that she has had recurring nightmares even several decades after the war. To remember and recreate the intact family of her childhood must have been at least as painful as it was to remember and recreate Daniella's story of imprisonment in the camps. To talk openly of prejudice in Alberta, where Brewster still lives, must also have meant some pain, especially since in telling her son's story she is writing of another child who has died (in an accident as a young adult). One cannot make the historical narrative necessary to the act of testimony without entering into a therapy of the self that, while it may empower the survivor, also relives the suffering. Cathy Caruth observes that "the ability to witness the *event* fully" is won "at the cost of witnessing oneself" (7). It is a more complete witnessing to herself, her life, her community, before and after the experience of the Holocaust, that Eva Brewster achieves in her second text, which stands as a testimony, one that speaks "for others and to others."

Creating the scenic language that brings history and self together in the act of testimony is a linguistic effort that should not be underestimated. Importantly, it involves not only the struggle to speak out so as to be part of the healing of self and community but also a struggle for the formal elements of language that will make the testimony happen. Jane Lazarre, in her account of overcoming personal trauma, illness, and grief in *Wet Earth and Dreams*, describes this very real process[1]: "And here

---

[1] Lazarre's title does not include the word "memoir"; however, she calls the book "this memoir" in her acknowledgements.

in these pages, I shape and reshape the structure, the language. On the printed draft I design new connections and more precise descriptions with a dark black pen. Frequently, my newest, best insights are made in the margins, between the lines, continuing onto the back of the page. Then, on this computer, I work them into the text as if they had always been there. Something shifts inside me. I am saved by form" (20). Eva Brewster speaks in her acknowledgements of her gratitude to her editor for being "long-suffering" with her "frequent doubts and resistance to changes" (viii). It is ironic that memoirists, practising a discourse that is so often dismissed as lacking in artfulness, often credit revision of the manuscript, involving a search for the right writing strategies, with giving them a breakthrough in understanding their own content. Particularly when the writing is seeking to search through a traumatic past, writers note the hard work of finding what Marie Cardinal calls "the words to say it" (in her book of that title). Because of the healing elements involved in shaping and making testimony, memoirists are truly "saved by form," as Lazarre puts it. When Elie Wiesel speaks of "testimony" as "a new literature" comparing it to the highly formalized expressions of the sonnet, tragedy, and epic, he emphasizes, for me, the importance of critical inquiry that does not pass over the form of memoir because of our illusion that non-fiction, autobiographical writing is somehow a "natural," artless expression. Eva Brewster's search for form through two texts illustrates the art of memoir writing.

Jane Lazarre's book is deliberately self-conscious of this artfulness. Lazarre writes of discovering a formal solution to the problem of how to write about the traumatic event of her mother's death from breast cancer when she was eight, an event that cripples her with anxiety and illness in middle age. Because her family has had to get on with living, she has never really come to terms with her mother's death. In middle age she becomes depressed and obsessively anxious about her own children and herself. When career reversals strike, her mental health is also threatened. Then she is diagnosed with breast cancer. At this low point, a reckoning with the past suddenly begins. But Lazarre realizes that she cannot write a linear narrative reaching back to the originating trauma because her mother's death has been too long untold for it to find an appropriate linguistic form. She must approach the originating trauma indirectly by first working through other associated tragedies and setbacks. Lazarre chooses to begin her book with a brief enactment of her own awakening in a "recovery" room after cancer surgery, illustrating the turning point in her life that begins her search through the past. She is able to face her own situation by first entering into a detailed re-enactment of how she was affected by the death of her longtime therapist, a woman who also died of breast cancer, and who, in many ways, had become a surrogate mother for Lazarre. In telling the story of this death, as well as in narrating the death of her brother-in-law from AIDS, she is able to finally approach the remembrance of her mother's death, to recreate it and learn about her own emotional life from that recreation. She says of this linguistic therapy that there was a need "to relive my early powerful emotional ambivalence toward my mother's memory as well as her absence [which] had influenced my entire life story, rubbing it, slowly scraping away at it, polishing it" (9). We speak of polishing a fictional story, but in a memoir the story is one's own life; it too must be polished, through the painful and difficult, but finally "exhilarating" (9) act of writing that the trauma at the heart of many life stories requires.

That "polishing" can be further informed through an understanding of the nature of trauma and its linguistic consequences. According to the 1987 version of *The Diagnostic and Statistical Manual* of the American Psychiatric Association, a traumatized person is one who "has experienced an event that is outside the range of human experience" (Brown 100). However, considerable research has widened our understanding of trauma since that definition was established. In "The Intrusive Past," researchers Van Der Kolk and Van Der Hart question the definition of trauma as "outside the range of human experience" by emphasizing the linguistic implications of those words. Since the events that cause the trauma did happen, and therefore are factually within human experience, what really mark trauma are events that are outside our linguistic experience. When people suffer trauma they often experience a loss of language that amounts to a "'speechless terror'....The experience cannot be [entirely] organized on a linguistic level, and this failure to arrange the memory in words and symbols leaves it to be organized on a somatosensory or iconic level, as somatic sensations, behavioral reenactments, nightmares and flashbacks" (172). Since 1987 the emphasis in definitions of trauma has moved from "trauma" as originating "wound," whether physical or psychic or both, to "trauma" as the individual's "perceptions of fear, threat, and risk to well-being" (Brown 111). Therefore, long-term conditions as well as single events are now recognized as contributing to trauma. Occurrences such as personal tragedy, gender or race oppression, the intergenerational effects of devastating natural disasters, or large-scale historical events that directly or indirectly influence future lives are now recognized as degrees and kinds of traumatic experiences. As Laura Brown observes, this broadening definition foregrounds the idea "that personality develops in a complex web of interaction between the internal, phenomenological experiences of the individual and the external, social context in which that person lives" (103). We are also beginning to understand how we may have misnamed traumatic symptoms in the past. In recent times, because of certain kinds of symptoms occurring in men as a result of their war experiences, a similar constellation of symptoms, formerly named hysteria in women, has now come to be understood as post-traumatic stress disorder (PTSD). As a result, the phenomenon is now broadly researched and described. Cathy Caruth in *Trauma: Explorations in Memory* defines PTSD as

> a response, sometimes delayed, to an overwhelming event or events, which takes the form of re-peated, intrusive hallucinations, dreams, thoughts or behaviors stemming from the event, along with numbing that may have begun during or after the experience, and possibly also increased arousal to (and avoidance of) stimuli recalling the event...[t]he event is not assimilated or experienced fully at the time, but only belatedly, in its repeated *possession* of the one who experiences it. To be traumatized is precisely to be possessed by an image or event. And thus the traumatic symptom cannot be interpreted, simply, as a distortion of reality, nor as the

lending of unconscious meaning to a reality it wishes to ignore, nor as the repression of what once was wished....[I]t cannot be understood in terms of any wish or unconscious meaning, but is, purely and inexplicably, the literal return of the event against the will of the one it inhabits....[I]t is not a pathology...of falsehood or displacement of meaning, but of history itself. If PTSD must be understood as a pathological symptom, then it is not so much a symptom of the unconscious, as it is a symptom of history. The traumatized, we might say, carry an impossible history within them, or they become themselves the symptom of a history they cannot entirely possess. (4–5)

It is at the point of the interplay between this more complex sense of personal trauma, the location of its symptoms in a linguistic and historical context, and the broadened sense of its social context that my designation of the trauma memoir is located. This link between trauma and memoir is important to my concern with "repossessing the world." Since suffering from the symptoms of trauma is like being "possessed" by them, writing can become a way of repossessing the trauma and its consequences, of moving from a condition in which one is possessed by the past to a condition in which one possesses the past (Caruth 157). I am particularly intrigued by Caruth's statement that the traumatized carry a "symptom of history." This implies that some other discourse, in addition to the traditional discourse of history, must be employed to address traumatic events. As I have emphasized throughout this study, contemporary memoir is a discourse that is a social as well as a linguistic practice. It is a discourse that brings together factual history and imaginative representation to serve some social function. When concerned with representing a traumatic past, it often imitates the linguistically associative, elliptical, and incremental nature of psychiatric talk therapy while grounding itself in the public history of its times. Concerned with the self as living in, and as a product, of its communities, it is a facilitating form for the re-enactment of personal and collective trauma, the witnessing to its reality and the process of its healing.

In order to illustrate the connections between formal arrangements, early trauma and, its effect on a life story, and the memoir form, I turn to Alice Kaplan's *French Lessons: A Memoir*. I find as a critic and a memoir writer that when it comes to memoirs that re-enact trauma, understanding formal solutions leads me to understand the nature of trauma itself and how it shapes human memory and human thought. Early in her text Kaplan observes that "listening to my childhood...what I hear first are scenes of language" (5). I propose that an important part of recovery from the psychic effects of trauma involves making scenes in language that the trauma sufferer finds to be a satisfactory reconstruction of the traumatic events. This could be compared to what Suzette A. Henke calls "scriptotherapy," "the unexpected eruption of repressed tales of traumatic experience in feminist life narratives" (*Shattered Subjects* xiii). However, I am less concerned, in my study of the contemporary memoir form in the hands of women, with the "unexpected eruption" than with the more predictable literary devices and techniques that the memoir writer adapts to perform the trauma in language. In addition, I am concerned with the specific place of the reader in the reading contract with a writer who uses the memoir for the purposes of constructing a self while making a testimony. For making testimony is not only a literary activity carried on by a writer, but it is also an activity carried on by the reader. I propose that a large part of the reading process of such texts requires a reader who is willing to accept a literature that claims to be more than a fictive construct. It requires a reader who recognizes a form of literature that claims to be testimony, what Shoshana Felman describes as "a conflation between text and life." The reader must be willing to accept that "textual testimony...can *penetrate us like an actual life*" (2). Many general readers are prepared to allow a text to operate in this way. However, many of us trained in literary studies, dominated as that discourse is by texts that claim their status as fiction, are taught that the text is to be considered as separate from the writer and her life. The study of memoir requires not a return to being the so-called "naïve" reader, but a further sophistication of our critical sense that understands the literature of testimony as similar too, but in important ways different from, the texts that are normally a part of academic study.

As readers we must move with the memoirist's text, through "scenes of language" that the writer attests to as the re-enactment of her own life. These include re-enactments of trauma, sometimes presented in the stark clarity of "factual" language, which is a highly detailed recounting of events marked by the emotionless, disassociative reaction typical of many single-incident trauma victims. Conversely, enactments can be fragmented and half absent under conditions of partial amnesia, the state manifested by many victims of long-term, not easily identified or accepted states of trauma such as childhood sexual abuse (Van Der Kolk and Van Der Hart 168). The reader must work with the writer as a kind of psychoanalytic detective with a good grasp of historical and cultural contexts and the linguistic consequences of trauma. The reader moves with the narrator/writer from a condition in which one is possessed by the past, to a condition in which one possesses the past.

Alice Kaplan does not call her book a "trauma" memoir, but I find that an understanding of trauma is essential to my understanding of the form of *French Lessons*. In an interview about being a member of a workshop writing group, Kaplan herself emphasized the importance of form in the writing process. Disparaging the "let-it-all-hang-out" ethic that is often attributed to any writing labelled "personal writing" makes her assert that "[w]hat we've found again and again in our work in the group is that you have to find a formal solution to the problem of writing about yourself" (164–65). Her fellow workshop participant Marianna Torgovnick adds: "If there is going to be exposure, it needs to be exactly the right kind of exposure for you as a writer and to your audience. It's a really disciplined form of writing" (Williams 164). I find that part of the "discipline" of writing that emerges from the trauma of one's past experience is finding a way to imitate the process of trauma and the changed conditions of life that result from having experienced trauma. While trauma is often written about as a site of debilitating illness, it can also be a source of great wisdom and a factor in great achievement. Kai Erikson views the person who has experienced trauma as having access to a special truth: "Traumatized people calculate life's chances differently. They look at the world through a different lens....They evaluate the data of everyday life differently, read signs differently, see omens the rest of us are for the most part spared" (194). Eva Brewster has certainly used the traumatic events of her life to become a reader of "signs" in a community that would prefer she stay silent. It is this ability to read signs differently, to see our culture in a different light, that makes the way in which trauma is expressed of particular interest to me in my study of the memoir form.

The condition that contributes to Alice Kaplan's situation involves a continuing presence in her life of elements that contradict her safe, upper-middle-class, Middle-American upbringing. Her trauma cannot at once be identified by either an easily recognized originating event or the well-known pathological effects of trauma induced in victims of "beyond the range of human experience" types of trauma. The opening scenes of *French Lessons* do not introduce any traumatic events directly. Instead, in imitation of the associative linguistic process of psychiatric therapy combined with a subtle theorization of language making, it circles around the idea of language at the centre of the memoir's concerns as we watch little Alice showing off her language skills to her family. We move with Kaplan though the homey details of her life in her comfortable fifties suburb. It is a Jewish household in which the parents have "made the transition from Diaspora Yiddish to American English in a quick generation" (9) and where language is so key to their status that the dinner table becomes the locale where being American is practised and perfected. "We spoke American in that house," Kaplan declares: "My mother still corrects my English....Now I write in the staccato Midwestern style she taught me." (9). Her Jewishness seems to exist only as a kind of joke. Hearing her mother's occasional use of colloquial Yiddish expressions such as "schlemiel" when speaking to others (not her children), she concludes: "I heard just enough Yiddish in childhood to imagine a world of awkward, foolish people with wild plans that turned to buffoonery" (4).

But among the linguistic details of this nostalgic evocation of a safe Minneapolis suburb there are hints of darker realities in a series of scenes that at first seem incidental but which builds in intensity as the first chapter ends. On the day that the Kaplans move into their prosperous Republican neighbourhood they find that the former owners have left a detective report in the empty house. In it the Kaplans read of how the former owners had them investigated and found that "although we were Jews, our general comportment was in line with the gentility of the neighborhood." Kaplan adds that this "episode sat in the back of my mind as I grew up. I watched us. We were on trial, being upright for the neighborhood" (6). I propose that the appearance of this document, naming the family as "Jews" in this negative manner, is the kind of significant naming that Judith Butler describes in *Excitable Speech*: "One is not simply fixed by the name one is called. In being called an injurious name one is derogated and demeaned. But the name holds out another possibility as well: by being called a name, one is also, paradoxically, given a certain possibility for social existence, initiated into a temporal life of language that exceeds the prior purposes that animates that call. Thus the injurious address may appear to fix or paralyze the one it hails, but it may also produce an unexpected and enabling response" (2).

To find no sign in a house of its former owner except an official-looking document, which the adults do not dismiss out of hand but take seriously, must have a profound impact on a child. She is named a Jew in a way in which she has never before understood Jewishness. This naming is both a derogatory name-calling and a potential "opportunity" for self-naming. Its immediate effect on Kaplan is to make her watchful. Watchfulness is like the "hypervigilance" (Brown 100) of the traumatized. Part of Kaplan's general sense of watchfulness is her ability to observe the differences around her. This ability is demonstrated by the more lengthy language scene in which Kaplan constructs the life of her grandmother. Beginning as a remembrance of her grandmother's homey and comic ethnic world, the anecdote moves quickly to a hint of traumatic events only temporarily buried by American acculturation. In style this section is understated, the humour, for a time, comfortably containing the traumatic story. The young Alice is amused by her grandmother's warnings about the dangers of boys and men and her ethnic eccentricity of her refusal to sign social security forms or voter registration documents. Alice knows this is because of the suspicions bred into her grandmother in her childhood in Lithuania, "where her mother had hidden her in the closet so the Cossacks wouldn't rape her" (11). It is only as her grandmother ages into dementia that young Alice realizes the non-comic side of this trauma victim's linguistic framework. Kaplan puts it this way: "A fuse had blown in her head, making it impossible for her to control which language she was speaking" (12). Her description of her grandmother's condition reads like the diagnosis of a full-blown case of a traumatic crippling. It is awesome in its fragmentation, eerie in its belatedness, uncannily metaphoric in its location of traumatic effects in the inability to narrate a past that has been kept at bay, in the inability to make a healing narrative. Kaplan observes: "I had never heard my grandmother speak more than a sentence or two in a foreign language until she lost her mind. She had kept those past lives tight inside her, until they came out all jumbled up at the end" (12). Then she adds:

> Today I am a French teacher. I think about my Nanny, sliding from Hebrew to English to Yiddish. Sliding and pushing away bad memories. Nanny had a surfeit of memories, but there was no connection between one memory and the next. 'Il n'y avait pas de suite dans ses idées': 'there was no connection between her ideas.' Why does that sentence come to me in French, out of the blue. It flies into my head. No other sentence will do. I wonder why I switch like that—why I suddenly need to think in French. It is not like my grandmother's switching, but it feels disturbed. Like hers. French, for me, is not just an accomplishment. It's a need. I wonder if I could end up like her? (13-14)

It is in this accurate description of the belated effects of trauma creeping back into an elderly demented head, and in the implication of Kaplan's last question that she too may have unacknowledged traumas to deal with, that I find my permission to read this text as a trauma story. It is not one in which we can easily locate the originating event in the traumatic public events of our century, as with Eva Brewster's memoir of the Holocaust. In contrast, it is one that exposes the continuing unspectacular, but very real, traumatic conditions under which many individuals live today. It is a condition of trauma that requires us to link our personal lives with the public state of our collective experience; although our culture has not encouraged us to do so, this is precisely what contemporary memoir does in order to make its healing narrative.

The personal trauma that Kaplan highlights in her text and that starts her on her process of linking private and public events is the sudden death of her father just as she is turning eight. One afternoon he is fishing with her on the dock at their summer home. He leaves her to go inside for a glass of water. By the time she goes in search of him he has already left for the hospital. In the middle of the night her mother wakes her to tell her he is dead. Kaplan forgets nothing about the time surrounding the event, narrates it in the "flat matter-of-fact tone" (Kirmayer 173) typical of the disassociative, but detailed, memory of many trauma victims, who, rather than having trouble remembering, find they can forget nothing of the details around the event. Even seemingly unimportant details are vivid in recollection. Kaplan describes the gathering of family, the dress she wore to the funeral, how she had to sit very still because her chair squeaked when she moved. She knows exactly what her birthday cake looked like, the one the well-meaning adults presented to her at the end of the day of the funeral.

Kaplan performs memoir's typical narrative functions to accomplish her story. As witness and participant she imitates the traumatic discourse of accurate description combined with disassociation of the self from the memory in a language that is compelling in its scenic, dramatic quality. As reflective/reflexive consciousness of the memoir, she surrounds the incident with the contexts that help us absorb its symbolic significance. One of the ways she does this is by invoking the memory that stays with her as the marker of her father's death. At the summer place where the family stays on after the funeral, the parents' bedroom is a sleeping porch connected to Alice's bedroom. Alice's mother does not sleep there after the death. One night Alice opens the door to the sleeping porch and turns on the light, and the room is suddenly full of hundreds of bats circling and diving in panic. In times past, when an occasional bat entered the house, Alice watched her father chase it down with a tennis racket. After his death it takes an exterminator to get rid of them.

This literary trope of something terrifying being released into a little girl's world is magnified for Alice when, searching through her father's desk, a place forbidden to her in his life, she finds a frightening memory of her father's wartime service as a prosecutor at the Nuremberg trials: "There were black and white photographs of dead bodies....In several photographs hundreds of bony corpses were piled on top of one another in giant heaps. I had never seen a dead body, not even in a photograph" (29). Her mother tries to normalize the event by giving the children a happy memory of their father in the form of a memory book containing copies of his letters home from the war, his travel postcards from Europe, etc. Nevertheless, the Holocaust photographs become an integral part of Alice's memory of her father as the man who kept the bats at bay. I think that the photographs have, in the context of this memoir, a performative power similar to the moment of viewing the detective's report. As Butler would say, Kaplan is not only "fixed" by this discovery of Holocaust photographs as the prosecutor's daughter but also as part of a persecuted people. This "fixed" position is enhanced by her mother's actions of showing her she can make what Butler would call "a certain possibility of social existence" by doing a school report on the Holocaust. These events lay the groundwork for a lifetime in which schooling as well as the search for factual documentary evidence, and the intellectual activity of dealing with the personal experience in a public context, will become a reiterative performance of self. By her formal arrangement of the details in the memoir, Kaplan's future life work is once again tied to the childhood traumatic experience surrounding and including the death of her father. Her work as literary prosecutor of fascist writers is predicted in the formal arrangement of these early scenes in language.

Laurence Kirmayer says that part of constructing the trauma story is in giving "the reader the experience of complicity in seeking out and hiding from, memory" (174). Testimony requires an active reading process if it is to truly "penetrate us like a life." Kirmayer comments that it is not the "limits of memory but of language—the inadequacy of ordinary words to express all they have witnessed" (175) that often frustrates trauma victims. Kaplan describes her intensity in preparing her school report, how she disagrees with her mother, who took out some of the more horrific photographs as unsuitable for viewing by her school companions: "I believed my friends had no right to live without knowing about these pictures....They had to know. I had to tell them. Or was it just that I missed my father. I was trying to do what he would do, be like him" (31). As an active reader, I note that it is the mother who permits the daughter an intellectual mode for an ongoing processing of the trauma that starts her life as an intellectual, one that in important ways will imitate the father's role as Nuremberg prosecutor.

At the same time as this would seem to be the start of a healthy working through of the personal trauma, now unalterably joined for the child to the collective trauma of the Holocaust, the belatedness of traumatic reaction proves to be more subtle than the mother could anticipate. Typical of traumatized individuals, not long after her father's death Kaplan enters that latency period of trauma in which, consciously or unconsciously, the victim tries to ward off memory (Caruth 7). Forgetfulness, not of the event itself necessarily, but as a daily habit of the life that follows, is part of the interim solution. Kaplan remembers little after her father's death and the discovery of the photographs until adolescence. The bad news that she must leave childhood and become a woman proves too much of a burden for the girl who had to observe her birthday on the day of her father's funeral. To leave childhood is to leave the state where she last knew the father in the flesh and is similar to the trauma of turning eight on the day of his funeral. To become a woman is to be less like the father she adores.

The French language comes along as an opportunity for Kaplan to get on with her life. Yet, given the ambiguity with which trauma acts itself out in a lifetime, the French language ultimately acts as a linguistic location for re-experiencing the trauma of a world in which her father, the man who prosecuted evil, is no longer there. Kaplan's mother, reacting to her daughter's devastating experience of puberty—her inattention at school, her romantic obsessions, her denial of physical womanhood—sends her to Switzerland to study French at an upper-class boarding school full of "rich girls, daughters of exiled politicians, celebrities, army generals" (48). These young women all seem to be somewhat traumatized by lives that "involved embassies, revolutions, [and] transatlantic divorces" (50). The teenaged Alice loves the place. She feels much more at home among these quirky, displaced girls than in the safe suburb of her American home. She loves the rigorously ordered discipline of French-language instruction and the dependability of the routines of boarding-school life. Add to this her desire not to become an adult woman, and we come to understand that this is a location where the symptoms of traumatic reaction are both contained and strangely cultivated. Kaplan sums up her strategies for living: "For each bar of [Swiss] chocolate I didn't eat I learned a [French] verb. I grew thinner and thinner. I ate French. I had come from a house where the patterns had broken down and the death that had broken them was not understood. Now I loved the loudspeaker and the study hall and the marble floor because they made me feel hard and controlled and patterned; the harder I felt the more I felt the sorrowful world behind me grow dim and fake and powerless. In my stomach was an almost constant moaning, as though I were hollowed out inside. Before I got up in the morning I ran my hand over my hip bone, to feel my outlines" (53).

The study of the French language continues to be, paradoxically, both a discipline for surviving trauma, one that leads to Kaplan's career as a professor of French literature at Duke University, and a catalyst that reawakens the personal trauma of the father's death and its collective context of the Holocaust. Additionally ironic, many who suffer from unresolved trauma, feel a need to return to the site of trauma. Kaplan unwittingly encourages this through various life decisions, including her decision to study the French fascist writers of the 1930s for her Ph.D. studies. This prepares the ground of Kaplan's achievements as an intellectual, her scholarly work on the ways in which very good writers, through the interaction of individual acts in historical contexts, can become complicit in the doctrines of fascism.

The special ability to see the world in unconventional ways that comes from the experience of trauma needs to be carefully nurtured. The sufferer must be permitted to work through the healing process of making story in her own way, so that we do not lose the truth of her experience. T. Ribot's description of memory in *Les Maladies de la Mémoire* is significant in this regard: "A rich and extensive memory is not a collection of impressions, but an accumulation of dynamical associations, very stable and very responsive to proper stimuli....Consciousness is the narrow gate through which a small part of all this work is able to reach us" (quoted in Hacking 84). Kaplan's surrogate French mother, Dr. Micheline Veaux, a speech therapist, teaches her a similar lesson in psychoanalytic terms. She explains to her that "it is dangerous to cure someone of stuttering if the stuttering fulfills a psychic need that the person hasn't understood. Language is not a machine you can break and fix with the right technique, it is a function of the whole person, an expression of culture, desire, need." This particular "French lesson," is of a different kind than the rigorous purity of language instruction that Kaplan had subjected herself to. The knowledge that "language is our history, personal and political" (98) is what Kaplan's memoir exemplifies about traumatic testimony. In its unique temporally complex process lies its value as testimony and as art, both in terms of healing an individual and as a gift of knowledge to the collective culture. Kaplan is careful to note the inclusive dates of her memoir writing on its last page—"June 1987-Sept. 1992" (216)—and to note in her acknowledgements that some of the work of *French Lessons* is the result of being in an ongoing writing group (219). Working with trauma takes time and help from others, time to grow the scenes in language that heal the self and repossess the public world, allowing a healing of the self that can enable the individual to perform more effectively in her community.

Kaplan's contribution is in the form of various life "lessons," not named as such in the memoir, but rather performed through her portrayal of scenes from her own many lessons in the French language. There are lessons about fascism, about misogyny, and about the racism that can lie unseen in the very matter and method of language instruction. A hard lesson for Kaplan, as a lover of French literature, is the way in which one can discover fascism being performed in the language of a writer one admires. But one of the most valuable lessons she learns is that dangers and temptations lie in the path of one who chooses to become a literary prosecutor. She learns the horror of the allure of victim positions in academia, and the belated discovery, as Kaplan puts it, that "I've been willing to overlook in French culture what I wouldn't accept in my own, for the privilege of living in translation" (140).

For me, as an academic, this memoir teaches the importance of understanding the often traumatic terrain, both personal and collective, on which some academic intellectuals make their careers. Certainly, writing a memoir of my own childhood meant a growing understanding of the roots of my present self, and a reaffirmation of my career goals through understanding how intricately they have evolved from my past. It has helped me understand why, after some thought, I declined to include men's texts in this book. It has helped me understand why I refuse what would be a much more immediately effective strategy for validating women's memoirs, that is, by ranking them with men's texts and showing that they represent a valuable activity because men are doing something like what women are doing. It is my experience of gender as the most important difference in my own life that makes me hold to a position of highlighting the differences gender makes to women's writing. Reading Kaplan's memoir of her own evolution as an academic who would not follow the trend encourages me in my own chosen path.

Late in *French Lessons* there is a narrative that has made this memoir notorious among certain academics, and one that perhaps can be as emblematic of the positive results of examining the traumatic circumstances that underlie some of our life directions. Kaplan did her Ph.D. at Yale at the same time the father of deconstructive theories of reading, Paul de Man, taught there. Although as much entranced by the great man's ideas as her classmates, Kaplan doggedly insisted on carrying out her history-based study of the fascist writers of the thirties, writers no one else was interested in. She does not seek out de Man as a supervisor (although her best friend does) because she knows that her unfashionable topic will not interest a man who had taught that "it was more important to think in terms of rhetorical structure than historical periods, and I had chosen to work on material that made history impossible to ignore" (159-60). Kaplan understands that in bucking the deconstructionist trend she may be asking for a jobless future, but seeing the world differently has by now become a habit and it drives her in another direction. As she puts it, she could not resist the chance "to transgress a purity that I mistrusted in literary studies," so she takes up the challenge of her "imaginary conversation" (160) with her father about punishing war criminals. Taking up the traumatic circumstances that led her to define herself as the prosecutor's daughter uses that trauma in a positive way to strengthen her resolve to write her study of literary fascism.

For Kaplan, this positive use of her own past and its traumas leads to an academic's best dream coming true. As she puts it, when the secrets of de Man's fascist-tainted past were revealed, "I put my erudition to work with a vengeance. Suddenly this dissertation work, this topic that had seemed completely irrelevant to literary theory in 1978, was relevant. Every deconstructionist in the country wanted to know what fascism was, and I was in a position to tell them....My happiness was complete" (168-69). After a meditation on de Man, fascism, and her own life, Kaplan's memoir ends with a pedagogical insight. She regrets that de Man's "shunning [of] the illusion of the fully present communicative voice" prevented her interests ever coinciding with his. He would have been just the man to tell her a great deal about literary fascism, but de Man, she says, "covered his work with the clean veil of disinterestedness. Now I'm helping my own Ph.D. students write their dissertations, and I don't want to fail them the way de Man failed me. How do I tell them who I am, why I read the way I do? What do students need to know about their teachers?" (174). The answer to these questions, for Kaplan, is in her memoir's testimony to the "fully present communicative voice" and to the idea that a text (as Felman puts it) "can penetrate us like an actual life." *French Lessons*, through making "scenes of language" in which Kaplan's personal trauma connects with the larger life of her community and her intellectual work as a scholar, achieves this.

In "Landscapes of Memory," Laurence Kirmayer says that "telling a story of trauma occurs in a larger matrix of narrative and social praxis" and "the form of the narrative may also influence what can and cannot be recalled" (181). The memoir form, the word itself echoing the French word for memory, "*mémoire*," offers contemporary practitioners a site where this memory work can be done. Kirmayer describes the action of memory as a "cascade of experiences, eruptions, crevasses, a sliding of tectonic plates that undergird the self" (181). Through the acts of memoir, memory can be made into what Alice Kaplan calls "scenes of language," into writing that "is not a straight line but a process where you have to get in trouble to get anywhere" (Kaplan 194).

Kirmayer's geographical, seismic trope is a good one to evoke the formal challenges that are involved in the acts of memory that retrieve sexual abuse in childhood. It is typical that traumatic events of fairly short duration experienced by adults are retained in memory "unmodified...ten, twenty, or thirty years" because "myelinization"—a process of biochemical development that is complete by the end of puberty—allows for literal retention of traumatic memory. However, this is not the case with young children or people who have experienced long-term high-stress situations. Instead, "[m]odern research indicates that infantile amnesia is the result of a lack of myelinization of the hippocampus." As well, in adults "severe and prolonged stress can suppress hippocampal functioning, creating context free fearful associations, which are hard to locate in space and time" (Van Der Kolk and Van Der Hart 172). The image of "eruptions," of unseen forces moving like "tectonic plates," seeking the cause of present disability in the "crevasses" of memory, is a suitable trope for describing the action of memory in those who have suffered very early abuse. The image not only suggests the hidden nature of the trauma in the mind of the victim, but also its inaccessibility to a culture that often denies events it will not or cannot see. Kaplan's statement that one cannot go in a "straight line" in terms of such memory, but must "get in trouble to get anywhere," is descriptive of the kind of painful linguistic work that must be done if one is to make sense of traumatic symptoms. Sidonie Smith observes, in *Subjectivity, Identity and the Body*, that "the autobiographical subject carries a history of the body with her as she negotiates the autobiographical 'I,' for autobiographical practice in one of those cultural occasions when the history of the body intersects with the deployment of subjectivity" (23). The memoir subject not only has the subjectivity/body intersection to negotiate, but the culture/body as well, since memoir is a form that most explicitly addresses the way the larger body politic impacts the personal body. Janice Williamson, in her memoir CRYBABY!, seeks a form that will retrieve an experience that cripples, but is not consciously remembered, nor welcomed, either by the sufferer or her community, yet is a trauma that requires changes in community as well as the individual.[2]

Researchers Van Der Kolk and Van Der Hart note that infants record, in an "inactive" form of memory, the effects of events on their bodies, and very young children form "iconic" memories as "perceptual representations" that do not yet have the characteristics of "symbolic/linguistic" memory, which develops as they mature. In other words, traumatic events that occur before linguistic memory has developed cannot be narrated, but they can be re-experienced as "somatic sensations, behavioral reenactments, nightmares, and flashbacks" (172). Williamson's book is the record of putting into words what she intuits as painful sexual abuse from her father, abuse that would have occurred before linguistic memory was fully operational. She experiences crippling symptoms, physical illness, adverse reactions to adult sexual experience, obsessive fantasies and images, and adult infertility all of which she needs to make sense of, yet no linguistic memory exists that can help her make

---

[2] Williamson does not call CRYBABY! a memoir in her title, but the book is described on the back cover, as "a memoir of a woman struggling with the intimations of incest, her infertility, and the suicide of her father."

her story. More than any text I have read, in which trauma is a major motivating factor, this memoir imitates the process of trauma's belatedness of effects. As well, by foregrounding its formal composition—a poetic, postmodern series of meditations, narrations, quotations and poems—Williamson makes memory work to help heal the past.

When I say "makes memory work" I am quoting one of my students in the undergraduate class in memoirs that I taught in the fall of 1999. Because Williamson's text was more narratively complex then any other memoir we had studied, I took pains to talk about the typical strategies of postmodernism, the genre blending, the collage, the pastiche of forms, and the self-conscious examination of text making that went on in such art. At one point in the discussion, a student put up his hand and said, "Doesn't this book imitate the way Williamson makes memory work for her, since she was too young at the time of the trauma to retain a conscious memory?" His question brought everyone to life in a way my lecture on the poetics of postmodernism had not done. It turned out there were students in the class who had had experience in volunteer counselling, or were acquainted with the treatment of abuse victims and their symptoms through professional experience, or through feminist readings had knowledge of the debate over repressed memory. During our discussion over three classes that followed we touched on several points of form/content coherence in Williamson's text: making sense of symptoms in the present meant a need to seek imaginative links with an unremembered past. We noted how difficult it must be to distinguish flashbacks from fantasy. We began to understand that only repeated examination over time could help Williamson to gain understanding. We saw that somatic symptoms metaphorically imitate the original trauma in a way that resembles a process of poetic symbolization. We began to see that the trauma of sexual abuse, especially of incest, the knowledge of which is not welcomed in our culture, makes it difficult to find verification from significant others who don't want to talk about the past. The resulting rejection both stalls and drives the process of remembering. Given the difficulty of this remembering task, we understood Williamson's need to approach the trauma indirectly from many angles in a complex process of reflective/reflexive activity. Certainly, by the time we were through our discussions, it was obvious why a traditional arrangement of narrative was not possible for Williamson's text.[3]

Williamson makes her intention to be self-conscious about the textual and formal challenges of her book "obvious" from the beginning when she leads with quotations from Hélène Cixous, Virginia Woolf, and Marguerite Duras. The appearance of these three names establishes a kind of triangulated dialogic authority. Cixous is a theorist of language who believes that a new kind of writing "écriture feminine" can create a new subjectivity. Woolf is the feminist author of this century's most high-profile testimony to sexual abuse in the family as well as its most famous literary feminist. Duras is a more contemporary memoirist well known for her exploration of female sexual identity and postmodernist approaches to language. But the fact that each quotation is in a different typeface and font also draws our attention to Williamson's use of visible markers to aid understanding. In this case I found the effect of the visible difference was to draw attention to the difference of each woman's observation on the same subject, the difficulty of writing about what is most important in their lives. Cixous says that "the only book that is worth writing is the one we don't have the courage or the strength to write" (6). Woolf comments on the problem of the "I" in writing, how it "lie[s] like a shadow on the page," commanding a certain obedience to traditional identity "polished for centuries by good teaching and good feeding" and how the power

---

[3] When I say "obvious," I can only speak for the members of the class that actively joined in the discussion. The fact that they had seen the coherence of form and content was illustrated by the substantial number who answered a question on that topic on a class test with a large degree of success. However, a significant number of class members remained silent during discussion, or spoke as little as possible when asked to join the discussions. I did not wish to force the issue of participation in discussion on a topic that might be so charged for some students. In the anonymous class evaluations that each student completes (and to be opened by the instructor only after marks are official), a minority of students commented to the effect that if a course was going to contain "feminism" then this should be noted in the calendar so that students could avoid it if they so chose. Since the Williamson text was the book that most required an openly feminist discussion, I suspect that there was a silent backlash in my class that I was unaware of at the time of teaching.

of such conventional identity patterns makes other important realties "shapeless as mist" (6). Duras speaks of wanting her writing to resemble "a motorway going in all directions at once" but realizing that it "will merely be a book that tries to go everywhere but goes to just one place at a time" (7). My students and I took these foregrounded quotations as guides to our reading. As we read each seemingly separate section of the text we talked about the difficulties of writing such a story, the courage it must take in the face of opposition and how that affects the telling. We spoke often of how Williamson deals with the problem of "I," and I often asked them how one section (one part of the motorway) related to the others.

I would like to briefly examine some of the formal approaches Williamson makes to tell her difficult story. One of the ways that the testimonies of childhood sexual abuse victims are often denied is through pointing to the lack of what our culture calls "evidence." Williamson introduces an ironic kind of evidence: pictures from her childhood that seem to witness to a happy little girl. Such evidence could contradict her suspicions of incestuous sexual abuse by her father at an age when she was too young to make linguistic memories. But these pictures also have on their backs such seemingly harmless captions as "Push me some more, Daddy" for a picture of the little girl on a swing. As the text evolves, the captions seem less benign. Williamson does not assert the captions as traditional evidence, but uses them to destabilize our faith in pictorial evidence, to highlight the very impossibility of "evidence" in such a situation.

In the section entitled "Swing Memory" she uses the photograph of her childhood self in a garden swing to construct her text as moving between "evidence" and "denial" in a series of "waking dreams" that imitate her memory process as an adult when she tries to make sense of a recurring swing of belief and doubt in the reality of the incest. At one moment she is impressed by the "evidence" of a novelist she meets at a party who has done research on the brain in order to write about a character who experiences disassociation. The novelist tells her that "even *Scientific American* has something to say about child sexual abuse and memory" (67): "We are unable to remember traumatic events that take place early in life because the hippocampus has not yet matured to the point of forming consciously accessible memories. The emotional memory system, which may develop earlier, clearly forms and stores its unconscious memories of these events. And for this reason, the trauma may affect mental and behavioral functions in later life, albeit through processes that remain inaccessible to consciousness" (68). The passage is italicized in the text, as if to give it evidential authority, as does the mention of *Scientific American* and the citing of the reference to the June 1994 edition of the magazine.

Yet each assertion of textual "evidence" is followed by a textual "denial" as this scientific statement is followed by the following "denial":

> She reads it [sexual abuse] everywhere. In a postcard titled "Snake Club, Sarasota Florida, 1944," a row of pubescent children sit along the soda bar caressing their snakes. One girl sucks a popsicle suggestively. Or is she merely sucking? Is the "merely" in a world where to suck means nipple or cock? The soda jerk smiles into his faucet.
>
> The image is edgy, fishy, ambiguous, unsettling, fascinating: as mesmerizing and hypnotic as we imagine the snakes to be. (68)

While in the same moment as science seems to confirm her own experience, the pictorial image reminds her that she lives in a very subjective traumatic situation, where she suspects her own interpretative world is far from the "merely" world of others. Both the scientific quotation and the pictorial image are characterized as part of the "waking dream" that is her life, as if she is obsessed by a nightmare that she cannot wake from. For the reader the effect of the hypnotic, ambiguous, yet fascinating swing from "evidence" to "denial" through fifteen pages of text is powerfully emotional. However, it is not lacking in terms of an argument, since as this chapter moves toward its close, more tangible "evidence" emerges. There is the testimony of a best friend who, once she sees that Williamson is actively pursuing the idea of incest, tells her that thirty years ago Williamson's father molested her as well. Ironically, "denial" also becomes tangible as memory becomes more real and Williamson speaks out: "[H]er father denies everything, she is marginalized as 'hysterical,' a crisis that splits the family asunder" (79). Yet, even in the moment of family "denial" of the incest victim, new "evidence" in the form of testimony of a "former childhood neighbour of the family" comes to the surface. This woman, "[o]n hearing of the turmoil...bursts into tears, confessing the accused father molested her many times as a child when she was too afraid to tell" (80). The argument of the chapter imitates traumatic memory's recovery process as a swing between doubt and assertion. It is a swinging that is increasing in force, "gaining altitude" as Williamson puts it, in order to swing the writer and reader into a mutual movement toward belief in the sexual abuse and a trajectory of healing.

In each of the chapters of this text, formal arrangements such as the swing of "evidence" and "denial" are used to suggest the nature of the trauma, the extent of its effect on the grown woman's life, and the way healing must perform itself "somewhere between imagination and history" (11). And while healing enacts itself in the private centre of one woman's life, the memoir that results is public testimony. Williamson reinforces this necessary public part of the process—despite the suggestions of other people that she not write about incest at all—by asserting that her book "is also about a collective history longer than my own—one that begins with Freud's Dora" (11). One of the formal arrangements of this text is to imitate the disassociative illness of the childhood victim of sexual abuse in order to turn that crippling into a strength. Williamson constantly uses the pronoun "I" as if it were in the third person, disassociated from herself, and also uses "she" to speak of herself in the third person. Late in the text she takes on the persona of Freud's most famous patient, Dora, writing a diary through this figure, making the otherness that memoir cultivates serve as part of the healing process.

This memoir sees the self in others' experiences, not only in the recreation of Dora's voice, but through the critical, creative, and theoretical texts that are quoted and the personal letters and accounts of experiences of friends and relatives that are included. The variety of its sources is part of the dialogic form that breaks down artificial boundaries between private and public and is essential to this memoir's formal arrangement. This arrangement reflects the experience that Williamson's life has been, not only as professional writer and literary critic (all the quotations are sourced at the end of the text), but also as an abuse victim, as a family member, as a woman among other women who are suffering, as a feminist, and as an artist healing herself.

The memoir form's ability to bring together self and other, private life and public history, imaginative construction and factual testimony, is perhaps best illustrated in the final chapter, named "Fragments of an Analysis." One might expect from this title a very personal story of a therapeutic psychoanalytic "analysis," but true to Williamson's serious wordplay throughout the text the "analysis" is not only a reference to her personal healing process, but refers to her intellectual acts as well. The thirteen "cases" make up a feminist casebook of stories of self and other. The first cases construct an ongoing critique of the limitations of some therapists' approaches to treatment, illustrated by personal experience. In the first case, the therapist "dismisses" her concern with realizing the full imaginative possibilities of the concept of "the child within," by saying it is "only a metaphor." It is as if the therapist, while believing in the "talking cure," has not understood that the linguistic form that "talking" takes is central to healing. As a literary critic, Williamson insists on taking metaphor much more seriously, understanding that the "child" stands for "the woman who speaks into the wind," unheeded (176). The therapist in the second case says to Williamson: "[Y]ou're not very confident of your boundaries are you?" As a trauma victim who has learned to value the qualities obtained from her injuries, Williamson decides to validate the usefulness of her own vulnerability by arguing: "My world won't be bounded by the prefab equivalent of a fortress wall, or a garden gate" (177). Each attempt to contain her in the constraints of traditional psycho-social linguistic stereotypes is resisted by linguistic recasting of the binding language. Like Erikson, who wants us to recognize the positive uses of the "different" voice of the trauma victim who reads signs we cannot read, Williamson insists that healing is not about forgetting the hard-won abilities that trauma has given her.

Sometimes, lightening her intense text with humour, she allows psychobabble to condemn itself. This is illustrated in the forth case where she reprints a portion of the University of British Columbia's "Mood Disorder" description, which advises the victim of depression to avoid anything more intellectual than "light novels and *People* magazine" (179). Making visual comedy of the list in "Depression: What You Need to Know," Williamson shades the list in a depressing grey. This case marks the gradual movement outward from the personal story to the community story that takes place as we move through the cases. The text has become a "testimony" that "speaks for and to others," the use of the pronouns "us" and "our" attesting to the joining of self and other. The eighth case contends with what has become the sexual abuse victim's most crippling foe: the "False Memory Syndrome Foundation." Williamson includes in her testimony, the testimony of Dr. Jennifer Freyd, herself an author of a book on the trauma of childhood sexual abuse, whose mother and alcoholic father began the Foundation: "Is my father more credible than me because I have a history of lying or not having a firm grasp on reality? No, I am a scientist whose empirical work has been replicated in laboratories around this country and Europe....Am I not believed because I am a woman? A "female in her thirties" as some of the newspaper articles seem to emphasize? Am I therefore a hopeless hysteric by definition? Is it because the issue is father-daughter incest and, as my father's property, I should be silent?...Indeed, why is my parents' denial at all credible? In the end, is it precisely because I was abused that I am to be discredited despite my personal and professional success?" (184-85).

The building effect of the case studies on this reader is to demonstrate the continuing need for linguistic vigilance, a vigilance that includes careful attention to a formal arrangement that allows the survivor to participate, through her artful testimony, in the fight for others' survival. Williamson widens the circle of criticism and exposure of cultural denial in the eleventh case by showing government complicity in denial and in the twelfth case by commenting on how publishers and even other writers discourage the writing of childhood sexual abuse trauma. In the thirteenth case she comes back to the victims and survivors as a group, and in criticizing a therapist leading a group for asking for the re-enactment of trauma on demand, she advises women to be "true to each other, in confidence, we speak" (192). Although speaking "for others" as a survivor, Williamson insists that the "details" of these stories are not hers to tell.

In a brief epilogue chapter, "Where Does the Misery Come From," Williamson describes her return to the cottage that her father once owned, where she brings her linguistic task home "to edit the galleys of her book" and "remake the cottage in her own image" (193). Repossession of the body and the mind that have been crippled by the incest takes linguistic (through the editing process) and even geographical form, through repossessing the cottage as a place she can be. This homecoming, and her commitment to the future, after so much necessary preoccupation with the past, takes the form of a decision to adopt a child. In such ways the writing, which erupted from the damaged life, which was worked and shaped into testimony, comes back into the life to make it more whole. These writing acts allow Williamson to repossess the private world as a habitable space for the future, as well as to repossess her more public roles as teacher and writer in ways that can help other victims.

I considered a number of narratives of childhood sexual abuse to include as support for my views in this chapter. They are moving and effective and their formal styles are close to what Henke describes as "scriptotherapy" in which "the act of life writing...carries through the work of reinventing the shattered self as a coherent subject capable of meaningful resistance to received ideologies and of effective agency in the world" (xix). While each of the books I read exhibits "meaningful resistance" and varying degrees of "effective [personal] agency in the world," Williamson's book most vigorously pursues the public agenda of speaking to the need for public health professionals, politicians, writers, and other public intellectuals to take proactive stances. In this way she fulfils the naming on her book as memoir on the back cover. Her text is not only "scriptotherapy" but is "memoir" in the way I find contemporary women's memoirs are, a text with a recognizable mandate that involves finding ethical writing strategies for "speaking for [as well as] speaking to others" in order to facilitate more than self-survival. Such texts speak for the survival of others who do not have the linguistic opportunities that a writer of Williamson's experience and ability can make for herself in the public world.

6

Joining Heart and Head

Contemporary Academic Women's Uses of the Memoir Form

> I prefer the term memoir for literary reasons but for etymological ones as well. By its roots, memoir encompasses both acts of memory and acts of recording—personal reminiscences and documentation. The word record, which crops up in almost every dictionary definition of memoir, contains a double meaning too. To record means literally to call to mind, to call up from the heart. At the same time, record means to set down in writing, to make official. What resides in the province of the heart is also what is exhibited in the public space of the world.
>
> —Nancy Miller, *Bequest and Betrayal*

NANCY MILLER'S comment that "what resides in the province of the heart is also what is exhibited in the public place" (*Bequest* 2) refers to her own experiment in melding her writing as critical reader of a series of elegiac memoirs with the personal writing of her memoir of her parents. She, like a number of academic women I will consider in this chapter, uses the memoir form to bring together what is "called to mind" with what is "call[ed] up from the heart." There is a desire on the part of many women in the academy to seam together the seemingly dichotomous identity situations in which they find themselves. As practitioners of the traditional and honoured modes of reasoned and objective argument that the academy teaches, women working in the humanities and social sciences do not always find a way to value and legitimize what they learn as practitioners of the many experiential modes of women's lives. In such lives the skills of reason and objectivity are of little use by themselves, and effective ways of knowing must evolve from complex interrelationships of reason and emotion, self and others, private and public experience. Memoir is a mode by which such women can value both sides of their experience. However, while Miller and I think similarly about the usefulness of the memoir form in bringing together head and heart, she would not necessarily agree with me in my gendered emphasis in this book. Miller is well known in my field as a distinguished feminist critic and theorist of personal writing and autobiographical forms as used by women. In an article in the women's studies journal *Signs* in 1997, she reports on the "avalanche of published memoirs by women in recent years" (heralded by the *Women's Review of Books* in July 1996). Miller makes it clear that she is not ready to identify the "avalanche" as a gendered phenomenon:

> Ten years ago I would not have hesitated to explain why the memoir has become the genre of choice for so many women writers and academic critics, how women's writing differs from men's. Today, rather than construct a poetics of women's fin de siecle memoirs, I am more inclined simply to describe a dozen or so examples of this particular mode of storytelling by women, comparable only, I think, to a parallel explosion in feminist biography (and again [as in the explosion of men's memoirs] in biography in general). In

some important way, the proliferation of auto/biographical writing by women is reminiscent of the exuberant years of 1970s feminist fiction. There seems to be a renewed urgency to add the story of our lives to the public record. ("Public Statement, Private Lives" 981-82)

While recognizing that something is happening to women and the memoir form, Miller hesitates to identify this phenomenon as specific to women or to speculate on what particular attributes of the form are useful to women. She seems not up to her usual daring feminist departures of the 1980s and early 1990s, undertaken in works such as *Subject to Change: Reading Feminist Writing* and *Getting Personal: Feminist Occasions and Other Autobiographical Acts.* Perhaps she is having her own "fin de siecle" letdown, one that may well be pandemic in feminism at the moment, a retreat from the insistence on the differences of women's texts because of the fear of "gender essentialism" (Smith and Watson 40). However, as Diana Fuss teaches us in *Essentially Speaking*, essentialism is neither good nor bad in and of itself, but rather has a value dependent on its deployment. To consider gender as a factor in the formation of a new discursive form is not, to my mind, an example of gender essentialism. I insist on examining female difference not because I believe the difference is an essential and exclusive one, but because I see women in the lead of a complex change in life-writing practice. We need to explore what female gendering has to do with that change.

And yet I sympathize with Miller's hesitancy in naming memoir as a female gendered act. Works such as Tobias Wolff's *This Boy's Life* or Henry Louis Gates, Jr.'s *Colored People* reveal what an excellent stage memoir is for performing masculinity and all its complexities. While most contemporary male memoirists still assume their experience of gender is the norm of human experience rather than a specifically masculine experience, a minority of men do take up the form to explore the complex formation of their masculinity. This merely reinforces the important presence that female gender has in most women's memoirs. Contemporary men have their own good reasons to write memoirs, and these may well become the subject of someone else's critical inquiry. I am interested in the way in which female gendering is facilitated, complicated, subverted, and reinvented through the memoir's elastic form.

Miller's hesitancy to identity the gendered aspect of women's memoirs may well also stem from the fact that she has written her own memoir, *Bequest and Betrayal: Memoirs of a Parent's Death*, in which she reads her own relationships to her parents through the literary critic's acts of reading other peoples' memoirs of their parents. Some of these memoirists are men. Yet I find Miller's autocritical memoir is very intensely female gendered throughout. In a very obvious way, in terms of the sheer number of women's memoirs that she explores compared with men's memoirs, Miller's gender interests are highlighted. While she does take up men's accounts (for example, Philip Roth's *Patrimony* and Art Spiegelman's *Maus*), what interests Miller most often in women's accounts seems to be the ways in which women write of their relationships with their mothers. Miller is particularly fascinated with Carolyn Steedman's troubled relationship with her mother in *Landscape*, as I have been in my chapter on mother/daughter memoirs. She finds that "Steedman's attempt to separate from her mother displays an almost ontological resentment" (83), and interweaves Steedman's identification problems concerning her mother with Miller's own difficult relationship with her own. In the same way, Miller undertakes readings of autobiographical texts by Annie Ernaux, Vivian Gornick, and Simone de Beauvoir, all of whom concern themselves with the mother/daughter relationship. Even when discussing the men's texts and their connection to her own life, her discussion tends towards a female gendering of the issues of a parent's death.

When writing of Roth's *Patrimony* she meditates on the fact that "there is no easy equivalent of patrimony, since matrimony leads away from the mother and since it's always less clear what, under patriarchy, a daughter can inherit from her mother, let alone pass on or return" (41). Miller understands matrimony as it has been defined by patriarchy, as the act of giving a daughter in marriage to another family, rather than how matrimony might be understood in a more equal world in which women would have some gift of "power and humanity" (as Chesler puts it) to give to their daughters. When analyzing Susan Cheever's memoir of her famous father, John Cheever, it is the "silent web of the daughter's seduction" (129) into the myth of the father that fascinates Miller. She concludes that Cheever's effort "is the book of a daughter in thrall to her father, to his self-construction as a writer" (160). Perhaps the condition of being "in thrall" with fathers is a consequence of a lack of a tradition of "matrimony" in the sense Chesler understands it. Miller seems fascinated with the kind of ambiguous inheritance that daughters might receive from fathers. Indeed, the treatment of fathers in her memoir is not the kind one would find in a man's book, but rather a female gendered writing act. In saying her final word on her own father's life it is once more the gendered aspects of the situation that are highlighted. After her father's death she finds some prayer shawls and traditional Jewish religious accoutrements among his belongings. This surprises Miller, as her father was not part of a conservative Jewish congregation where he would use such items. At first she plans to give them away, then changes her mind:"Instead, I packed everything into a small suitcase and stowed it on the top shelf of my hall closet. To whom were they destined? I know only that the contents of the suitcase were never meant for a daughter" (188). Miller does not explore further her own motivations in keeping this unusual patrimony, which she obviously can make no use of, but in some strange way perhaps she feels it was meant for her, since she does not give it away. Such scenes make this a memoir that could never be mistaken as a son's memoir of his parents' deaths. Even without the central chapter "Mothers and Daughters: The Price of Separation," the book is performed as a daughter's book throughout.

In her analysis of Alice Kaplan's *French Lessons* in an article on recent women's memoirs, Miller says: "Seventies feminism...had everything to do with finding the words in which to say it—emotions with no name. In the nineties, naming is not the problem, it's about *doing* something with the words" ("Public Statements, Private Lives" 984). Miller herself is "doing something" in her integration of memoir and close textual study of others' memoirs, an act of autocritography for which her training as an academic woman has prepared her. I would also add that just as "finding the words" for all sorts of activities, emotions, and ways of thinking important to women has been an important part of second-wave feminism, "doing something with the words" is as gendered an occupation as "naming." In fact, naming and doing cannot be separated, binarized into two different modes. Academic women today are "naming" the memoir form as a way of "doing" their lives that does not exclude important parts of their experience; they are becoming aware that they must perform "non-sacrificial" discursive acts to maintain the complex identities that being women in the academy has given them.

I can also witness that actually writing a memoir can pull you up short in terms of easy theorization of other people's attempts in the same genre. I discovered this when, in trying to figure out what the memoir form was and why contemporary women wanted to write memoirs, I found myself writing my own memoir, which I have quoted from in my preface. That act did make me aware of how much more complex the form is than I ever dreamt, and incidentally delayed the writing of this critical study of women's memoirs by years. While I began to realize how complex and subtle was the gendering of memoir, the act of writing a memoir also increased my desire to understand the special ways in which women take up the form. One of the things I discovered about memoir is that it does not need to make a demand for the kind of feminized, confessional autobiographical acts that are stereotypically associated with women. While many memoirs do deal with very personal and intimate details of the memoirist's life that concern sexuality, family relationships, and experiences of shame, other memoirs do not. And when they do, the memoir form's requirement that the personal be set in the broader context of the culture can avoid the exploitation described by the essayists in *Confessional Politics*, in which such revelations are ripe for appropriation for the purposes of further victimization. For example, I found that much of the intimate detail that I wished to explore in my memoir called for a setting that allowed me to place such subjects as sexual exploitation in the larger setting of the ideology in which I was brought up. I found that my training as a cultural critic allowed me to see my personal life as tied to larger cultural phenomena. As Irene Gammel has observed, it is possible for "women [to] creatively dodge and escape confessional snares" (2). Miller herself cannily sets her own complex and often negative experience of family life in comparison and contrast with the lives of the memoirists she reads as a literary critic, so that revelations about family life become part of a cultural critique rather than a confession that reappropriates her into a feminized powerlessness.

In offering this analysis of Miller's memoir I wish to make the point that this is not the moment to give up on women's difference. Reading with gender in mind has much to teach us as readers. As a way of doing that, I offer my own readings of academic women's memoirs to demonstrate why being female and academic is a difference that mandates the memoir form as a particularly appropriate vehicle of self-expression for women whose training has taught them various modes of cultural critique. There is a sense that these women are artfully shaping the experience in which they have participated and which they have witnessed in a form that they wish to stand as an ethically informed statement of what they believe to be true. As well, in choosing the memoir form, these women refuse the typical strategy of traditional autobiography as it has been defined in the last two hundred years. They refuse what Lee Quinby calls the "totalizing individuality of the modern era" (297), one which privileges separation of the self from others as a maturation process. In addition, they refuse the acquisition of authority through the guise of objectivity that humanistic academic discourses (in imitation of scientific method) have pretended to in the twentieth century. For these women, self-performance is always located in relationships with others, often with many significant others. For these human subjects, their lives as writers and intellectuals and as women in the academy have problematized a multiplicity of often painfully conflicted identities, which, ironically, make them seek the academic life as a place where they can accommodate this multiplicity. Their texts are attempts to bring the intellectual process of critical thinking to bear on their own various self-identities and to hold these in balance without oppressing any aspect of what or who has made them. The relationship of life and academy is inevitably fraught with the ambivalence that many of these women feel as the result of perceiving themselves as subjects from the margins. These margins are often as multiple as their identities and range anywhere from a sense of ethnic, racial, or class marginalization to a sense of marginality to do with sexual orientation. There is, as well, a deeply felt sense of being marginal because of women's necessarily ambivalent relationship with scholarly and intellectual activity, given the masculine history of intellectual life in most disciplines.

Academic women who choose the memoir often want a form that allows the story of their professional lives to be informed by the conditions of their personal lives. Two examples of this are Jill Ker Conway's *True North: A Memoir* and Jane S. Gould's *Juggling: A Memoir of Work, Family and Feminism*. When she published *True North* Conway was already well known for her memoir *Road to Coorain*, which recounts her Australian outback childhood, her close working relationship with her father, and her conflicts with her mother. *True North* relates the development of her intellectual pursuits as a historian and as an administrator at the University of Toronto before she became president of Smith College. The elasticity of the memoir form allows Conway to write of the development of her intellectual and administrative skills at the same time as she relates her part in the larger communal developments in education, such as the new directions in social historiography and the impact of feminism and student activism on the academy. She sets these public features in the context of the life of a woman who, in true 1960s superwoman style, also serves as hostess and caregiver to a successful husband who was also a university administrator.

In the chapter entitled "Historian," Conway is able in the space of three pages to move through a history of the full range of identities that construct her sense of her self. She begins with a discussion of how learning "to love the essay as a literary form" (161) changed her approach to writing history. Her interest in the interdisciplinary use of the essay allowed her to "track[ ] down some of the more recondite themes" (161) not usually taken up in the narratives of history, such as the fact that the endocrine system in humans shows more differentiation between individuals than between males and females. This causes her to meditate on her mother's life, not in the ways she did in *Road to Coorain*, as the daughter of a difficult and mentally unstable mother, but as a scholar realizing how gender roles can limit the scope of females whose energies are inappropriately used. This insight turns her away from her original focus on collective biography to an interest in the "more general history of the experience of women in the process of urbanization" (161). In the same paragraph as she tells her readers that she has signed a book contract to work on the new area, Conway relates how she made room in her busy life for such work. She details how she and her husband arranged to stay late at their offices three nights a week to accomodate essential library time for research. Since Conway's day is taken up by commuting, teaching, and responsibility for all household work, including the cooking and entertaining that is the result of her husband's administrative position, these evenings are especially valuable. The couple work at keeping their relationship close by making evenings at home alone into special celebratory moments. Conway's ability to use the style of the serious personal essay allows the mundane details of the arrangements of a woman's life to fit well with the more public account of her accomplishments, and in doing so it reinforces the connections she is making regarding women's private/public balancing act.

Conway observes that her multiple roles have made her the kind of professor who finds herself "making up shopping lists with one part of her mind, while the other functioned apparently smoothly to deliver the lecture of the moment on the causes of the Civil War" (162). She is able to move, within the space of a paragraph, from an account of serene evenings of poetry readings with her husband to the specifics of life for women in the academy in the 1960s. This precedes and leads into an observation that "my daily academic activities kept reminding me that my field of research was of direct immediate relevance to women's lives" (163). To emphasize the difficulty women have entering academic life, she recounts an anecdote of her experience as head of a search committee. Her position as chair occasioned more that one referee to begin his letter by observing "I would not normally nominate a woman for a position at Toronto, but seeing that the Committee Chair is a woman..." (163). Incidents from her personal life, her research life, and her life as an administrator combine to teach her more of women's situation in the academy. The facility the memoir form offers to contain this diverse experience (in this case in the space of several paragraphs) is enabled by the way a memoirist like Conway can take up the form of the personal essay, in which crafted anecdotes of diverse life activities can be drawn together to illustrate a particular theme or motif. While narrative, descriptive, and analytical writing work together in both the essay and the memoir forms, it is the special characteristic of the memoir to always connect its themes to a substantial ongoing self-performance. This Conway does with a skill that does not allow her personal reference to become a mere confession of the difficulties of a life lived with the realities of the career woman's doubled duties.

This ability of the essayistic memoir to allow the writer to move in her text, in a continuing and integrated manner, between personal life and public activities is nowhere more graphically illustrated than in Jane Gould's *Juggling*. The title of the memoir itself speaks to the lives of those women memoirists who took up careers in a time when married women had no cultural permission to give up any of the domestic roles that others expected of them and that they expected of themselves. It also speaks to the style of the memoir in which various issues of private/public, self/family, career/community are juggled in the multiple discursive possibilities of the form. Gould's memoir describes the difficult passage of a woman who is typical of the white, middle-class woman of the 1930s and 1940s. She first accepts the inevitability of giving up her education and becoming a stay-at-home mom. Later, very gradually, she emerges from that cocoon, fighting the claustrophobic role expectations of the 1950s to get a toehold in the job market. Eventually, because of her experience and know-how in women's career difficulties (she has made a profession of helping thousands of women return to the job market) and the coincidental arrival of the women's movement, she gains a position at one of the central intellectual engines of that movement as director of the Women's Center at Barnard.

Jane Gould would seem to be the ultimate insider, as white, well-educated, well-married, well-heeled career woman, yet she expresses a sense of marginality quite typical of many contemporary women memoirists: "Throughout my life I've had ambivalent feelings about belonging. Sometimes the ache to be accepted was so strong that I would actually pray to be invited to a party where I knew I would be bored if I went. When I married a doctor, had two children, and was 'just like everyone else,' I took a distinct pleasure in 'doing the right thing.' But nothing was ever enough, and I never outgrew the strong feeling that I was different—an outsider. Gradually, I learned to trust my judgment, while at the same time, admitting that if I was to be effective as an innovator, I could learn to work within a traditional setting. Coming to Barnard brought back these old feelings with intensity" (99).

Gould's reasons for feeling marginalized may seem trivial when compared with some of the material marginalities that affect people of colour, the disabled, and the economically deprived, but she speaks to a malaise that is not untypical of privileged middle-class, white women in the academy. Having grown up in the full expectation that she would "belong" if only she carried out the proper activities of girls in the dominant culture, she finds herself in the late twentieth century undertaking a number of conflicting roles for which little in her confined and relatively privileged upbringing has prepared her. Such a subject position is not generally viewed with much sympathy. However, the memoir form allows Gould to show us white privilege from the inside. It allows her to relate the subtle, yet very real, culture shock of growing up wealthy only to find herself in a tighter, lower-middle-class existence as a teenager and working college girl. Writing from the inside of a class identity, Gould describes the apparent safety of the "married a doctor" existence, which becomes suddenly less safe when her husband's heart attack at age thirty-six predicts an earlier death than normally expected. The memoir allows the writer to write from inside the stereotype and to find the specifics of a material reality that shows privilege as a complex blend of opportunities and prohibitions, keeping the reader from too easily dismissing a woman simply because she has been privileged.

Like Conway's memoir, Gould's is also able to show the important factor of the husband's health in nuancing the patriarchal definitions of the white, bourgeois marriages these women take on. Conway's career becomes more and more central to the life of the couple because her husband is considerably older than she is and suffers increasingly from manic-depressive disorder as he ages. The death of Gould's husband in mid-life leaves her able to focus on career and later to form a marriage with a man who, because of his own complete devotion to work, wants a wife who is preoccupied with her own career. These personal factors, woven into the pattern of memoir because of the continuing demand the form makes to link the events and issues of private life with that of the career life, helps us see an important but subtle factor in such women's self-performance. The memoir form points to the effect of the weakened authority of the husband, due to some incapacity to continue his dominant role in the marriage, on a middle-class woman's independence.

Seemingly in direct contrast to these white women's negotiations within the tight boundaries of role definition in mid-to late-twentieth-century North America are the memoirs of two post-colonial women whose multiplicity of margins has also found a place in the academy. Meena Alexander, poet and professor at Hunter College and author of *Fault Lines: A Memoir*, and Shirley Geok-Lin Lim, author of *Among the White Moon Faces: An Asian-American Memoir of Homelands*, both make use of the memoir's ability to translate multiple histories and identities into a life. Interestingly, Alexander only alludes to her life as a scholar and teacher, being much more concerned with finding a sense of self that will turn her fragmented life as a South Asian woman living as a wife and mother in a North American marriage into the poetry that she yearns to write. After a rich life in an intellectual and politically active family in India, marriage to an American academic brings her to the suburban life of a young mother in Minneapolis. She is "chilled by this strange new world: baby food in jars and shopping malls and at home books stacked high in piles with no time to read them." In the moment of an accident, a cigarette igniting a wastepaper basket, Alexander finds the image of her dislocation and her yearning: "I am this basket, this burning thing, how shall I bear my life here?...[I walked] around and around the sidewalks of the neat suburban area and watched other wives lay out the washing and roll out their carpets and thought, I am a wife like that, I am, I am....But in my mind's eye I kept seeing that basket burning, filled with waste paper from writings that never had time or space to come to anything, torn pages of a Sears catalog, fourth-rate junk mail, bits of soiled tissue paper. Where was the life I had led? Who was I?" (147). Although memoirs by academic women often work argumentatively and narratively, blending the instructive voice of the essayist with the anecdotal recounting of events that support thesis-like statements of positions, it is interesting to see the memoir of a poet working more imagistically and descriptively. The incident of the waste paper basket comes late in the text in the chapter called "Long Fall," which relates Alexander's "falling" into life in America, motherhood, and eventually academic life. However, the chapter is also filled with the life left behind in India, and mentions many journeys, to Sudan as a child, to England as a student, that have made the life of this woman. The style of the chapter (indeed, of the entire book) requires the reader to work associatively rather than in a linear manner, making the image of the flaming basket a symbol of Alexander's move through locations, ethnicities, and identities to the psychic emergency that can find its resolution only in writing to halt disintegration of the self. Alexander's memoir speaks to the plethora of rhetorics and stylistics that the form can encompass—from this memoir, which works like a long narrative poem, to Conway's and Gould's blending of anecdote and argument in the form of the personal essay.

Among the White Moon Faces works out of a range of memoir styles. It is richly evocative and poetic in the narrative of a

Malaysian childhood and carefully analytical when describing how the colonizer's culture is made into the vehicle of personal liberation for the ethnic Chinese schoolgirl. In its narrative of the horrors of adjusting to the eccentricities of North American life as a university student, it is comically anecdotal. It also brings the full voice of the personal essay's assertive narrator to an account of women's marginalization in the academy. Lim's memoir is exemplary as a stylistic paradigm of the memoir form. It also illustrates that, in the multiplicity of subject positions that post-colonial women experience, it is women's discursive skill that sustains their balancing act. As Lim says in her summary chapter, "Moving Home:"

> I write this on the morning of my fiftieth birthday. A mile away the waves of the Pacific Ocean are in an unusual swell....My life rushes me toward a shore, in full motion; only my skills keep me on my feet, not drowning.
>
> How do I reconcile these two different yet simultaneous images—the ropes that my mother and father have cunningly woven, invisible like spirits and ghosts, that tie me to the ancestral altar table which presides in every Confucian home; and the crashing surf that knocks me off my feet and throws me onto a beach, which is never the same from moment to moment? (231)

Lim brings together her training in the British romantic tradition of life viewed through nature's glass with her post-colonial concern for melding opposing traditions in a subjectivity of balanced artistry, and poises them—by the use of the question mark—on the border of the present and the future autobiographical moment.

Lim's memoir is concerned with both the construction of personal subjectivity and, as is typical of the memoir form, the wider implications of her own story. She narrates an anecdote about becoming the advisor for a Jewish-American student who was uninterested in her Jewish heritage because "my parents didn't want me to grow up burdened by a Jewish identity" (230). Seeing that the student's imminent marriage into a conservative Jewish family will make her lack of interest a disadvantage, and having had the personal experience of marrying a Jewish man,

Lim encourages the student to do independent studies in Jewish-American literature. Lim uses the anecdote to assert her own vision of what a university should be, not a place to merely nurture careers in "Fortune 500 companies" but one where a multi-ethnic "world-civilization" might begin (230). Having moved from the specific to the general, Lim moves back to the specific and the personal to observe: "Setting out from a nation that denied people like me an equal homeland, I find myself, ironically, making a home in a state that had once barred people like me from its territory" (230). For Lim, repossessing the world means not only performing in words the multiple pasts for the purpose of her self-understanding in the present, but also repossessing the world in an intellectual sense so that she may help effect a "world-civilization." This combination of a personal, intellectual, and ethical agenda for self-performance is typical of memoirs by academic women.

The memoir form is a useful form to express the movement of those with subject locations on the gender, racial, and national margins of a dominant society to the central "intellectual machinery" (Lim 230) that the university represents. This is part of the phenomenon of the academy finally becoming open, with some universities actively welcoming non-male, non-white subjects. However, once inside, other marginalizations besides race, gender, and class may well make the individual feel oppressed and ineffective because of less easily addressed fraudulent fronts they feel forced to adopt. It is only in very recent years that women who are lesbians have been able even to contemplate living their gender orientation as a conscious part of their daily lives as teachers, writers, and intellectuals in the academy. In *I Dwell in Possibility, A Memoir*, Toni McNaron speaks of the debilitating effects that being in the closet had on her intellectual life. After an early life as a brilliant academic achiever, successful in obtaining a university appointment, tenure, and an associate professorship, McNaron finds that the hidden nature of her life as a lesbian has led to unhealthy habits. She has affairs with women who are basically "kept" lovers, develops a serious drinking problem, and, most terrifying of all, experiences a resulting inability to read and write well. Hitting the bottom, McNaron finds herself unable to communicate with even her most intimate friends: "What I wanted most was someone to tell what it felt like to live inside my skin, lonely, hung over much too often, scared of being out as almost anything I really was—Southerner, lesbian, drunk, writer, passionate human being with dreams of a feminist world" (171).

The first step back on the road to health is multiple and is typical of women who find the memoir form expresses the range of their multiple identity, in its personal, communal, and career expressions. McNaron realizes that stopping drinking alone will not do it, nor will both coming out as a lesbian *and* stopping drinking do it (even though coming out gives her a real sense of community for the first time in her adult life and being sober makes her healthy and alert). To preserve her health, she decides that she must also bring her lesbian identity to her work. She confronts the problem head on and tells her department head that staying on in the academy means, for her, living, teaching, and writing as a lesbian. For McNaron, "occupying space as a lesbian at the university has changed virtually everything about working there" (182), as her productive scholarly output indicates. Interestingly, part of the multi-step process of emerging from her debilitating self-hatred was a process of journalizing that eventually led to her memoir. This process allows her to speak, in the very specific and historicized ways that the memoir form encourages, of her childhood as a privileged, Southern girl, her break with traditional roles, and her life as an academic, a feminist, and a lesbian in a time of enormous change in the academy.

The pain and pleasure of "coming out" is a memoir narrative we have now become accustomed to in a world a little more willing to recognize the variety of subject locations on the continuum of gender identity. Yet what kind of narrative can express the amazement and consternation, the spectacular dislocation of oneself and one's significant others, that comes with the sudden realization—at close to fifty, after a lifetime as a female heterosexual—that one is falling in love with another woman? This is the challenge that Elspeth Cameron takes up in

No Previous Experience: A Memoir of Love and Change. As an experienced, prize-winning biographer and a distinguished teacher of Canadian literature and culture for decades, Cameron is well aware that formal choices are at the heart of writing well. The choice of the memoir allows her to bring together the diverse strands of her complex life and that of her partner, while neglecting no part of the great destabilization of relationships that their love brought. Given its effects on their spouses, children, parents, and friends, as well as on both of their academic careers in two different cities, this memoir has a lot to handle. One of the things that Cameron does to relate the various strands is to appropriate the language of romance to a lesbian story. Romance has often been negatively viewed by feminists in terms of its effect of narrowing women's lives to male-defined uses, but romance has also received some lively rewritings as part of lesbian literary production, and Cameron is now part of that tradition. The flexibility of the memoir—its ability to accommodate scholarly argument and documentation as well as various experiments in essayistic and biographical narrative, its allowance for the poetic alongside the historical—proves as welcoming to romance as to other discourses. Cameron's preface signals her conscious performance of romance conventions to make her memoir:

> It can happen on a hike. You round a woody corner and suddenly you're in the clear on the brink of a pale limestone bluff, your stomach clenched, breath held as you stare straight down into the lush damp valley you never suspected was there....
>
> They used to tell it in books. A ride on a magic carpet through the midnight blue of Arabian nights....You knew there was another reality behind closed doors in strange places. It was scary. You needed a password. Open Sesame.
>
> I dimly recall an old movie. Was it Shangri-La?...a green valley, pastoral peace, a village of incomparable beauty, spread splendid in the sun.
>
> Later I recognized it with an upwards rush of the hair on my neck. I knew without being told what stout Cortez, with his eagle eye, felt as he stood, silent, upon his peak in Darien....
>
> It can happen anytime, anywhere. (3-4)

Calling up all the signals of the archetypal, from the use of nature imagery to connote the "lush damp valley" of love, through appeals to our history of romantic images from exotic literary Arabias, Shangri-Las, and Dariens, to a hyperbolic warning that "you can miss the whole thing. You can be blinded by blizzards, forget the password" (4), Cameron constructs a world well lost for love. The tactic may make some feminists squirm, understanding as we do the way that romance conventions have been used to imprison women in patriarchal scripts. Nevertheless, the decision to perform a romantic version of the event works, as this memoir, in the cause of lesbian love, becomes one of those page-turners that evoke all the romance scripts we have internalized, but to a different lesbian-gendered purpose. Being as fair as desire can be to all the people that stand in its way, Cameron also weaves a romantic tale of stolen meetings, family rejection and acceptance, spouses that are cruel and spouses that behave stoically. She alludes to colleagues that ignore, cut, oppress, or accept, in a book that manages to make even the academic conference an occasion of lively romance. Cameron's refusal to censor her discovery that being a lesbian also involves learning how to make physical love in a whole new way is facilitated by her emphasis on the romance of lesbianism. She repossesses the literary expression of romance to put it to the new use of "coming out." Cameron and McNaron's books are both about finding an identity as a lesbian, yet they are very different in style, philosophy, and narrative route. This is because they come from two very different lives. Yet the books are both called memoirs. These two memoirs illustrate the form's stylistic elasticity.

It is ironic to note that the contemporary women of whom I write, whose non-traditional lives have been associated in one way or another with the academy—a place where the streamlining of discourse into standardized formats has become a fine art—have chosen the form of the memoir. Each of these academic women memoir writers, intuitively or self-consciously, have chosen to foreground the word "memoir" in the title of their books. Their choice of the form reflects the integration of matters of the heart and the head that made them the intellectual beings they are. They have also chosen the memoir when they have all mastered the "objective" formats of the academy that turn discourse into a hegemony of power. In writing memoir they not only choose to deconstruct their own privilege as academics, to work against the established discursive authority to which they have access, but they also choose to use that discursive authority to practise new formats, to speak about what has been forbidden in academic discourse. By writing memoirs they have refused to use, or have found that it was impossible for them to use unmediated, authoritative academic discourse. At the same time, in taking up memoir, these writers work at "dodging the conventional readings designed to contain them in traditional confessional paradigms" (Gammel 2) by placing the personal life in its institutional and cultural contexts.

Perhaps the best example of this inability of the academic discourse to perform the very subjects who use the academy's discursive modes is found in Alice Kaplan's book *French Lessons: A Memoir*, which I have already discussed in my chapter on trauma and the memoir form. Her accomplishment is also relevant to my point about women in the academy making new uses of the memoir form. Her memoir is the undoing of the ways in which her culture, and especially her education in that culture has turned her against herself as woman, as a Jew, as an intellectual. Kaplan's anecdote about her experience of Paul de Man as a teacher is central to her deconstructive technique, in which the master's tools are turned against the master. Her condemnation of the way she and other young academics were taught to read in the 1970s is an indictment of the literary academy as we have known it:

> What a waste! Taking apart meaning, looking at words, shunning the illusion of the fully present communicative voice—these aspects of deconstruction theory as we absorbed it *may* have been part of de Man's intellectual struggle against the manipulative tendencies of fascist propaganda. *May* have: I'll never know, because de Man covered his work with the clean veil of disinterestedness. Now I'm helping my Ph.D. students write their own dissertations, and I never want to fail them the way that de Man failed me. How do I tell them who I am, why I read the way I do?
> What do students need to know about their teachers? (174)

Each of the women I have written about might answer Kaplan's questions about their identities as teachers differently, but for all of them the need to bring the personal back into intellectual activity, to create a balance of subject positions from all the margins that have made them, to speak in a "fully present communicative voice," has manifested itself in the writing of a memoir. It has served their purposes well, allowing them to use the writing skills that life in the academy has taught them, but to use them subversively by taking up the many discursive strands that allows a memoir writer to powerfully join the heart and the head. Each has constructed a memoir discourse of the personal, political, and professional that an innovative intellectual career requires and repossessed the world of hard-won personal wisdom in order to join it with the life of a public intellectual.

Conclusion

Repossessing a Relational Autonomy That Resists Appropriation

IN 1998 Sidonie Smith and Julia Watson published an anthology, *Women, Autobiography, Theory*, that collects many of the critical and theoretical contributions concerned with women's autobiographical production in the last two decades. In their introduction they devote a short section entitled "The Future of Women's Autobiography" to the worrisome argument that their subject of study, women's autobiography, "may itself have become suspect" (40). I believe that this suspicion results from the fact that all of the ways of thinking and being that feminists have evoked and practised are in the process of being appropriated by the larger culture for its own purposes. When we appropriate the ideas of others we do not perform the same action as when we make legitimate use of them. Intellectual appropriation is the act of using the ideas of others while ignoring the fuller context of those ideas. It also involves not giving due credit for these ideas. This appropriation is sometimes achieved by actively misconstruing the originators and their purposes, while presenting their ideas as one's own. Such appropriations mandate acts of repossession by feminists, acts that detail the contribution of feminist knowledge to any given field of study. My book has such a repossession as its goal. Feminist theorists of life writing and women who write memoirs need to claim their place in the history of the field, or else their contributions will be minimized and eventually go unrecognized. More importantly, appropriation robs ideas of their ethical context and thus their fullest effect.

I have argued that women are well placed at present to be profoundly influenced by changes in how we define ourselves as human subjects, how we balance the working of autonomous and relational desires in our performance of self. This is why I advocate the continued study of women's autobiographical production as necessary to the broader study of changes in the performance of human subjectivity. Smith and Watson assert that "while we recognize the need to continually critique cultural constructions of 'woman' and 'difference,' we also recognize the utility and importance of continuing to focus on the cultural production of women" (41). I have found that to discover the "utility and importance" of women's autobiographical production in the present moment, a genre study of a principle mode of that production, the memoir form, is necessary. To undertake that study in a way that avoids a limiting essentialism, genre must be understood as both writing strategy and social discourse. Studying women's life-writing production at the turn of the twenty-first century without taking into account the fact that the genre of memoir has become central to women's performances of self would be like trying to study nineteenth-century women's life-writing production without taking into account the genre aspects of the diary and letter forms that were so often the vehicle of those women's self-performance.

The memoir genre is coming into its own not only as an important mode of performing subjectivity, but also as a mode in which women's works are leading the way, both in number and quality of autobiographical texts. I have chosen to take up primarily texts that their authors identify as memoirs to emphasize that writers' choices are an important part of naming genre locations. Writers who self-consciously work within a set of writing strategies, who practise and experiment with a generic tradition, are as important a component of changing social discourse as readers who are conscious of the genre's history and innovativeness. It is my hope that this book will help to increase this consciousness in both readers and writers. Since the memoir form is becoming a popular as well as a literary practice, I expect that other studies will be produced to expand our consciousness of the possibilities of the form.

In my introduction I emphasized that the memoir form is a "discursive practice that brings together material realities and imaginary possibilities." Memoir therefore has the ability to become a satisfying aesthetic practice for many writers. Throughout this study I have tried to show that memoir has the capacity to be very specific to the local as well as theoretical about the writing act it uses to perform the self of the memoirist. This capacity should also increase the memoir's attractiveness for literary study. But the most important function of memoir is its role in an "evolving feminist sense of subjects in process" (Smith and Watson 40). I find that many women's memoir texts, even when they do not subscribe to an announced feminist philosophy, are feminist in their impulse in the same way that present-day changes in subjectivity formation are feminist in their impulse. At the present time we are all becoming more conscious of the need to bring together rather than to dichotomize the diverse strands of identity. Feminism asserts that the aspects of living and being that women have always practised because of their roles in society are elements we need to integrate into all of our ways of becoming and being in the world. While women memoirists' concerns with performing selves that have agency in the world require that their texts be vitally concerned with autonomy, in their very structure as accounts of alterity they also emphasize the relational and the communal as the ongoing grounds of our self-performance. I believe that the pervasive desire of our times for less binarized versions of human subjectivity finds one of its most commodious expressions in the memoir form—just as other eras have found the epic, the sonnet, the novel, and other modes as most suitable.

Contemporary women's memoirs, while concerned with the life of the individual, are also able to make more general statements about the nature of community life. Through its blending of styles—dramatic, narrative, essayistic, descriptive, and imagistic—and its practice of combining factually based testimony and fictive anecdote, the memoir form bridges the typical strategies of historical and literary discourses in order to establish necessary connections between the public and the private, the personal and the political. With these characteristics it is not surprising that memoirs have become popular with a wide range of intellectual and creative contemporary women. Indeed, the memoir form, practised in English since medieval times and often denigrated as the reserve of amateurs, from retired generals to unemployed courtesans, is becoming, in new hands, a radicalized and professionalized generic expression democratically available to a wide range of practitioners.

The great strength of the form is in the elastic modes it makes available for our fuller repossession of the cultural world in which we perform our lives. It requires that the writer understand her writing acts as performative of a subjectivity that will give her more agency in the world. To do that requires the growth of personal autonomy through the acts of reflective/reflexive writing. Part of that autonomy is the writer's realization of herself as a consequence of its matrix in the other—the other of history, family, career, of all life's relevant relational contexts. Some might argue that many books that call themselves autobiographies do this as well. That may be so. However, I have argued that the word "autobiography," invented in the Romantic period of literature, was an attempt to prescribe a particular kind of autobiographical subjectivity—that of the ego-centred, romantic, bourgeois rebel, professionally career-centred, bound on rising above the relational dictates of a mundane society to the place of the exceptional man, the autonomous man. I do not advocate the abandonment of the term "autobiography," but rather a continuing critique of its construction as a category (just as we feminists continue to critique the category "woman"). Part of that continuing critique is to recognize that while critical history has been naming "autobiography," there have been in existence writing practices that reflect more ancient ways of being and becoming in the world. Those practices are described by the word "memoir." Memoir has required a human subject whose autonomy is compellingly intertwined with relationships, and community, a human subject that does not seek to disentangle herself from those compelling ties, but builds autonomy based on them. For such a subject, memoir is the much older and more appropriate form, going back to the Middle Ages, written by all sorts of people, most of them not professional writers, some of them women, whose lives were not as neatly organized as the newer term "autobiography" might require.

It is ironic that as modernity's emphasis on autonomy fails to satisfy the identity needs of the inhabitants of the global village, we may be returning to something similar to the "traditional" communal subject of the past. However, it would be a tragic irony, given modernity's positive emphasis on the possibilities for responsibility and freedom of each human being, if we were also to return to the kind of institutional oppressions of the individual subject that former times required. If autobiographical practices are to produce agency for human subjects to resist conformity while performing constructive and multiple connections to the world, memoir discourse needs to continue to be the lively art of balancing the self and the other. If women's memoirs can help show that such balancing acts are workable and performable, they will have truly repossessed a cultural world where we can be our fullest human selves.

I began this book with reference to my own memoir writing, which has been so much a part of my learning process as a critic and theorist. I would also like to end with it. I knew as I wrote *Memoirs from Away* that, like many memoirists, I too had a guilty secret, in my case an undisclosed sexual incident of molestation that was central to my gender consciousness, but of which I found it impossible to write. I knew intuitively as a woman experienced in my culture, as well as consciously as an academic feminist, that the disclosure of anything sexual in nature by a woman is always viewed as confessional, and any confessional act by a woman tends to make the writer vulnerable to the appropriation of the pornographic, victimizing, and blaming gaze that the essayists in *Confessional Politics* describe. I delayed a long time before writing about this event in my life, and yet knew that it was important enough, central enough to my growing up, that to leave it out would be to have not gone the distance with the memoir acts I had undertaken.

While I worked at finding a form, an incident from my childhood, one seemingly tangential and unrelated to sexual molestation, kept reiterating itself in my memory work. In the memory/fantasy, I stood beside the roadway in front of my childhood home, where my older brother, his friend, and I had stationed ourselves to watch the prime minister of Canada drive by. This was an actual event, remembered by my brother and others, as well as myself. Even though it had no connection with the molestation, but kept reiterating itself whenever I thought about how I would write of the molestation, I wrote it down. I even named my chapter "My Brother Dave, His Friend Sid and Louis St. Laurent," the names of the three males involved in our neighbourhood's brief moment of celebrity. Beginning the chapter in this way was experimental on my part, for I did not know where this naming would lead. As I wrote I realized that the experience of almost meeting the prime minister of Canada symbolized my own continuing problematic relationship to the patriarchal elements of the society in which I have lived. When I finished the chapter I realized that the personal reference of my first title was really the description that comes after the colon in articles of cultural critique. My primary title became "History and Politics," indicating my turn to a discourse in which I felt that the personal "confession" did not act simply to allow intrusion into my vulnerable, intimate life, but instead performed a discourse that could use that vulnerable, remembered childhood self to make connections to the larger ideology while not being appropriated by it. These are connections that many in our society do not want women to make. I think as a memoirist I was willing to take risks, but I also directly asked my readers to take similar risks in understanding my story in the larger, feminist reading of my culture. I know the piece was successful in serving my need to perform a more effective, autonomous, relational self inside the memoir form. However, I have proposed that for memoir to be successful the form needs readers who enter a text with an "attitude" that does not seek to appropriate, judge or colonize, but that mandates that readers risk their own vulnerabilities in reading the memoir text. I hope that this study of contemporary women's memoirs can help prepare the readers of memoirs to take those risks. If it does, then I will have been successful in repossessing the discourses of the academy for my own and other women's empowerment. After many years of both desiring the power of the academy's discourses, and finding that they cancelled out whole parts of my learned knowledge, that is a repossession I dearly desire.

Works Cited

Adams, Kate. "The Way We Were." *Women's Review of Books*, xvi, 12 (Sept. 1999): 8-9.

Adams, Timothy Dow. "Talking Stories/Telling Lies in *The Woman Warrior.*" *Approaches to Teaching Kingston's* The Woman Warrior. Ed. Shirley Geok-lin Lim. New York: MLA, 1991. 151-58.

Alexander, Meena. *Fault Lines: A Memoir.* New York: Feminist at CUNY, 1993.

Barrington, Judith. *Writing the Memoir: From Truth to Art.* Portland, OR: Eighth Mountain, 1997.

Bateson, Mary Catherine. *With a Daughter's Eye: A Memoir of Margaret Mead and Gregory Bateson.* New York: Washington Square, 1984.

Belenky, Mary Field, Blythe McVicker Clinchy, Nancy Rule Goldberger, and Jill Mattuck Tarule. *Women's Ways of Knowing: The Development of Self, Voice, and Mind.* New York: Basic, 1986.

Benstock, Shari, ed. *The Private Self: Theory and Practice of Women's Autobiographical Writings.* Chapel Hill: North Carolina UP, 1988.

Bernstein, Susan David. "Confessing Feminist Theory: What's 'I' Got to Do with It." *Hypatia* 7, 1 (1992): 120-47.

Beverly, John. "The Margins at the Center: On *Testimonio* (Testimonial Narrative)." *De/Colonizing the Subject: The Politics of Gender in Women's Autobiography.* Eds. Sidonie Smith and Julia Watson. Minneapolis: Minnesota UP, 1992. 91-114.

Billson, Marcus. "The Memoir: New Perspectives on a Forgotten Genre." *Genre* 10 (1977): 259-82.

Bové, Paul A. "Discourse." *Critical Terms for Literary Study.* Eds. Frank Lentricchia and Thomas McLaughlin. Chicago: U of Chicago P, 1990. 50-65.

Brewster, Eva. *Progeny of Light / Vanished in Darkness.* Edmonton: NeWest Press, 1994.

———. *Vanished in Darkness: An Auschwitz Memoir.* Edmonton: NeWest Press, 1986.

Brodski, Bella, and Celeste Schenck, eds. *Life / Lines: Theorizing Women's Autobio-graphy.* Ithaca: Cornell UP, 1988.

———. "Mothers Displacement and Language in the Autobiographies of Nathalie Sarraute and Christa Wolf." *Life / Lines: Theorizing Women's Autobiography.* Eds. Bella Brodzki and Celeste Schenck. Ithaca: Cornell UP, 1988. 243-59.

Brown, Laura. "Not Outside the Range: One Feminist Perspective on Psychic Trauma." *Trauma: Explorations in Memory.* Ed. Cathy Caruth. Baltimore: Johns Hopkins UP, 1995. 100-12.

Bruss, Elizabeth. *Autobiographical Acts: The Changing Situation of a Literary Genre.* Baltimore: Johns Hopkins UP, 1976.

Bunkers, Suzanne, and Cynthia Huff, eds. *Inscribing the Daily: Critical Essays on Diary Literature.* Amherst: Massachusetts UP, 1996.

Buss, Helen M. (a.k.a.) Margaret Clarke. *The Cutting Season.* Edmonton: NeWest Press, 1984.

———. *Mapping Our Selves: Canadian Women's Autobiography.* Montreal: McGill-Queen's UP, 1993.

———. "Memoir with an Attitude: One Reader Reads *The Woman Warrior: Memoirs of a Girlhood among Ghosts.*" *a/b: Auto/Biographical Studies* 12, 2 (Fall 1997): 203-24.

———. "Memoirs Discourse and William Godwin's *Memoirs of the Author of* A Vindication of the Rights of Women." *Mary Wollstonecraft and Mary Shelley: Writing Lives.* Eds. Helen M. Buss, D.L. Macdonald, and Anne McWhir. Waterloo, ON: Wilfrid Laurier UP, 2001.

———. *Memoirs from Away: A New Found Land Girlhood.* Waterloo, ON: Wilfrid Laurier UP, 1999.

———. *Mother and Daughter Relationships in the Manawaka Works of Margaret Laurence.* Victoria: Victoria UP, 1985.

Butala, Sharon. *The Perfection of the Morning: An Apprenticeship in Nature.* Toronto: Harper Collins, 1994.

Butler, Judith. *Bodies that Matter: On the Discursive Limits of "Sex."* New York: Routledge, 1993.

———. *Excitable Speech: A Politics of the Performative.* New York: Routledge, 1997.

———. *Gender Trouble: Feminism and the Subversion of Identity*. New York: Routledge, 1990.
Cameron, Elspeth. *No Previous Experience: A Memoir of Love and Change*. Harmondsworth, UK: Viking Penguin, 1997.
Cardinal, Marie. *The Words to Say It*. Trans. Pat Goodheart. Cambridge, MA: VanVactor and Goodheart, 1983.
Carlson, Kathie. *In Her Image: The Unhealed Daughter's Search for Her Mother*. Boston: Shambhala, 1990.
Caruth, Cathy. "Introduction." *Trauma: Explorations in Memory*. Ed. Cathy Caruth. Baltimore: Johns Hopkins UP, 1995. 183-99.
Chesler, Phyllis. *Women and Madness*. Garden City, NY: Doubleday, 1972.
Chin, Frank. "This is Not an Autobiography." *Genre* 18 (1985): 109-30.
Chodorow, Nancy, and Contratto, Susan. "The Fantasy of the Perfect Mother." *Rethinking the Family*. Eds. Barrie Thorne and Marilyn Yalom. Boston: Northeastern UP, 1992. 191-214.
Conway, Jill Ker, ed. *In Her Own Words: Women's Memoirs from Australia, New Zealand, Canada, and the United States*. New York: Vintage, 1999.
———. *True North: A Memoir*. Toronto: Vintage Random, 1995.
———, ed. *Written by Herself, Autobiographies of American Women: An Anthology*. Introduction and Notes by Jill Ker Conway. New York: Vintage, 1992.
Culley, Margo. "Introduction." *A Day at a Time: The Diary Literature of American Women from 1764 to the Present*. New York: Feminist at CUNY, 1985.
de Certeau, Michael. *The Practice of Everyday Life*. Trans. Steven F. Rendall. Berkeley: California UP, 1984.
Dillard, Annie. "To Fashion a Text." *Inventing the Truth: The Art and Craft of Memoir*. Ed. William Zinsser. Boston: Houghton Mifflin, 1987. 54-76.
DuPlessis, Rachel Blau. "Reader, I Married Me: A Polygynous Memoir." *Changing Subjects: The Making of Feminist Literary Criticism*. Ed. Gayle Green and Coppélia Kahn. London: Routledge, 1993. 97-111.
Eakin, Paul John. *How Our Lives Become Stories: Making Selves*. Ithaca: Cornell UP, 1999.
Egan, Susanna. *Mirror Talk: Genres of Crisis in Contemporary Autobiography*. Chapel Hill: North Carolina UP, 1999.
———. *Patterns of Experience in Autobiography*. Chapel Hill: North Carolina UP, 1984.
Ehrlich, Elizabeth. *Miriam's Kitchen: A Memoir*. New York: Viking, 1997.
Erikson, Kai. "Notes on Trauma and Community." *Trauma: Explorations in Memory*. Ed. Cathy Caruth. Baltimore: Johns Hopkins UP, 1995. 183-99.
Felman, Shoshana, and Dori Laub. *Testimony: Crises of Witnessing in Literature, Psychoanalysis, and History*. New York: Routledge, 1992.
Freedman, Aviva and Peter Medway. "Introduction." *Genre and the New Rhetoric*. Washington: Taylor and Francis, 1995.

Freedman, Diane P., Olivia Frey and Frances Murphy Zauhar. *The Intimate Critique: Autobiographical Literary Criticism.* Durham: Duke UP, 1993.

Fuss, Diana. *Essentially Speaking: Feminism, Nature and Difference.* New York: Routledge, 1989.

Gammel, Irene. "Introduction." *Confessional Politics: Women's Self-Representations in Life Writing and Popular Media.* Ed. Irene Gammel. Carbondale: Southern Illinois UP, 1999. 1-10.

Gates, Henry Louis, Jr. *Colored People: A Memoir.* New York: Vintage, 1994.

Gilmore, Leigh. *Autobiographics: A Feminist Theory of Women's Self-Representation.* Ithaca: Cornell UP, 1994.

———. "The Mark of Autobiography: Postmodernism, Autobiography, and Genre." *Autobiography and Postmodernism.* Eds. Kathleen Ashley, Leigh Gilmore, and Gerald Peters. Amherst: U of Massachusetts P, 1994.

Gornick, Vivian. *Fierce Attachments: A Memoir.* New York: Simon and Schuster, 1987.

Gotera, Vicente F. "'I've Never Read Anything Like It': Student Responses to *The Woman Warrior.*" *Approaches to Teaching Kingston's* The Woman Warrior. Ed. Shirley Geok-lin Lim. New York: MLA, 1991. 64-73.

Gould, Jane S. *Juggling: A Memoir of Work, Family and Feminism.* New York: Feminist at CUNY, 1997.

Granofsky, Roland. *The Trauma Novel: Contemporary Symbolic Depictions of Collective Disaster.* New York: Peter Lang, 1995.

Gusdorf, Georges. "The Conditions and Limits of Autobiography." *Autobiography: Essays Theoretical and Critical.* Ed. James Olney. Princeton: Princeton UP, 1980. 28-48.

Hacking, Ian. "Memory Sciences, Memory Politics." *Tense Past: Cultural Essays in Trauma and Memory.* Eds. Paul Antze and Michael Lambek. New York: Routledge, 1996. 67-88.

Hampsten, Elizabeth. *Read This Only to Yourself: The Private Writings of Midwestern Women 1880-1910.* Bloomington: Indiana UP, 1988.

Hart, Francis Russell. "History Talking to Itself: Public Personality in Recent Memoir." *New Literary History* 11, 1 (Autumn 1979): 193-210.

Heilbrun, Carolyn G. *The Last Gift of Time: Life Beyond Sixty.* New York: Dial, 1997.

———. *Writing a Woman's Life.* New York: W.W. Norton, 1988.

Henke, Suzette A. *Shattered Subjects: Trauma and Testimony in Women's Life-Writing.* New York: St. Martin's, 1998.

Herrman, Anne. *Menopausal Memoir: Letters from Another Climate.* New York: Haworth, 1998.

Hinz, Evelyn J. "Mimesis: The Dramatic Lineage of Auto / Biography." *Essays on Life Writing: From Genre to Critical Practice.* Ed. Marlene Kadar. Toronto: Toronto UP, 1992. 195-212.

Hirsch, Marianne. *The Mother/Daughter Plot: Narrative, Psychoanalysis, Feminism.* Bloomington: Indiana UP, 1989.

hooks, bell. "Narratives of Struggle." *Critical Fictions: The Politics of Imaginative Writing.* Ed. Phiomena Mariani. Seattle: Bay, 1991.

Jay, Paul. *Being in the Text: Self Representation from Wordsworth to Roland Barthes.* Ithaca: Cornell UP, 1984.

Jelinek, Estelle C. "Introduction: Women's Autobiography and the Male Tradition." *Women's Autobiography: Essays in Criticism.* Ed. Estelle C. Jelinek. Bloomington: Indiana UP, 1980. 1-20.

———. *The Tradition of Women's Autobiography: From Antiquity to the Present.* Boston: Twayne, 1986.

Juhasz, Susanne. "Maxine Hong Kingston: Narrative Technique & Female Identity." *Contemporary American Women Writers: Narrative Strategies.* Eds. Catherine Rainwater and William J. Schenk. Lexington: UP of Kentucky, 1985.

Kadar, Marlene. "Coming to Terms: Life Writing." *Essays in Life Writing: From Genre to Critical Practice.* Toronto: Toronto UP, 1992. 3-20.

Kaplan, Alice. *French Lessons: A Memoir.* Chicago: U of Chicago P, 1993.

Kaplan, Caren. "Resisting Autobiography: Out-Law Genres and Transnational Feminist Subjects." *Decolonizing the Subject: The Politics of Gender in Women's Autobiography.* Eds. Sidonie Smith and Julia Watson. Minneapolis: U of Minnesota P, 1992. 115-138.

Karr, Mary. *The Liars' Club: A Memoir.* New York: Penguin, 1995.

Kaufman, Linda S. *Discourses of Desires: Gender, Genre and Epistolary Fictions.* Ithaca: Cornell UP, 1986.

Kazin, Alfred. "Autobiography as Narrative." *Michigan Quarterly Review* 3 (1964): 210-16.

Kennedy, Colleen, and Deborah Morse. "A Dialogue with(in) Tradition: Two Perspectives on *The Woman Warrior.*" *Approaches to Teaching Kingston's* The Woman Warrior. Ed. Shirley Geok-lin Lim. New York: MLA, 1991. 121-30.

Kingston, Maxine Hong. "Cultural Mis-readings by American Critics." *Asian and Western Writers in Dialogue: New Cultural Identities.* Ed. Guy Amirthanayagam. London: Macmillan, 1982. 55-65.

———. "Personal Statement." *Approaches to Teaching Kingston's* The Woman Warrior. Ed. Shirley Geok-lin Lim. New York: MLA, 1991. 23-25.

———. *The Woman Warrior: Memoirs of a Girlhood among Ghosts.* 1975. New York: Vintage, 1989.

Kirmayer, Laurence J. "Landscapes of Memory: Trauma, Narrative and Dissociation." *Tense Past: Cultural Essays in Trauma and Memory.* Eds. Paul Antze and Michael Lambek. New York: Routledge, 1996. 173-98.

Komenaka, April R. "Autobiography as a Sociolinguistic Resource: Maxine Hong Kingston's *The Woman Warrior.*" *International Journal of the Sociology of Language* 69 (1988): 105-18.

Laurence, Margaret. *Dance on the Earth: A Memoir.* Toronto: McClelland and Stewart, 1989.

Lazarre, Jane. *Wet Earth and Dreams: A Narrative of Grief and Recovery.* Durham: Duke UP, 1998.

Lejeune, Philippe. *On Autobiography.* Ed. Paul John Eakin. Trans. Katherine Leary. Minneapolis: Minnesota UP, 1989.

Lerner, Gerda. "Introduction." *The Female Experience: An American Documentary.* Ed. Gerda Lerner. Indianapolis: Bobbs-Merrill, 1977.

Li, David Leiwei. "The Naming of a Chinese American 'I': Cross-Cultural Sign/ifications in *The Woman Warrior.*" *Criticism* 30 (1988): 497-515.

Lidoff, Joan. "Autobiography in a Different Voice: *The Woman Warrior* and the Question of Genre." *Approaches to Teaching Kingston's* The Woman Warrior. Ed. Shirley Geok-lin Lim. New York: MLA, 1991. 116-20.

Lim, Shirley Geok-lin. *Among the White Moon Faces: An Asian-American Memoir of Homelands.* New York: Feminist at CUNY, 1996.

———, ed. *Approaches to Teaching Kingston's* The Woman Warrior. New York: MLA, 1991.

———. "Part One: Materials." *Approaches to Teaching Kingston's* The Woman Warrior. Ed. Shirley Geok-lin Lim. New York: MLA, 1991. 3-15.

Lionnet, Françoise. *Autobiographical Voices: Race, Gender, Self-Portraiture.* Ithaca: Cornell UP, 1989.

Mason, Mary. "The Other Voice: Autobiographies of Women Writers." *Autobiography: Essays Theoretical and Critical.* Ed. James Olney. Princeton: Princeton UP, 1980. 207-35.

McDonnell, Jane Taylor. *Living to Tell the Tale: A Guide to Writing Memoir.* New York: Penguin, 1998.

McNaron, Toni. *I Dwell in Possibility, A Memoir.* New York: Feminist at CUNY, 1992.

Meigs, Mary. *The Box Closet.* Vancouver: Talonbooks, 1987.

"Memoir." *The Compact Edition of the Oxford English Dictionary.* Oxford: Oxford UP, 1987. 828-29.

Miller, Nancy K. *Bequest and Betrayal: Memoirs of a Parent's Death.* New York: Oxford UP, 1996.

———. *Getting Personal: Feminist Occasions and Other Autobiographical Acts.* New York: Routledge, 1991.

———. "Public Statements, Private Lives: Academic Memoirs for the Nineties." *Signs* 22, 4 (Summer 1997): 981-1015.

———. *Subject to Change: Reading Feminist Writing.* New York: Columbia UP, 1988.

Misch, Georg. *History of Autobiography in Antiquity.* Vol. 2. Trans. W.W. Dickes. Cambridge: Harvard UP, 1998.

Mitchell, Emily. "Thanks for the Memoirs." *Time* 153, 14 (April 12, 1999).

Mittman, Elizabeth. "Christa Wolf's Signature in and on the Essay: Woman, Science and Authority." *The Politics of the Essay: Feminist Perspectives.* Eds. Ruth-Ellen Boetcher Jores and Elizabeth Mittman. Bloomington: Indiana UP, 1993. 95-112.

Modjeska, Drusilla. *Poppy.* Ringwood, Victoria, Austral.: McPhee Gribble Penguin, 1990.

Myers, Victoria. "The Significant Fictivity of Maxine Hong Kingston's *The Woman Warrior.*" *Biography* 9 (1986): 112-25.

———. "Speech Act Theory and the Search for Identity in *The Woman Warrior.*" *Approaches to Teaching Kingston's* The Woman Warrior. Ed. Shirley Geok-lin Lim. New York: MLA, 1991. 131-37.

Neuman, Shirley, ed. *Autobiography and Questions of Gender.* London: Cass. 1991.

———. "From a Different Poetics to a Poetics of Difference." *Essays on Life Writing: From Genre to Critical Practice.* Ed. Marlene Kadar. Toronto: Toronto UP, 1992.

Nussbaum, Felicity A. *The Autobiographical Subject: Gender and Ideology in Eighteenth-Century England.* Baltimore: Johns Hopkins UP, 1989.

Olney, James. "Autobiography and the Cultural Moment: A Thematic, Historical, and Bibliographical Introduction." *Autobiography: Essays Theoretical and Critical.* Ed. James Olney. Princeton: Princeton UP, 1980. 23-27.

Perreault, Jeanne. *Writing Selves: Contemporary Feminist Autography.* Minneapolis: Minnesota UP, 1995.

Petrey, Sandy. *Speech Acts and Literary Theory.* New York: Routledge, 1990.

Pratt, Mary Louise. *Toward a Speech Act Theory of Literary Discourse.* Bloomington: Indiana UP, 1977.

Probyn, Elspeth. *Sexing the Self: Gendered Positions in Cultural Studies.* London: Routledge, 1993.

Quinby, Lee. "The Subject of Memoirs: *The Woman Warrior*'s Technology of Ideographic Selfhood." *De/Colonizing the Subject: The Politics of Gender in Women's Autobiography.* Eds. Sidonie Smith and Julia Watson. Minneapolis: U of Minnesota P, 1992. 298-320.

Rabine, Leslie W. "No Lost Paradise: Social Gender and Symbolic Gender in the Writings of Maxine Hong Kingston. *Signs: Journal of Women and Culture and Society* 12 (1987): 471-93.

Rainer, Tristine. *Your Life as Story: Writing the New Autobiography.* New York: Putnam, 1997.

Rich, Adrienne. *Of Woman Born: Motherhood as Experience and Institution.* London: Virago, 1984.

Robertson, Adele Crockett. *The Orchard: A Memoir.* Foreword and epilogue by Betsy Robertson Cramer. New York: Metropolitan, 1995.

Rousseau, Jean-Jacques. *Confessions.* 1781. Translated and with an introduction by J.M. Cohen. Harmmondsworth, Eng.: Penguin Classics, 1953.

San Juan, Jr., E. "Beyond Identity Politics: The Predicament of the Asian American Writer in Late Capitalism." *American Literary History* 3 (1991): 542-65.

Scott, Joan W. "Experience." *Women, Autobiography, Theory: A Reader.* Eds. Sidonie Smith and Julia Watson. Madison: U of Wisconsin P, 1998. 57-71.

Shulman, Alix Kates. *Drinking the Rain.* Penguin, 1995.

Smith, Sidonie. "Performativity, Autobiographical Practice, Resistance." *a/b Auto/biography Studies* 10, 1 (Spring 1995): 17-33.

———. *A Poetics of Women's Autobiography: Marginality and the Fictions of Self-Representation.* Bloomington: Indiana UP, 1987.

———. *Subjectivity, Identity, and the Body: Women's Autobiographical Practices in the Twentieth Century.* Bloomington: Indiana UP, 1993.

———, and Julia Watson, eds. *De/Colonizing the Subject: The Politics of Gender in Women's Autobiography.* Minneapolis: Minnesota UP, 1992.

———. *Women, Autobiography, Theory: A Reader.* Madison: Wisconsin UP, 1998.

Sommer, Doris. "'Not Just a Personal Story': Women's Testimonios and the Plural Self." In *Life / Lines: Theorizing Women's Autobiography.* Eds. Bella Brodszki and Celeste Schenck. Ithaca: Cornell UP, 1988. 107-30.

Stanley, Liz. *The Autobiographical "I": The Theory and Practice of Feminist Auto/biography.* Manchester, Eng.: Manchester UP, 1992.

Stanton, Domna C., ed. *The Female Autograph: Theory and Practice of Autobiography from the Tenth to the Twentieth Century.* Chicago: U of Chicago P, 1987.

Steedman, Carolyn. "Autobiography and History". *Past Tenses: Essays on Writing, Autobiography and History.* London: Rivers Oram, 1992.

———. *Landscape for a Good Woman: A Story of Two Lives.* London: Virago, 1986.

Suleri, Sara. *Meatless Days.* Chicago: U of Chicago P, 1989.

Thompson, Phyllis Hodge. "This Is the Story I Heard: A Conversation with Maxine Hong Kingston and Earll Kingston." *Biography* 6 (1983): 1-33.

Thurer, Shari L. *The Myths of Motherhood: How Culture Reinvents the Good Mother.* Boston: Houghton and Mifflin, 1994.

Van Der Kolk, Bessel A., and Onno Van Der Hart. "The Intrusive Past: The Flexibility of Memory and the Engraving of Trauma." *Trauma: Explorations in Memory.* Ed. Cathy Caruth. Baltimore: Johns Hopkins UP, 1995. 158-82.

Veeser, H. Aram. *Confessions of the Critics.* New York: Routledge, 1996.

Watson, Julia. "Shadowed Presence: Modern Women Writers' Autobiographies and the Other." *Studies in Autobiography.* Ed. James Olney. New York: Oxford UP, 1998. 180-89.

Weir, Allison. *Sacrificial Logics: Feminist Theory and the Critique of Identity.* New York: Routledge, 1996.

Williams, Jeffrey. "Writing in Concert: An Interview with Cathy Davidson, Alice Kaplan, Jane Tompkins and Marianna Torgovnick." *Confessions of the Critics.* Ed. H. Aram Veeser. New York: Routledge, 1996. 156-76.

Williamson, Janice. *CRYBABY!* Edmonton: NeWest, 1998.
Wong, Sau-ling C. "Representations of Caregivers of Color in the Age of 'Multicul-turalism.'" *Mothering: Ideology, Experience and Agency*. Eds. Evelyn Nakano Glenn, Grace Chang, and Linda Rennie Forcey. New York: Routledge, 1994. 67-94.
Wolff, Tobias. *This Boy's Life: A Memoir*. New York: Harper and Row, 1990.
Woolf, Virginia. "A Sketch of the Past." *Moments of Being: Unpublished Autobiogra-phical Writings*. Edited and with an introduction and notes by Jeanne Schulkind. London: Triad Grafton, 1978.
Wylie, Philip. *Generation of Vipers*. New York: Holt, Rinehart and Winston, 1942.
Yalom, Marilyn. "*The Woman Warrior* as Postmodern Autobiography." *Approaches to Teaching Kingston's* The Woman Warrior. Ed. Shirley Geok-lin Lim. New York: MLA, 1991. 108-15.
Zinsser, William. "Writing and Remembering: A Memoir and an Introduction." *Inventing the Truth: The Art and Craft of the Memoir*. Ed. William Zinsser. Boston: Houghton Mifflin, 1987. 9-30.

Index

Adams, Henry, 4
Adams, Kate, xvi, 1
Adams, Timothy Dow, 28
Alexander, Meena, 174-75
Anderson, Benedict, 67
anecdote. *See* memoir and other genres
American-feminine, 45-46
Augustine, Saint, 3-4, 8, 10, 13
autobiography. *See* memoir and autobiography
autocritical: discourse, 100; reading practice, 28, 43; writing practice, 36, 40-41, 166
autocritography, 168; (*see also* memoir and other genres)
autograph, 5

Barthes, Roland, 8
Bateson, Mary Catherine, 106-109
Belenky, Mary Field et al., 59

Benstock, Shari, xx, xxi
Bernstein, Susan David, 17, 41
bildungsroman. *See* memoir and other genres
Billson, Marcus, 10, 16, 31-32, 82
biography, 19, 37, 171. *See* memoir and other genres
Bové, Paul, 7
braiding (métissage), 34, 37; pleating, 39; weaving, 63, 166
Brave Orchid, 30, 33, 42, 51-53
Brewster, Eva (Daniella Raphael), 123-26, 128, 130-38, 141, 144
Brodski, Bella, xx, 4
Brown, Laura, 136-37, 142
Bruser, Fredelle Maynard, 101
Bruss, Elizabeth, 4, 6
Bunkers, Suzanne, 9

201

Buss, Helen, xii-xiv, xvii-xxii, 9, 79, 87-88, 168, 187-88
Butala, Sharon, 82
Butler, Judith, 61, 64-65, 142

Cameron, Elspeth, 178, 180
Cardinal, Marie, 135
Carlson, Kathie, 102
Caruth, Kathy, 134, 137, 146
Cheever, Susan, 167
Chesler, Phyllis, 85-87, 112, 167
Chin, Frank, 28, 37
Chodorow, Nancy, and Susan Contratto, 104-105
Cixous, Hélène, 154
Cockshut, A. O. J., 28
collage in memoir, 68-69, 71-72, 153
Contratto, Susan, and Nancy Chodorow, 104-105
confessional politics (Gammel), 53, 188
confessions. See memoir and other genres
Conway, Jill Ker, 7, 170-74
Cook, Christine, 29
crucified woman, 116
Culley, Margo, 9

Daniella Raphael. See Brewster, Eva
de Beauvoir, Simone, 60, 62, 166
de Man, Paul, 150, 181
de Montaigne, Michel, 23-24
diary. See memoir and other genres
Dillard, Annie, 18, 23
discursive voice of memoir, 18
drama. See memoir and other genres
Duras, Marguerite, 154-5

Eakin, Paul John, 13, 20
Egan, Susanna, 5

Ehrlich, Elizabeth, 66-79
endings of memoirs, 36-37, 47, 124, 131
enunciative position: in Probyn, 86-87
Erikson, Kai, 141, 159
Ernaux, Annie, 166
essay. See memoir and other genres
essentialism, 114, 117, 165, 184

Faulkner, William, 87
Felman, Shoshana, and Dori Laub, 22, 139, 151
Flax, Jane, 20
Foucault, Michel, 31, 39, 41
Franklin, Benjamin, 8
Freedman, Aviva and Peter Medway, 7
Freud, Sigmund, 21, 157
Fuss, Diana, 113-14, 165

Gammel, Irene, 53, 169, 181, 188
Gates, Henry Louis, Jr., 165
genres. See memoir
genre theory, 6-7
Gilmore, Leigh, 5-6, 9
Godwin, William, 19
Gornick, Vivian, 110-12, 166
Gotera, Vicente F., 38
Gould, Jane S., 170, 172-75
Gusdorf, Georges, 9

Hampsten, Elizabeth, 9
Hart, Francis Russell, xi-xii, 10, 34-36
Henke, Suzette A., 139, 160
Heilbrun, Carolyn G., 83
Herrman, Anne, 82-83
Hinz, Evelyn, 20
Hirsch, Marianne, 101
history. See memoir and other genres
Hitler, Adolph, 126-28

Huff, Cynthia, 9
hysteria in women, 157, 159

Jay, Paul, 9
Jelinek, Estelle, xx, 9
Johnson, Diane, 29
Joyce, James, 40
Juhasz, Suzanne, 28

Kadar, Marlene, 6
Kaplan, Alice, xiv, 139-52, 167, 181
Karr, Mary, 112-13
Kazin, Alfred, 3
Kemp, Margery, 110-11
Kennedy, Colleen, 50-52, 97
Kingston, Maxine Hong, xx, xxii, xxiv, 10, 21, 27-56, 58, 60, 62, 65, 79, 80, 97, 109
Kirmayer, Laurence J., 144, 146, 151
Komenaka, April R., 28
Kristeva, Julia, 70, 105

Laub, Dori, 22, 121
Laurence, Jocelyn, 115
Laurence, Margaret, 87, 99-101, 113-18
Lazarre, Jane, 134-6
Lejeune, Philippe, 4-5
Lerner, Gerda, xvii
Levy, David, 103
Li, David Leiwei, 38
life writing, xv, xxii, 2-9, 11, 18, 118, 165, 184
limit attitude (in Probyn), 41-42, 87
Lionnet, Françoise, 9, 34
Lim, Shirley Geok-lin, 28-29, 174-77
literary non-fiction, 18
literary technique, 18
lyric poetry. *See* memoir and other genres

Lutkenhaus, Almuth, 116

McDonnell, June Taylor, 25
McNaron, Tony, 177-78, 180
Malcolm X, 8
Mason, Mary, 9
matrimony, 87, 95, 99, 106, 112, 119, 166-67
Mead, Margaret, 106-109
Meigs, Mary, 110
memoir: and active readership, xxiii, 47-48, 113; as art, xvi, 135; and attitude in reading, 27-55, 72, 189; and author's reading process, 28, 31; and autobiography, xxii, 2-19, 23, 28-29, 31-32, 34-35, 37-38, 89, 96, 125, 152, 164-65, 169, 183, 186-87; and auto-critical reading, 28; as balancing act, xxiv, 18, 57-84, 97, 103, 124, 184, 187; and contemporary academic women, xxi, xxv, 17-19, 89, 149-51, 163-82, 189; and contemporary male writers, 165-66; and contemporary women writers, xx, xxi, 3, 12, 28, 30, 72-73, 83, 89, 161, 184, 186; and critical reading assumptions, xiv, xv, 28, 31; definitions of, xi, xiv, 1-2, 5-7, 106, 163-64, 185; and fantasy, xix, xx, 116, 153; father-daughter/son relationships in, 167; form, xiv, xv, xxiv, 8, 63-65, 68, 91, 100, 115, 121, 135, 140, 145, 166, 168, 171-72, 176-77, 179-81, 185-86, 189; gender in, xii, xiv, 3, 6, 13, 20, 33, 39-40, 42, 149, 164-68; historicizing of the personal in, xi, 125; and iden-

tity-making, xvi, xvii, 17, 57-84; and the Internet, 7; as marginal form, xiv; memorializing the other in, 37; and memory, xii-xvii, xxii, 14-15, 106, 109, 148, 151-59, 188; mother-daughter relationships in, xxii, xxiv, xxv, 25, 29, 39, 44-45, 50-55, 74-75, 83, 85-119, 123, 146, 166, 171; narrator of, xvi, xxiii, 16-18, 32, 51, 55, 89, 112; narrative voice in, 16-17, 19; and other genres, xxiv, 4, 6, 8, 29, 49, 108-109, 112, 114, 151, 153, 181, 186-87; autocritography, 89, 113; bildungsroman, 44; biography, 19, 109; confession, 8, 10-14, 34, 40, 53, 103, 168, 188; diary, 6-9, 109, 114, 184; drama, 21, 23, 40, 114, 121, 125; essay, xv, 18, 23, 35, 114, 171-72, 176; epistle, 121, 184; history, xiv, xv, xvii, xxii, 2, 11, 19, 23, 31-35, 96, 123, 127-28; lyric poetry, xv, 14-16, 22, 121-22, 125; non-literary, as travel accounts, business records, genealogies, 11; novel and short story, xv, xxii, xxiii, 6, 11-12, 19-20, 23, 38; parables, 40, 176-77; pornography, 34, 54; satire, 35; testimony, 11, 135; and performance of self, xiv, xxi-xxiv, 20-22, 26, 29, 31-32, 35, 37, 41, 51, 53, 63-65, 71, 76, 81-83, 94, 97-100, 109, 114, 119, 125, 145, 169, 174, 184-85; reiterative performance of self, 65-66; sacrificial logics of performance of self, xxiv, 60, 62, 65-66, 68, 76, 83, 86, 90, 92, 98, 112-13, 168; and (reader/writer) participant, 16-17, 19, 32, 33, 35, 41, 47, 49, 51, 63, 69, 91, 109, 119, 144, 160; personalizing of history, xi, xxi, 125, 158; and reading strategies, xxii-xxiv, 26, 35, 44, 53, 175; re-emerging of self process in, 87-89, 98, 118; and reflection, 16-17; reflective/reflexive consciousness in, 16-17, 32-33, 35, 41, 47, 49, 51, 63, 69, 76, 91, 107, 109, 125, 130, 133, 144, 186; and reflexivity, xxiii, 16-18, 41; relational aspects of, 13-14; and repossession, 183-84, 189; of childhood, xii; of cultures, 3, 55, 62-86, 100; of history, xii, 46, 96, 109; of public world, xii, 68, 96, 105, 133, 138, 148, 177, 182, 186-87; and rhetorical strategies, xxiv, 25, 32, 35, 48, 115, 175; as social discourse, 6-7; tasks of, 18; as therapy, 15, 21 (*see* therapy); and trauma, xvii, xxv, 22-23, 121-37; tripartite narrator of, 16-17, 32-33, 35, 41, 47, 49, 51, 63, 69, 87, 91, 107, 109; witness (reader/writer) in, 16-17, 32-33, 35, 41, 47, 49, 51, 63, 69, 91, 109, 122, 126, 129, 133-34, 144; and women's common reality-making process, xv, xx, xxiii

métissage, 9, 34
Miller, Nancy, 85, 87, 163-69
Misch, Georg, 3, 9

Mitchell, Emily, 7
Mittman, Elizabeth, 24
Modjeska, Drusilla, 109
Myers, Victoria, 21, 28, 38

naming: of genres, 5-6; of matrimony/patrimony, 86, 167-68
Neuman, Shirley, 9, 62-63
No Name Woman, 43-49
Nussbaum, Felicity, 12

objectivity, xv
Olney, James, 9

performative language, 21
Perreault, Jeanne, 9, 20
Petry, Sandra, 21
polishing a fiction, 136
postmodernism, 153
post-traumatic stress disorder, 137, 138, 157, 159
Pratt, Mary Louise, 21
Probyn, Elspeth, 39-42, 46, 87

Quinby, Lee, 10, 31-34, 169

Rabine, Leslie W., 28, 36
Rainer, Tristine, 13
reality (nature of), xvi
reminiscence, 15-6
reportage, 18
research, 18-9
revision: of history, xiii, 2; of memory, xiii; of revision, xv, xxiii; of self, 17
Ribot, T., 148
Rich, Adrienne, 23, 86, 104-105
Robertson, Adele Crockett, 83
role models, 45-6
romantic movement, 15, 186
romantic conventions, 179-80
Roth, Philip, 166
Rousseau, Jean-Jacques, 4, 8, 11-13, 40

Said, Edward, 101
San-Juan, E., Jr., 28
scenic language, 121, 134, 140
scenes of language, 140, 151
Schenck, Celeste, xx, 4
Scott, Joan W., 40
self, 40, 46, 55, 57; -collage, 71; and community, 13; -construction (self-making), xiv, 8; divided, xx; and emotion, 15; and imagination (imagining, imaginary), 19, 32, 44, 48, 153, 185; narration of, 64; negation of, 58-59; performing the, xiv, xxi, 20-21; problematize and define the, 62; reconstruction of, 21; revision of, 17; repossessing the, 34, 160; therapy of, 134 (*see* therapy)
Shulman, Alix Kates, 79-82
Smith, Sidonie, xx, 9, 20, 63, 65, 103, 152, 165, 183-85
Sommers, Doris, 5
speech acts, 21
Spiegelman, Art, 166
Stanley, Liz, 9
Stanton, Domna, xx, 5, 9
Steedman, Carolyn, 89, 90-98, 166
Suleri, Sara, xxi, xxii

testimonio, 5
testimony, 33, 122-61
therapy, 15, 21, 134, 136, 136, 138, 148-49, 158
Thompson, Phyllis Hodge, 27
Thurer, Shari, 103
Torgovnick, Marianna, 140

Van Der Hart, Onno, and Bessel Van Der Kolk, 136, 140, 151-52
Veeser, H. Aram, 36, 89

Watson, Julia, 9, 25, 62, 165, 183-85
Weir, Allison, xxiv, 57, 60, 62-63, 65-66, 70, 80, 90, 105
Wiesel, Elie, 121, 135
Williams, Jeffrey, 140
Williamson, Janice, 152-61
Wolff, Tobias, 165
Wong, Sau-ling C., 39

Woo, Deborah, 28
Woolf, Virginia, xviii, xix, xxi, 118, 154-55
Wordsworth, William, 8-9
Wylie, Philip, 103

Yalom, Marilyn, 28

Zinsser, William, 22

Books in the Life Writing Series Published by Wilfrid Laurier University Press

Haven't Any News: Ruby's Letters from the Fifties
Edited by Edna Staebler with an Afterword by Marlene Kadar
1995 / x + 165 pp. / ISBN 0-88920-248-6

"I Want to Join Your Club": Letters from Rural Children, 1900-1920
Edited by Norah L. Lewis with a Preface by Neil Sutherland
1996 / xii + 250 pp. (30 b&w photos) / ISBN 0-88920-260-5

And Peace Never Came
Elisabeth M. Raab with Historical Notes by Marlene Kadar
1996 / x + 196 pp. (12 b&w photos, map) / ISBN 0-88920-281-8

Dear Editor and Friends: Letters from Rural Women of the North-West, 1900-1920
Edited by Norah L. Lewis
1998 / xvi + 166 pp. (20 b&w photos) / ISBN 0-88920-287-7

The Surprise of My Life: An Autobiography
Claire Drainie Taylor with a Foreword by Marlene Kadar
1998 / ISBN 0-88920-302-4
xii + 268 pp. (+ 8 colour photos and 92 b&w photos)

Memoirs from Away: A New Found Land Girlhood
Helen M. Buss / Margaret Clarke
1998 / xvi + 153 pp. / ISBN 0-88920-350-4

The Life and Letters of Annie Leake Tuttle: Working for the Best
Marilyn Färdig Whiteley
1999 / xviii + 150 pp. / ISBN 0-88920-330-X

Marian Engel's Notebooks: "Ah, mon cahier, écoute"
Christl Verduyn, editor
1999 / viii + 576 pp. / ISBN 0-88920-333-4 cloth / ISBN 0-88920-349-0 paper

Be Good Sweet Maid: The Trials of Dorothy Joudrie
Audrey Andrews
1999 / vi + 276 pp. / ISBN 0-88920-334-2

Working in Women's Archives: Researching Women's Private Literature and Archival Documents
Helen M. Buss and Marlene Kadar, editors
2001 / vi + 120 pp. / ISBN 0-88920-341-5

Repossessing the World: Reading Memoirs by Contemporary Women
Helen M. Buss
2002 / xxvi + 206 pp. / ISBN 0-88920-408-X cloth / ISBN 0-88920-410-1 paper

www.ingramcontent.com/pod-product-compliance
Lightning Source LLC
Chambersburg PA
CBHW051427290426
44109CB00016B/1461